THE RAPES OF LUCRETIA

A Myth and its Transformations

THE RAPES OF
LUCRETIA

*A Myth
and its Transformations*

IAN DONALDSON

CLARENDON PRESS · OXFORD

1982

Oxford University Press, Walton Street, Oxford OX2 6DP

London Glasgow New York Toronto
Delhi Bombay Calcutta Madras Karachi
Kuala Lumpur Singapore Hong Kong Tokyo
Nairobi Dar es Salaam Cape Town
Melbourne Auckland

and associates in
Beirut Berlin Ibadan Mexico City Nicosia

Published in the United States
by Oxford University Press, New York

© Ian Donaldson 1982.

British Library Cataloguing in Publication Data
Donaldson, Ian
The rapes of Lucretia.
1. Lucretia 2. Mythology, Classical
3. Rape (in religion, folk-lore, etc.)
I. Title
292'13   BL820.L/
ISBN 0-19-812638-7

Library of Congress Cataloging in Publication Data
Donaldson, Ian.
The rapes of Lucretia.
Includes bibliographical references and
index.
1. Lucretia, in fiction, drama, poetry, etc.
I. Title.
PN57.L8D6   809'.93351   81-21731
ISBN 0-19-812638-7   AACR2

Set by Oxford Verbatim Limited
and Printed in Great Britain
at the University Press, Oxford
by Eric Buckley
Printer to the University

PREFACE

The story of the rape of Lucretia is one of the most familiar of all stories from the ancient world. It tells of events which supposedly occurred more than two and a half thousand years ago, leading to the expulsion of the last of the Roman kings and the establishment of the Roman Republic. To the Romans, it was a story of great political and moral importance, which helped to keep alive certain crucial ideas about the nature of kingly rule, wifely conduct, and personal and political liberty. In later times, the story became widely celebrated throughout Europe, forming the subject of many poems, tragedies, romances, novels, operas, and paintings. It also came to be seen as a contentious story, whose moral and political assumptions were often sharply attacked. Under the pressure of criticism, however, the story was subtly adjusted: new episodes were added, new constructions put upon action and motive. And in a variety of ways the story continued to grow.

I have called this story a myth; and have chosen this word to indicate not simply its dubious historicity but also its capacity to endure and to adapt to changing social contexts, accumulating power, significance, and narrative complexity with the passage of time. This book sets out to explore the myth, examining its origins and changing fortunes, and looking at some of the ways in which, over many centuries, it has been interpreted, criticized, elaborated, and transformed. Its aims are (in turn) interpretative, not encyclopaedic. It is not intended to be an exhaustive survey of all versions of the Lucretia story in European art, literature, and controversial writing, but a critical examination of certain decisive stages in the evolution of that story, and of certain versions which have seemed to be of particular interest either in their own right or for their bearing upon the larger questions which the book pursues.[1]

The first part of the book concentrates upon the actions and dilemmas of Lucretia herself, and upon the debate set in train by Augustine's remarks about her decision to take her own life after being raped by Sextus Tarquinius; a debate which in turn reflects changing ideas about the distresses and stigmas of rape, and about the ethics of suicide. Part Two looks at the role of Lucius Junius Brutus, at the various ways in which the story has been politically interpreted, especially during periods of revolution, and at changing attitudes to the character and motives of Brutus himself. The final section attempts to place the whole story in a wider context, and to suggest that changing interpretations of the story are to be seen in relation to much larger shifts of thought about Roman ideas of heroism and moral conduct; glancing at the analogous case of Cato of Utica, whose story becomes curiously intertwined with that of Lucretia and Brutus.

In examining this story, I have been especially interested in the close relationship that may exist between the creative and the philosophical processes of mind; between art and argument; and that should ideally exist also between those secondary activities conventionally known as literary or art criticism, on the one hand, and history of ideas, on the other. I have attempted to show how writers and artists have been affected, for better or for worse, by their knowledge of contemporary debates about the story; and how their works may in turn be seen to contribute to such debates, often with a subtlety which may be absent from more purely discursive writings. Conversely, I have been struck by the extent to which such discursive writings may sometimes aspire to the condition of fiction, their authors being led – sometimes seemingly unawares – into speculative fantasies about the story of Lucretia, constantly refashioning it according to their own preoccupations and assumptions.

This book itself aims to present a narrative, a story about a story; and it is therefore written in such a way as to be easily and consecutively read by general readers as well as specialists in particular fields of study.

ACKNOWLEDGEMENTS

I am greatly indebted to the many friends and acquaintances who have generously helped me with particular problems in this book, and commented upon early drafts. Some of these helpers are acknowledged in my notes; others will recognize in the text the influence of their criticism and ideas; none is responsible for the errors and deficiencies which remain. I should like to thank David Alston, Jan Białostocki, Bernhard Fabian, Sasha Grishin, Jocelyn Harris, Jennifer Montagu, Elaine Moon, Luisa Quartermaine, Jacques Sherer, J. B. Trapp, and Dale Trendall for particular guidance and advice; H. D. Jocelyn, Juliet Mitchell, Alwynne Mackie, and R. M. Ogilvie for their more extended commentaries; J. C. Eade, Julie Barton, and the editorial staff at Oxford University Press (especially Phoebe Allen, Elaine Koss, and Susan le Roux) for their help in preparing the typescript. My deepest debt is to Tamsin Donaldson, who has criticized, encouraged, and helped to shape my ideas from start to finish.

Humanities Research Centre
The Australian National University
Canberra

CONTENTS

PLATES

I

LUCRETIA

Leibniz, the founder of optimism, and a great poet as well as a profound philosopher, writes somewhere that in a temple at Memphis there was a great pyramid of globes placed one on top of the other. A priest, who was asked by a traveller what this pyramid of globes represented, replied that these were all the possible worlds and that the most perfect of all was at the summit; the traveller, who was curious to have a closer look at this most perfect of all possible worlds, climbed to the top of the pyramid, where the first thing he saw was Tarquin raping Lucretia.

Diderot to Sophie Volland, 20 October 1760[1]

The Shaping of the Myth (1):
Victims and Victors

The story of the rape of Lucretia is not one story but many
stories. The earliest surviving accounts differ from each other
on many details; and as time goes by, new variants appear, new
episodes are added. Running the earliest versions freely together, however, we may reconstruct a story that goes like this.

I

One night during their siege of the city of Ardea in the year 509
BC, a group of Roman noblemen – amongst them the sons of
the Roman king, Tarquinius Superbus – began to boast about
the virtues of their various wives. There was plenty to drink,
and boasting soon turned to argument. Tarquinius Collatinus
(a kinsman of the king) insisted that his wife, Lucretia, sur-
passed the wives of all his friends; and proposed at last that
they all ride then and there the twenty-odd miles back to Rome
and thence nine miles on to Collatia to test the point, calling
upon each wife in turn to see how she was behaving that very
night. 'Whereuppon', says Livy (in the Elizabethan translation
of William Painter), 'they rode to Rome in post'.

At their comming they found the kinges doughters, sportinge
themselues with sondrye pastimes: From thence they went to the
house of *Collatinus*, where they founde *Lucrece*, not as the other
before named, spending time in idelnes, but late in the night occupied
and busie amonges her maydes in the middes of her house spinning of
woll. The victory and prayse whereof was giuen to *Lucretia*, who
when she saw her husband, gentlie and louinglie intertained him, and
curteouslye badde the *Tarquinians* welcome.[2]

But the story was of course to have a graver outcome. On seeing this exemplary wife, Livy continues, 'Sextus Tarquinius the sonne of Tarquinius Superbus (that time the Romaine king) was incensed with a libidinous desire, to construpate and defloure Lucrece.' Tarquin's motives are variously described by several of the early narrators of the story: in Ovid's account, he is simply smitten with love; in that of Livy, less simply, he is aroused as much by Lucretia's chastity as by her beauty; for Dio Cassius, 'it was rather her reputation than her body that he desired to ruin'.[3] Tarquin returned later to Collatia. As the king's son and Collatinus' kinsman, he was courteously and unsuspectingly received by Lucretia, and given food and a room for the night. When the household was asleep, Tarquin entered Lucretia's bedroom, armed with a sword. At first he attempted to seduce the startled Lucretia by promising that he would marry her and make her his queen; then he threatened her with death if she did not let him have his way. Finding her adamant, Tarquin then tried another tactic. If she continued to resist him, he said, he would kill not only her but also his own slave (who in certain versions of the story is black), and place his naked body beside hers in the bed, swearing that he had found them together, and killed them in anger.[4] At the thought of this posthumous disgrace, Lucretia was at last overcome, and submitted to Tarquin's rape. And Tarquin went his way back to Ardea.

Next morning, Lucretia summoned her father Lucretius and her husband Collatinus, asking them each to come at once to the house with a trusted friend. Lucretius arrived with Publius Valerius; Collatinus, with Lucius Junius Brutus, a kinsman of his and of the king. Brutus was generally regarded as a half-wit; in fact his idiocy was assumed for reasons of safety: the king had murdered Brutus' father and brother to obtain their wealth, and Brutus was awaiting an opportunity for revenge. To these four men (and, in some versions of the story, to other men besides)[5] Lucretia told her story, pledging them to avenge her rape. Taking a knife from beneath her garments, she then stabbed herself in the breast. While the other men wept helplessly, Brutus, the apparent idiot, was quick to act, pulling

the bloody knife from her body and swearing by her blood –
'none more chaste till a tyrant wronged her'[6] – and by the
gods that he would drive the family of Tarquins from Rome.
Lucretia's body was displayed at Collatia and at the Forum in
Rome, where Brutus amazed the Romans with his transformed
personality and the power of his oratory, eloquently reminding
them of the tyranny of the Tarquins and of their many crimes,
of which this rape was the most recent and most outrageous.
The people rose in anger against the royal family, driving them
from Rome and vowing to have no more kings. Brutus and
Collatinus were installed as the first consuls of the Roman
Republic, Collatinus being replaced before long by Publius
Valerius; the very name, Tarquinius Collatinus, being considered by the people an intolerable reminder of the banished
race of kings.

What kind of story is this? Is it, to begin with, a true story, or
is it merely a fiction? How did it originate, how did it grow, and
how did it acquire its particular narrative shape? What is its
purpose, and what are its underlying assumptions? What kind
of imaginative power fuels the story, carrying it on its long,
now gently declining, trajectory across so many centuries? The
questions are easily multiplied, but not always easily answered.
In approaching them, we shall have to rely not simply on
historical deduction but also at times on a measure of speculation.

II

The main classical accounts of the story of Lucretia appear to
derive ultimately from older sources which survive only in
fragments or not at all.[7] The most important surviving narratives are those of Livy, published between 27 and 25 BC; of the
Greek rhetorician Dionysius of Halicarnassus, in about 7 BC;
of Ovid, a few years later; and of Plutarch, a century or so later
still. The story is also recounted by a handful of other narrators, such as Diodorus of Sicily in the first century BC and
Valerius Maximus, Florus, and Dio Cassius in (respectively)
the first, second, and third centuries AD.[8] The earliest surviving

accounts were thus all written down many centuries after the occurrence of the events they purport to describe.

This fact in itself is enough to arouse suspicion. Some historians are more suspicious than others. One extreme view is that the entire story is a fiction invented in the third century BC (by Fabius Pictor, the earliest Roman historian) in order to conceal the unpleasant fact that the last king of Rome was expelled not by a civil uprising by a foreign power.[9] Another is that it is not really a Roman story at all, but rather an elaboration of a legend belonging to certain religious cults in Ardea, which were brought to Rome only in the second half of the fourth century BC.[10] Neither of these views has won universal acceptance amongst historians. R. M. Ogilvie, the leading authority on the early books of Livy, takes a more eclectic approach, not denying that the story may conceivably have grown out of actual events, but noting also the way in which it has been shaped and improved by the passage of time, incorporating elements of fiction, folklore, and transferred fact.[11] Lucius Junius Brutus, for example, may have been a real person, though his character as presented in this story is evidently the product of much fictitious elaboration, and contains a number of logical and chronological oddities.[12] Other characters in the story – Lucretia's father, Lucretius, for example – seem to be pure invention. The story as a whole is rather too carefully arranged to be altogether convincing. Livy's narrative in particular is so strikingly dramatic as to have aroused speculation about an actual theatrical source, and to have eased many a later adaptation of the story for the stage. The men's debate about the wives and their surprise visit at night – episodes that occur in some, but not all, versions of the story – have seemed to some commentators to be suspiciously like scenes out of New Comedy.[13] The picture of Lucretia and her women busy at the hearth is a familiar classical idyll of a kind to be found elsewhere, for example, in the writings of Tibullus.[14] In Ovid's account, the scene is sentimentally elaborated: Lucretia is discovered making a cloak for her absent husband, and weeping as she imagines the dangers of war to which he may be exposed. 'Fear not, I've come,' says Collatinus, and takes her in his arms.

Such features may be largely a matter of narrative heightening, the familiar liberties and elaborations of the early historians and poets. More perplexing and intriguing is the existence of a number of analogues to the story of Lucretia. The fundamental feature of the story, that of a tyrant unexpectedly endangered or overthrown because of a sexual transgression — his own, or that of a close relative — recurs in several other ancient tales of Greece and Rome. There is the story of the friends Harmodius and Aristogeiton, for example, who in about 514 BC attempted to deliver Athens from the tyranny of the brothers Hipparchus and Hippias, the sons of Pisistratus. Hipparchus tried to seduce Harmodius; finding himself unsuccessful, he then tried to bring public disgrace upon Harmodius' sister by summoning her to take part in a religious procession, and then declaring her unworthy of this honour. Angered by these sexual insults, Harmodius and Aristogeiton conspired to murder Hipparchus; Hippias, in attempting to avenge this murder, was himself driven from Athens not long afterwards. These events are contemporary with those related in the story of Lucretia.[15] Or again, there is the story of Virginia, stabbed to death by her father Virginius in Rome in 450 BC so that she might not fall into the hands of the decemvir Appius Claudius; her death triggered off the plebeian uprising that was to end the tyranny of the Decemvirate. These stories are all closely intertwined: the story of Lucretia may owe much to that of Harmodius and Aristogeiton, and the story of Appius and Virginia appears to be merely a reworking of the story of Lucretia.[16]

And there are other, tantalizingly similar, stories, in which the steadfastness of a woman serves as a moral example to an oppressed people, inciting them to revolt. There is the story of Xenocrite of Cumae, for example, and the tyrant Aristodemus. Aristodemus forced the people of Cumae to undertake humiliatingly menial labours, just as the Tarquins had done in Rome when they ordered the construction of the Great Sewer; in each case it was felt that the tasks were more suited to slaves or conquered people than to those who were free. Aristodemus took sexual advantage of Xenocrite with the same seignorial spirit that Sextus Tarquinius displayed towards Lucretia. One day another woman of Cumae, seeing the tyrant coming, stepped out of his way and covered her face, saying that he was the only man of Cumae. The remark shamed the men of Cumae, and stirred Xenocrite to urge them to rebel against Aristodemus and recover their lost freedom.[17]

Though the existence of such analogues may cast a further shadow of doubt over the literal credibility of the story of Lucretia, it does nothing to diminish the story's historical interest and significance. True or false, the story remains, as Pierre Bayle puts it, 'one of the hinges on which the history of the Romans turns'.[18] That the story takes the form it does – a form shared to some extent by other, rather similar, stories – may indicate that from earliest times it has been subjected to a certain deliberate narrative shaping; a shaping that is satisfying not merely in aesthetic terms, but in other ways as well. Though the story may well contain elements of historical fact, these elements – along with others which are clearly fictitious – appear to have been fashioned into a powerful aetiological myth, intended to rehearse and to explain the origins of certain fundamental Roman ideals. It is a story about public and political behaviour, and about private, sexual behaviour, and about the relationship between these two kinds of behaviour. It is a story about the nature of liberty: liberty for the state, and liberty for the individual. Certain correspondences between political and domestic events are implied. The political tyranny of Tarquinius Superbus is mirrored in the sexual tyranny of his son, Sextus Tarquinius.[19] Lucius Junius Brutus – *liberator*, as Livy calls him – achieves political liberty for Rome, as Lucretia by her suicide achieves personal liberty (in a sense that Seneca, and later, David Hume, would have understood and approved);[20] it is significant that Brutus vows to free Rome while holding the dagger with which Lucretia has killed herself.

The private and public aspects of the story are intimately related and carefully balanced; yet those who reworked or commented on the story in later times often tended to ignore one aspect and highlight the other. Those who saw the story as primarily concerned with questions of sexual behaviour saw Lucretia as its central actor. Those who saw the story as primarily political in meaning, on the other hand, saw Brutus as the central actor, sometimes curtly dismissing what an eighteenth-century English adaptor called *'that excrescent Action* of Lucretia'[21] as marginal to the main point and interest of the story. In those versions in which Brutus is the principal figure, the focus often shifts to events which occurred after the death of Lucretia: to the discovery in the new Republic of a plot to restore the Tarquins, and the involvement in this plot of Brutus' own sons, Titus and Tiberius, whom Brutus rigorously condemns to death. The character of Brutus – dark, wounded, fiercely single-minded, hiding his deeper feelings under masks of stupidity and Stoicism – exercises a particular spell upon writers and artists. In the second section of this book we shall look at some of the ways in which Brutus was regarded, and in which the story was shaped and reshaped as a political fable and myth of revolution. But for the present our focus is on that part of the story which principally concerns Lucretia.

So far from being 'excrescent' to the political part of the story, the rape of Lucretia is intricately related to it by a series of formal analogies and correspondences. In many versions of the story, the political symbolism is plain: Lucretia is not simply Lucretia, but the figure of violated Rome; the rape epitomizes the wider tyranny of the Tarquins. The symbolism of the story runs two ways: if Rome is like Lucretia, Lucretia is also like Rome and its neighbouring cities. Tarquin lays siege to her in much the same spirit as he besieges Ardea, infiltrating himself into her confidence in much the same manner as he had once infiltrated himself into the confidence of the people of Gabii – enemies who, to their cost, gave him a friendly welcome when he came to them pretending to be a fugitive from the cruelty of his father, and allowed him command over their military forces. *Cepimus audendo Gabios quoque*, says Tarquin to himself in Ovid's version of the story, 'By daring we captured Gabii too'. These correspondences are to become particularly prominent in Shakespeare's version of the story. Shakespeare's Tarquin, thinking of Collatine, speaks of 'This siege that hath engirt his marriage'. Shakespeare's

Lucrece is reminded of Tarquin's treacherous· behaviour towards her when, after her rape, she looks at a tapestry depicting the fall of Troy, and sees the figure of Sinon, who entered Troy through an act of military deception similar to Tarquin's deception of the people of Gabii.[22]

That we talk of the rape of a country as well as of the rape of a woman is more than a matter of mere lexical coincidence; the linguistic and metaphorical association hints at other deeper associations of a psychological and behavioural kind.[23] The symbolic equations lend the story a certain symmetry, yet at the same time possibly diminish it in human terms. By converting a woman into a symbol (or an object of veneration), you may partly obscure the fact that her story is actually a dispiriting one, her real sphere of activity sharply delimited. It is through women, writes Simone de Beauvoir, that certain historical 'events have been set off, but the women have been pretexts rather than agents. The suicide of Lucretia has had value only as a symbol.'[24] The agent in this story is a man, Brutus; Lucretia, the woman, merely suffers. The classical narrators praise her to the extent of saying that she is like a man, but also make it clear that her possibilities of action are circumscribed by the fact that she is a woman. For Ovid, Lucretia is *animi matrona virilis,* a matron of manly courage. Valerius Maximus calls her one who, through an unhappy error of fortune, has a masculine spirit in a female body. In Dio Cassius' account, she knows precisely what her sex permits her to do and restrains her from doing: 'Now I, because I am a woman, will treat my case as becomes me,' she says before her death; 'but do you, if you are men and care for your children, avenge me, free yourselves, and show the tyrants what manner of men you are and what manner of woman of yours they have outraged.' Brutus disdains the tears of Collatinus and Lucretius as womanish, and taunts the Romans by reminding them that they have become effeminate, urging them (in Livy's version) to take up the sword 'as befitted men and Romans, against those who had treated them as enemies'. Lucretia, though she is also a Roman, is a Roman woman, and may not act in such a way. In certain late versions of the story, Lucretia pursues Tarquin with her dagger in hell; but this is a rare touch, and quite at odds with the main emphasis which is found in all early versions of the story.[25] Revenge, retaliation, hitting back at the enemy – all these are tasks for men, not for the injured woman; male pride is offended by the rape, and must be satisfied by an answering act of male aggression. The Old Testament heroine Judith boldly goes to the tent of her enemy Holofernes and returns with his severed head; Lucretia, on the other hand, takes up the sword only against herself. Totally without blame, she nevertheless diverts her energies inwards, inflicting upon herself the ultimate punishment.

The fact that Lucretia should find it necessary to kill herself may seem explicable partly in terms of the status of women in Roman society. Searching for a possible modern parallel, we may think of the many Muslim women who killed themselves after being raped during the recent war in Bangladesh, knowing that their men would not take them back.[26] In a society in which a woman is regarded as a subordinate and property of her husband, her rape, even if she has resisted and detested it, may seem to bring disgrace not merely upon her, but – more importantly – upon her husband. The woman kills herself rather in the same spirit in which a junior minister, innocently caught up in a public scandal, might resign rather than bring down his prime minister and government.

There are hints in some versions of the story that might support an interpretation along these lines. In Shakespeare's *The Rape of Lucrece*, Lucrece's husband Collatine and her father Lucretius actually squabble over the question of their relative proprietorial rights in the dead woman; in Nathaniel Lee's *Lucius Junius Brutus* (1680), Collatinus likewise contends with Brutus:

> For who has that propriety of sorrow,
> Who dares to claim an equal share with me?
> (I. 421–2)

Furthermore – taking a broader view of the matter – we might notice that the story is much concerned with the idea of transferred shame and transferred penalties. Sextus Tarquinius rapes Lucretia, and his father Tarquinius Superbus loses his kingdom. Tarquinius Superbus is a bad king, and his kinsman Tarquinius Collatinus suffers on that account by losing his consulship, the bonds of kinship again unexpectedly pulling down someone who is not the main agent of the action. Lucius Junius Brutus, despite his relationship to the Tarquins, manages to survive this chain reaction purely because of his fierce and lonely moral integrity, his ability to sever all bonds of kinship, all family feelings, in the interests of the larger family of the state, going to the lengths of condemning his own sons to death, and being celebrated after his own death as the father of his country.[27] By a similar act of heroic self-abnegation, Lucretia also prevents moral pollution passing along a family line.[28] Similar, but radically different: for while the innocent Brutus punishes his guilty sons, the equally innocent Lucretia punishes her innocent self. Brutus, being a man, sacrifices his feelings; Lucretia, being a woman, sacrifices her life.

Yet such an explanation, whatever its value in sociological terms, does not fully account for the way in which the story has traditionally been perceived and mythologized. In most versions of the story Lucretia is scarcely presented as though she were a natural subordinate, or as a figure at all comparable to the suiciding women of Bangladesh. On the contrary: many who deal with this subject choose rather to highlight the paradoxical power which Lucretia manages to wield, while being the victim of two violent acts, one performed by Tarquin, the other by herself. Lucretia's suicide is often presented as a moral triumph, an act which establishes her superiority not merely to her fate and ravisher, but also to her husband Collatinus, who in most versions of the story cuts a somewhat foolish figure, bragging of his wife's chastity without understanding or valuing its true worth, and being pushed aside (so to speak) by Brutus, Lucretia's champion and avenger.[29] Not merely that: her suicide is often seen — particularly in visual depictions of the subject — as an act which in some ways resembles, mocks, and counters the act which Tarquin himself has performed. To see how the story acquires this shape, we may turn to the painters.

III

Perhaps the best known of all the many paintings of this story is Titian's *Tarquin and Lucretia* (plate one), completed around 1570 when Titian was already over eighty. At the left of the painting is the slave whom Tarquin has promised to kill if Lucretia refuses to submit; yet here he has the air less of a possible victim than of an abettor, a fellow conspirator, holding back the curtains of Lucretia's bed to assist Tarquin and also, perhaps, to get a glimpse of Lucretia for himself. He remains, however, in the shadows; and the shadows are amongst the most remarkable features of this remarkable painting. The light spills from the top left of the painting across to the right, falling generously on Lucretia's face and body and upon the whiteness of her linen and of the mass of pillows that bolster her upright. The light catches the very tip of Tarquin's dagger, the tear on Lucretia's cheek, the bracelet on her right arm, which is held aloft as though appealing eloquently to heaven, and – at the exact vertical centre of the painting – the wedding ring on her left hand, which attempts forlornly to ward off her attacker. The dynamism of the moment is caught in the superb composition of limbs, the bodies seemingly locked together by a nervous intensity of gaze. Despite the high colour of her face, Lucretia is pale beside Tarquin's darker skin – a tonal contrast which possibly hints at the racial, as well as purely sexual, oppositions of the story: Lucretia is a Roman, Tarquin an Etruscan. Yet Tarquin is also dark in other ways: the shadow falls across part of his face, and there are depths of shadow behind him. The light catches his back: the scarlet of his stockings, the plum breeches, the ginger beard, the fiery reds that indicate his temperament. His clothes seem in a sense the important thing about him. A simple question must occur to many who look at this painting: why should Tarquin, moving from his bedchamber to Lucretia's late at night and bent upon rape, be depicted as wearing all those clothes? And why, for that matter, should the chaste Lucretia at this stage of the proceedings be in a state of total nudity? The problem recurs in numerous other paintings of the same subject. In a mid-seventeenth-century Florentine painting, for example (plate two), a naked Lucretia is assaulted by a Tarquin dressed in an elaborately buttoned garment whose pushed-back sleeves – like those of Titian's Tarquin – are the sole indications of déshabille. Other Tarquins are even more formidably and improbably clad in armour, spurs, and plumed helmets, with hefty swords belted to their sides. Naked Tarquins, such as Thomas Rowlandson's (plate three), are rarely encountered, and never, it would seem, in the company of clothed Lucretias.[30]

It is equally curious, if we continue to think in narrowly realistic terms, that Lucretia should so often be depicted by Renaissance artists as naked at the moment of her suicide. Take Lucas Cranach's drawing of c. 1525, for example, one of his many treatments of this subject (plate five: compare plates six, eight, and nine). Lucretia stands alone, gazing placidly towards us as though into a mirror, her fur gown falling from her shoulders to reveal a body adorned only by ringlets, a necklace, and tissues of gauze; her knife is just beginning to enter the body, but her face gives no hint of pain or even of discomfort. This is one of the commonest Renaissance ways of depicting Lucretia's suicide.[31] Yet Lucretia's nakedness and also her solitude at this moment are in direct conflict with the classical sources, which stress the fact that she killed herself not in private but before witnesses, all of whom were men, not all of them members of her own family. Most of the narrators refer specifically to the fact that Lucretia was dressed at the time; Ovid says that her last thought was to wrap her clothes about her modestly as she fell[32] – a touch which Chaucer liked well enough to borrow in his account of Lucretia's death in *The Legend of Good Women*, and which Addison was later to discuss with approval in *Spectator* no. 292.

The only known surviving depictions of Lucretia's suicide in classical art are on three Etruscan funerary urns of the first century BC. In one of these, Lucretia is shown not decorously draped as a Roman matron ought to be, but naked from the waist up. Lucretia's semi-nudity here has been taken as evidence that the representation is a hostile one, presenting an Etruscan rather than Roman view of the story: the half-naked

Lucretia is perhaps to be seen not as a model of virtue but as a woman who has sought out Tarquin as a lover and killed herself after being rejected or abandoned by him.[33] In Renaissance art, the nudity of Lucretia obviously has quite different implications. The painters evidently abandon the tradition of the modestly clothed Lucretia not out of lack of sympathy for their subject but for other reasons. Why?

One obvious explanation is that painters are seldom classical scholars, sticklers for getting things right; often they may be more interested in the technical challenges and aesthetic pleasures that may come from deviations out of the narrow traditions of the classical stories they illustrate. They may simply be delighting in the beauty of the naked female body, and tacitly inviting us to share that delight. Yet if such is the case, we may well feel our enjoyment tempered by an uncomfortable sense that we are being manoeuvred into a position similar to that of Tarquin's slave, gazing voyeuristically at Lucretia's nakedness, and that such enjoyment is very much at odds with the principal moral impulse of the original story. The difficulty is mitigated, though not entirely removed, by a second and equally obvious explanation. The painters are inviting us to look at their subjects not in entirely realistic terms, but with an eye to symbolic possibilities. The disposition of light in Titian's painting, the upright position of Lucretia's upper body, have a suggestiveness which reaches beyond naturalism. Lucretia's nakedness, both in Titian's painting and in other paintings, suggests not merely her beauty but also her vulnerability and her innocence. Tarquin's clothes seem to make him impregnable as his victim is not. His body, like his motives, is concealed: 'Thou art not what thou seem'st,' says Shakespeare's Lucrece. Where Tarquin is depicted as naked, as in Rowlandson's drawing (plate three), the effect is significantly different, the symbolism receding and the starkness of contrast between rapist and victim being sharply diminished. Despite the exaggeratedly bunched muscles of his back and shoulders, Rowlandson's Tarquin seems curiously, indeed almost risibly, vulnerable and lacking in menace.

The symbolism of nakedness is extended in an interesting way in Lorenzo Lotto's *A Lady as Lucretia* (plate seven). The subject of this painting is probably a Venetian lady named Lucrezia Valier, who in 1533 married Benedetto Pesaro; the painting is probably to be dated around 1534.[34] Lotto depicts Lucrezia Pesaro, by way of compliment and graceful allusion, in relation to her famous classical forebear. He wants to suggest that Lucrezia Pesaro has the same sort of chastity and courage as the Roman matron Lucretia, but at the same time naturally wishes to avoid any suggestion that she has suffered a similar fate. Thus Lucrezia Pesaro holds a picture of her name-sake, but holds it at arm's length, gesturing with her other hand towards it as though to indicate that she understands, but does not share, Lucretia's predicament, that she admires Lucretia's actions and the words which Livy tells us she uttered before her suicide, and which are here written on a scrap of paper beneath the picture of the suiciding Lucretia: NEC VLLA IMPVDICA LVCRETIAE EXEMPLO VIVET, 'Never shall Lucretia provide a precedent for unchaste women to escape what they deserve.' Lucrezia Pesaro looks us boldly in the eye, as though to assert plainly that she herself has no cause for shame. The Roman Lucretia in the inner picture looks only to heaven. She is naked, her hair falling loose and dishevelled about her shoulders. The Venetian Lucrezia wears her hair bound back and surmounted by a wig; despite her bare neck and shoulders, an important effect of the painting derives from the fact that she is dressed – dressed in a voluminous gown of dull gold and shining bottle green, whose sleeves are fashionably puffed and slit. The contrast between the clothed and unclothed figures is again striking. Part of the contrast, we might think, is that between an un-fallen and a fallen woman – the reverse of Eve and her fig-leaves. Yet the contrast does not reflect as severely as that upon the Roman Lucretia, who is instead, in the most literal of ways, being held up for our admiration and emulation. As in Cranach's paintings, her nakedness suggests her vulnerability, and also – symbolically – her purity and truth.[35]

Other features of these paintings also work in a symbolic rather than in a naturalistic way. Titian's painting, for example, depicts not the rape itself but the incident preparatory to the rape, in which Tarquin threatens to kill Lucretia if she does not give in to him. The raised knife is of great importance, and one needs no special schooling in Freudian psychology to understand its significance and to recognize how the painting works symbolically and analogically. The effect is more obvious in the cruder version of the painting (probably not by Titian himself) which is now at Bordeaux (plate four). One act of violence suggests another.

Much the same kind of symbolism is evident in many of the representations of Lucretia's suicide, such as those of Cranach. Michel Leiris in the first volume of his autobiography, *L'Âge d'homme,* discusses Cranach's Dresden panels of Lucretia and Judith (plate eight). His account is highly (and consciously) subjective: Leiris is exploring himself through the paintings quite as much as he is exploring the paintings themselves. Yet there is force in Leiris's suggestion that the knife which Cranach's Lucretia is holding seems to be sexually symbolic, and that in a curious way she appears to be preparing 'to cancel, by a parallel act, the effect of the rape which she has suffered'.[36] This impression is possibly even stronger in other versions of the same subject by Cranach which Leiris does not look at (plates six and nine). It is as though Cranach, with wonderful symbolic compression, is calling up simultaneously the two central events of the story, the rape and the suicide, which other artists – Botticelli, for example, and an anonymous German engraver of 1674 (plates ten and eleven) – sometimes presented side by side in different panels or sections of the same painting. (The German engraving shows in the inner scene at the left a naked Lucretia about to be raped by Tarquin, and, on the right, a clothed Lucretia killing herself in the presence of the men. At the open window hangs a parrot, emblem of talkativeness: the story is soon to be spread to the world beyond.)

But the symbolism of the knife is not merely sexual. Knives play a central part in the entire story of Lucretia. Tarquin menaces Lucretia with a knife, Lucretia kills herself with a knife, Brutus swears upon the same knife to drive the Tarquins from Rome, as do his companions.[37] In Gavin Hamilton's painting, *The Oath of Brutus* (plate twelve), we see the conspirators already beginning to draw their own daggers, preparing to move against the Tarquins. Botticelli's *Tragedy of Lucretia* (plate ten) shows a threefold scene: at the left, Tarquin threatens Lucretia with a knife; at the right, Lucretia is supported by friends, having stabbed herself with a knife which, in the central panel, is still to be seen protruding from her body. Brutus orates in the Forum in the midst of a veritable forest of weapons, slanting this way and that in apparent abandon as the men vent their grief and rage, but soon to move in concert against the family of Roman kings. The knife turns, one might say, against the original aggressors. Much of the beauty of the story consists in the paradoxical power and ultimate triumph of the apparent victim. Lucretia in Cranach's painting of 1533 stands alone and exposed: slim, frail, naked. Yet as her look of serene composure tells us, she is not defeated. Her knife is poised, ready to enter her body; when it strikes her, it also strikes her enemies, driving them from Rome for ever. In Cranach's Dresden panels Lucretia is paired, not contrasted, with Judith. In Botticelli's painting a statue of David holding the head of Goliath stands high above the dead Lucretia in the Forum; near David is Judith with the head of Holofernes. Judith and Lucretia are joined as women of power, who in their different ways manage, despite their apparent frailty, to bring down their enemies, as David brings down Goliath. What the painters accentuate here is an element already present in the earliest version of the story. *Quid victor gaudes? haec te victoria perdet*, writes Ovid in rhetorical question to Tarquin after the rape: 'Why, victor, do you rejoice? This victory will ruin you.' Despite her apparent passivity, subservience, and self-destruction, Lucretia is the ultimate victor.

In Tiepolo's painting *Tarquin and Lucretia* (plate thirteen) the ambiguities of the situation are brilliantly captured by means of a visual pun. Tarquin stands menacingly above and behind Lucretia, who sits upright, clutching apprehensively with her left hand the sheets of the bed, while her right hand reaches upwards to grasp the surrounding curtains. Tarquin's right arm half-circles Lucretia so that his dagger points at the front of her body; yet the painting is composed in such a way that it may also appear that it is Lucretia herself, not Tarquin, who grasps the knife, as she will shortly do when she kills herself.[38] Once again, several distinct episodes in the story (the threat, the rape, the suicide) have been conflated, prompting us to ask who holds the knife, who wields the ultimate power? Who is the victim, who the victor?

One last point needs to be added. What we are looking at here is a mythology, not real life; a mythology invented, sustained, and extended largely by men. It is significant that the number of women who have chosen to treat this subject in literature and the visual arts is exceedingly small. The covert excitements of the story, the exaltation of Lucretia as a symbol, the paradox of her inner power, seem – for obvious reasons – to have had a lesser appeal to the female than to the male imagination. 'The suicide of Lucretia has had value only as a symbol': and as Simone de Beauvoir's phrase implies, there must always be an appeal open from symbolism to life. In real life a woman who is raped is unlikely to feel any intimations of power or of triumph, especially if she is unfortunate enough to be driven to suicide by the event. In admiring the skill with which the myth is imaginatively elaborated, it is difficult not to be aware of the way in which those elaborations at times run counter to such familiar human truths.

One of the very few women painters to have tackled the subject is Artemisia Gentileschi, for whom the Lucretia story may well have had particular significance. In 1612 Artemisia Gentileschi's art teacher Agostino Tassi, a man notorious for his sexual and criminal escapades, was tried for the rape of Artemisia in the spring of the previous year. After a five-month trial in which Tassi blandly denied the charges and Artemisia was tortured with a thumb-screw during cross-examination, Tassi was finally acquitted. Artemisia's painting *Tarquin and Lucretia* (plate fourteen; *c*.1645–50) reveals little of the disturbance, or the individual strength, one might expect to find in her depiction of a subject of this kind. She works almost entirely within the conventions established by male artists such as Titian who had already treated the subject. A black slave draws aside the curtains of Lucretia's bed in much the same manner as the slave does in Titian's painting (plate one), disclosing the scene enacted within. A naked Lucretia, one hand held aloft like Titian's Lucretia, turns her body towards us, while her face looks back at Tarquin's upraised knife: she reveals herself to the spectator even as she attempts to conceal herself from her aggressor. The suggestion of display in the disposition of Lucretia's body and the tacit invitation to voyeurism in the painting as a whole (equally to be found in male treatments of the subject, and in many other male paintings of the nude female body)[39] hint at a central conflict of purpose which, in this context, may seem especially surprising. Tarquin stands above Lucretia in a pose reminiscent of Titian's Tarquin. Like Titian's Tarquin, he is elaborately clad, and his garments billow decoratively out behind him. The whole painting has a frozen, static quality, from which violence is curiously absent. (Contrast the relative forcefulness implied by the position of Tarquin's right knee in Titian's painting, and that of his left hand, in Gentileschi's.) Possibly by adopting this style of depiction Artemisia was attempting to place at some distance a subject painfully close to her own experience. Whatever the case, this female interpretation does not basically question, disturb, or refashion the predominantly male myth. A brutal experience is again ameliorated through art, and is transformed into an experience aesthetically pleasing to the beholder.[40]

But the story of Lucretia also presents and provokes quite other problems and transformations; to some of which we now may turn.

1. Titian, *Tarquin and Lucretia*, c.1570.

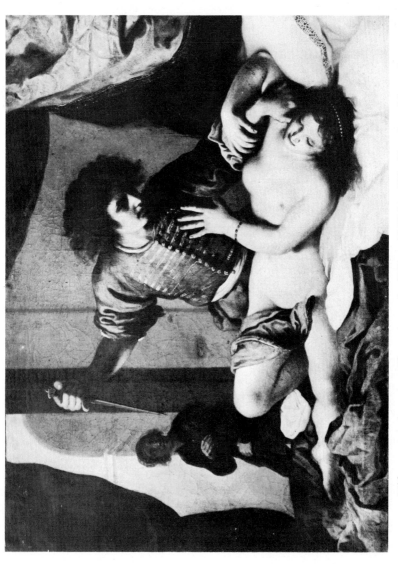

2. Mid-seventeenth-century Florentine artist (Biliverti? Ficherelli?), *Tarquin and Lucretia*.

3. Thomas Rowlandson, *The Rape of Lucrece*; watermark 181(6?). A majolica plate dated 1538 from Gubbio, now in the Musée du Petit Palais, Paris, bears a closely similar design, with Tarquin dressed and helmeted.

4. School of Titian, *Tarquin and Lucretia*.

5. Lucas Cranach, *Lucretia*, *c*.1525 (the date 1509 shown in the picture is a later addition).

6. Cranach, *Lucretia*, *c*.1525.

The Questioning of the Myth (1):
Augustine's 'Dilemma'

Why should a victim of rape, whose own moral conduct has been in every way beyond reproach, nevertheless feel obliged on account of this act to take her own life? Although today we may be in a better position to understand some of the psychological factors of shock, depression, and humiliation that might lead a raped woman to suicide, the idea of such a death being socially encouraged and admired is for most people today both perplexing and morally repellent. It is what chiefly makes the story strange for us, an alien myth; between our values and those of ancient Rome there seems to be an unbridgeable gap. This sense of strangeness and discomfort is not new; it has been expressed in one form or another – though not without contention – since at least the fifth century AD. How the gap opens, how the new sensibility shows itself, is the subject of this chapter.

I

Why does Lucretia die? This problem is raised in an indirect way in the classical versions of the story. It is not resolved, nor is it felt to be deeply troublesome. In Livy's account, Lucretia makes it plain to the men that she is not herself guilty. 'My body only has been violated,' she says, 'my heart is innocent: death will be my witness': *ceterem corpus est tantum violatum, animus insons, mors testis erit*. But if that is the case, say the men, then there is surely no need to die.

One after another they tried to comfort her. They told her she was helpless, and therefore innocent, that he alone was guilty. It was the mind, they said, that sinned, not the body: without intention there could never be guilt.

'What is due to him', Lucretia said, 'is for you to decide. As for me, I am innocent of fault, but I will take my punishment. Never shall Lucretia provide a precedent for unchaste women to escape what they deserve.' With these words she drew a knife from under her robe, drove it into her heart, and fell forward, dead.[1]

The men's remarks about Lucretia's innocence are intended to cheer her up, not to disconcert; the men want her to live, but do not see her readiness for death as morally questionable. The fact that she will kill herself despite their assurances that her death is not demanded by logic or necessity is a sign of Lucretia's moral perfectionism rather than her moral fallibility. Her death is indeed the ultimate sign of her innocence, her crowning act of virtue.

The principal reason which Lucretia offers for her death may seem curious, none the less. Her death, she says, will prevent other women who have willingly committed adultery from citing her case as a precedent and thus escaping the normal Roman punishment for adultery, death. It is as though Lucretia, while being convinced that she is unlike a common adulteress, nevertheless feels that it would be too complicated to distinguish her own case in terms of law or logic, and simpler just to kill herself. She moves unflinchingly to death with a heroism whose guiding principles seem to lie beyond the reach of logic. Much heroic behaviour, of course, is like this: grandly stupid, unamenable to logical analysis; the gratuitous and irrational element, the reckless abandonment of the opportunity to act safely and sensibly, are precisely what make such behaviour heroic. Yet to appreciate and admire it, we need to understand the force of other, more powerful, imperatives, whose demands may at exceptional moments override those of logic. In Lucretia's case, it may not at first be obvious what those imperatives are.

They stem, perhaps, from a basic sense that certain sorts of predicaments are more intolerable than death itself; and that certain sorts of disgrace, brought about by no fault of one's own, can be countered and effaced only by death. Dionysius of

Halicarnassus reports that Tarquin offers Lucretia 'death with dishonour or life with happiness': Lucretia rejects both alternatives. After the rape, Lucretia in this version of the story goes to her father and tells him that she has suffered 'worse things than death'. Her actions inspire Brutus to tell the Romans they must choose 'life with liberty or death with glory'; they declare 'that they would rather die a thousand deaths in defence of their liberty than suffer such outrages to be committed by the tyrants'. Lucretia's suicide reminds both men and women that certain values matter more than life itself; that there are fates worse than death.[2]

In seeking to explain Lucretia's suicide, it is necessary also to recall the way in which rape would have been regarded in the society in which Lucretia lived. Sexual intercourse between a wife and a man other than her husband was seen at this time as an act which mysteriously and irretrievably tainted the woman concerned. No distinction was made in this matter between adultery and rape, for the polluting effect of both acts was thought to be the same; hence the men's reassurances to Lucretia on the subject of intention and guilt might well have been seen by Lucretia as only partly comforting, and ultimately rather beside the point.[3] To the ancient Romans, the contamination of illicit sex was not confined to the parties immediately concerned. There was a strong sense of what a modern anthropologist has called 'transferred pollution'.[4] A woman's family was thought to be tainted by her adultery, in particular her husband and any children she might subsequently bear, whether to him or to her partner in adultery. In versions of the Lucretia story until at least as late as the eighteenth century, the issue of Lucretia's possible pregnancy as a result of the rape figures prominently and is sometimes offered as a principal reason why she should take her own life. In Hugh Downman's tragedy *Lucius Junius Brutus* (1779), for example, Collatinus comforts Lucretia after the rape and tells her that they can still have many happy years of life together; soon, perhaps, they may have children. The effect of this last remark upon Lucretia is electrifying:

Didst thou say children! –
Oh, 'tis a thought which darted cross my brain
Like to the blasting lightning – Children, saidst thou!
Who knows – how if – the ravisher! That thought
Would of itself determine.[5]

And at once Lucretia proceeds to stab herself. To Downman and his contemporaries, one of the problems about a pregnancy as a result of rape or adultery was that it posed a threat to the structure of the family, and hence to the question of succession and inheritance.

'Confusion of progeny constitutes the essence of the crime,' declared Dr Johnson roundly on the subject of adultery; 'and therefore a woman who breaks her marriage vows is much more criminal than a man who does it.'[6] To the Romans, however, something more than criminality was at issue; the pollution caused by rape or adultery was essentially a religious matter, affecting the woman and her immediate family in a deeper and continuing way. Such pollution could be removed only by the woman's death.

Under Roman law at that time, a husband had the right to kill an adulterous wife, after consultation with the family council; later, a father was vested with similar powers in respect of an adulterous daughter. (Unsurprisingly, a wife had no rights against an adulterous husband.[7]) Alan Watson has recently suggested that Lucretia's summoning of her husband and father and their friends may reveal the outlines of an actual legal situation: this group of men might be seen as constituting the *iudicium domesticum* or family council which could pass judgement upon Lucretia for her part in the events which have occurred.[8] An earlier commentator, Charles Appleton, has indicated other technical reasons why Lucretia may have felt compelled to take her own life, despite the fact that this council absolves her from blame. For one thing – a fact that was to bother a number of later adaptors of the story – Lucretia had actually *consented* to Tarquin's rape, as a witness to the act, Tarquin's slave, could testify. In order for the vendetta against the Tarquins to begin, it may have been necessary for an act of unambiguous physical violence to have occurred. With Lucretia's suicide, blood is shed, and blood may now be sought: vengeance is set in train.[9]

A pre-emptive suicide such as Lucretia's might be interpreted also as an attempt to restore a lost image of former virtue. By destroying her future, the raped woman is attempting simultaneously to destroy a part of her past. M. D. Faber has viewed the suicide of Shakespeare's Lucrece in much these terms. 'She is not interested only in dying,' says Faber, 'she is also interested in resurrecting through death the late-defiled honorable wife of Collatinus. That is to say, she is driven, in large measure, by what the suicidologist would probably call magical thinking.'[10] Though this motive is neither more nor less prominent in Shakespeare's poem than in most other versions of the Lucretia story, the general truth of this observation may be recognized. The ultimate act of physical violence administered by the woman to herself is intended to cancel the earlier act of physical violence, administered to her by another: an act which can apparently be digested or countered in no other way. Like a religious sacrifice, the suicide seems to cleanse the effects of pollution, and to restore lost purity and innocence.[11]

II

To the early Christians, there was evidently nothing very problematical about the death of Lucretia. The early Fathers of the Christian Church did not quarrel with the notion that a woman's honour is a treasure more precious than life, or with the notion that life should be laid down in order to save this treasure or atone for its loss. St. Jerome speaks with the warmest admiration of women who have valued their chastity so dearly as to kill themselves – and, in some cases, kill the men who have attempted to dishonour them as well – rather than live on in shame.[12] Roman and Christian ideals of female heroism are not at this stage fundamentally at odds here, and Lucretia takes her place in both Jerome's and Tertullian's lists of admirable women, pagan and Christian.[13] True, says Tertullian, Lucretia did not act from the same high motives that might inspire a Christian to take her life in similar circumstances, knowing nothing of the Christian God or Christian heaven; true, too, that we must not praise Lucretia at the expense of those who choose to preserve their chastity by taking holy orders: 'Easier it is to lay down your life because you have lost a blessing than to keep by living that for which you would rather die outright.'[14] Yet Lucretia was a virtuous heathen whose example might be remembered and emulated by Christians. The early Church could draw its inspiration for martyrdom from the ancient world in this way without any very obvious sense of strain.

The very high value placed upon virginity made female martyrdom a subject of particular interest to the Church, and there were many Christian women who were renowned for acting with Lucretia-like resolution. Eusebius reports that the Emperor Maxentius found it difficult to rape Christian women, who preferred to kill themselves rather than allow him any liberties. The best-known of these women was a matron named Sophronia, who, when approached by the Emperor's men, asked for a few minutes' privacy so that she might adorn herself suitably to meet the Emperor; when she did not reappear, the men entered her room and found her with a dagger in her breast.[15] A celebrated female martyr of the Church whose case was often compared with that of Lucretia was the virgin Pelagia, who, with her mother Domnina and sister had drowned herself (or, according to another version of the story, flung herself from a roof-top) in order to avoid being raped as a punishment for failing to throw incense to heathen idols.[16] Pelagia's death was celebrated in the Christian calendar; her predicament and actions, like those of Lucretia, were to be the subject of much agonized analysis in later centuries.

Lucretia's reputation as a virtuous pagan is never wholly eclipsed in later centuries. Dante sees Lucretia on the enamelled green in the company of other 'great spirits by the sight of whom I am uplifted in myself' – Plato, Socrates, Seneca, and others, and *quel Bruto che cacciò Tarquino*, 'that Brutus who drove out Tarquin'.[17] Chaucer in *The Legend of Good Women* goes further, presenting Lucretia almost as a Christian figure, whose actions prompt one to think of Christ's words on the stead-fastness of women, and who in Rome (he believes) was held to be 'A seynt, and ever hir day yhalwed dere/As in hir lawe'.[18] In Renaissance art Lucretia is sometimes presented as a quasi-Christian figure. Francesco Trevisani, for example (plate fifteen), depicts Lucretia in the posture of a dying Christian martyr, one arm flamboyantly aloft, eyes cast imploringly to heaven, her coronet of pearls discreetly suggestive of the crown of life her virtuous actions may have won her.[19] Marcantonio Raimondi's dying Lucretia (c.1511–12; plate seventeen) more daringly summons up a central Christian image. Lucretia's arms are widely outstretched, her head averted and eyes closed in a manner likely to remind us of the crucified Christ. As so often in these representations, Lucretia's death seems almost to take her unawares: the knife approaches Lucretia seemingly without her conscious knowledge or control, as though directed by some external force; it is as though her death, like Christ's, were essentially a matter of passive surrender rather than active self-destruction. Raimondi's representation gently deflects possible moral criticism of Lucretia's act, transforming her suicide into a Christian martyrdom. (Veronese's painting of c.1580–5 (plate sixteen), though lacking any explicit Christian reference, similarly shows Lucretia apparently ignoring the dagger which she holds to her breast; she looks downward as if from a gallery, seemingly absorbed in another, unseen, drama below.) In many of the Renaissance books about the lives of virtuous women, Lucretia's suicide is also ingeniously assimilated into the ethical and imaginative framework of the Christian religion. The Jesuit writer Pierre Le Moyne, for example, in *La Gallerie des femmes fortes* (1667), mystically contemplates the nature and significance of Lucretia's wound, musing whether a light may have issued from her blood to irradiate the cloud of her shame, and picturing Lucretia as forced, like Christ, to die more than once in order to convince unbelievers of her virtue.[20]

The Christianized Lucretia survives through into modern times. In André Obey's drama *Le Viol de Lucrèce* (1931; freely adapted from Shakespeare's poem), the nature of Lucretia's wound is again somewhat mystically regarded.[21] In Ronald Duncan's libretto for Benjamin Britten's opera, *The Rape of Lucretia* (1946; freely adapted from Obey's play), Lucretia's

suffering is seen in relation to that of Christ, and her wounds are
again likened to his:

> Here in this scene you see:
>   Virtue assailed by sin
>   But with strength triumphing;
> All this is endless
>   Crucifixion for him.
>
> Nothing impure survives,
>   All passion perishes,
>   Virtue has one desire
> To let its blood flow
>   Back to the wounds of Christ.[22]

In such works as these, Lucretia's suicide is seen to present no
major problem. The 'magical thinking' which drives her to her
death is assimilated to the more complex patterns of 'magical
thinking' which underlie Christian belief concerning the significance of Christ's crucifixion, another willing martyrdom intended (though in another way) to wash away the offences of
the past and restore an earlier image of pristine virtue.

III

Alongside this tradition, however, another and very different
one grows up. In this more sceptical and rigorously logical
view of things, Lucretia, like many other pagan heroes and
heroines, is seen as someone whose behaviour cannot easily be
accommodated to the Christian religion, but rather stands at
variance to it. A new and crucial sense of distance develops: a
sense that Roman and Christian ideas of moral conduct may be
founded upon radically different and irreconcilable principles,
and that the old Roman ideas as to what constitutes 'heroic'
behaviour need to be looked at more critically. The new scepticism is expressed initially and most influentially by Saint
Augustine.

In an early chapter of *The City of God* (probably written in
413 AD), Augustine draws attention to some of the difficulties
involved in the story of Lucretia. He begins by asking whether
or not it would be right to regard Lucretia as adulterous

because she submitted to Tarquin's rape. That would be unjust, he says, for Lucretia's mind did not go along with the act. There was a conjunction of bodies, says Augustine, but a diversity of minds; there was only one adulterer, and that was Tarquin. Yet if that is so, there is a further problem.

. . . how was it that she who did not commit adultery received the heavier punishment? For the adulterer was driven from his country, with his father; his victim suffered the supreme penalty. If there is no unchastity when a woman is ravished against her will, then there is no justice in the punishment of the chaste. I appeal to Roman laws and Roman judges. To execute a criminal without trial was, accorded to you, a punishable offence. If anyone was charged in your courts with having put to death a woman not merely uncondemned but chaste and innocent, ahd this charge had been proved, would you not have chastised the culprit with appropriate severity?

That is what Lucretia did. That highly extolled Lucretia also did away with the innocent, chaste, outraged Lucretia. Give your sentence. Or if you cannot do this, because the culprit is not present to receive the punishment, why do you extol with such praises the killer of the chaste and innocent?

Hence Augustine drives inexorably to his conclusion. 'There is no possible way out,' he writes; ' "If she is adulterous, why is she praised? If chaste, why was she put to death?" '[23] To subject the behaviour of a legendary heroine of the ancient world to such severely legal scrutiny may at first seem somewhat excessive and absurd. William Empson describes the attack simply as 'caddish', presumably distressed by Augustine's apparent failure to achieve a position of tolerant moral relativism.[24] But Augustine's questions had an immediate and pressing context. During the event which prompted the writing of The City of God, the sack of Rome by Alaric and the Goths in 410 AD, a number of Christian nuns had been raped. The nuns had chosen to live on after this event, rather than take their own lives. Augustine is asking why they should not have felt free to take this choice; what logical or moral basis there is for an older pagan mythology that glorifies the notion of a 'fate worse than death'; what justification there can be for suicide after rape. His questions are neither 'caddish' nor entirely theoretical. The problem which exercised Augustine was a continuing one: suicide after rape was such a common phenomenon that as late as 1184 it was a major factor leading to the Council of Nimes's condemnation of suicide under the Canon Law.[25]

The case of Pelagia and the virgin martyrs was not so easy. It was one thing to discard an outworn Roman mythology, and quite another to question the actions of a woman whose death was officially lauded and celebrated by the Christian Church. Augustine approached the question with circumspection. 'I would not presume to make a hasty judgement on their case,' he wrote; 'I do not know whether divine authority convinced the church by cogent evidence that their memory should be honoured in this way; it may well be so. It may be that they acted on divine instruction and not through a human mistake – not in error, but in obedience.'[26] This was to be Augustine's uneasy compromise: unlike Lucretia, Pelagia may possibly have had a direct message from God telling her to kill herself, just as Samson may have had a message from God telling him to pull down the temple on himself and upon the heathens. Yet Augustine was aware of the risks attendant upon such an argument. If anyone chooses to follow the example of Pelagia, he warned, she must be sure that the message comes indeed from God and not from her own imagination. Nor should one kill oneself simply to prevent the possibility of sin; that is merely committing one sin in order to avoid another.[27]

More radically still, Augustine warns his readers not to fall into the error of over-valuing chastity for its own sake. Chastity is not a 'treasure' that can be stolen, nor is it a possession in the common sense at all. One's body cannot be polluted by another's act, if one's mind does not go along with that act; purity is essentially a matter of the will, not of the body.[28] For Augustine, there is thus a crucial difference between rape and adultery. For the Romans, as we have seen, the two acts were not significantly differentiated; in his appeal 'to Roman law and Roman judges' Augustine is on shaky ground. Possibly, however, Augustine's distinction between mental and physical offences may contain a memory of

Lucretia's words in Livy's version of the story, 'My body only has been violated; my heart is innocent' (*corpus est tantum violatum, animus insons*), and of the consoling words of the men: 'it was the mind that sinned, not the body: without intention there could never be guilt' (*mentem peccare, non corpus, et unde consilium afuerit, culpam abesse*). Yet Augustine's argument, strengthened by memories of Christ's own words on adultery,[29] entirely reverses the conclusion of Lucretia's: in place of 'death will be my witness', *mors testis erit*, it insists on the legitimacy of continuing life. If will is the essential thing, then the accidents which overtake the body, however regrettable and distressing they may appear, are ultimately trivial. They are not fates worse than death or necessitating death. Life is not to be thrown away upon such trifling pretexts.

In reinterpreting the story of Lucretia, Augustine not only attaches quite a different value to the importance of will; he also proposes quite a different view of the significance of suicide. For Augustine, Lucretia's suicide is not a heroic act, but an act of murder. The notion of suicide as *self-murder* is central to the development of Christian opposition to the practice. Suicide was often regarded by Christians as being even more heinous than murder; for as Robert Burton puts it, 'he that stabs another can kill his body; but he that stabs himself kills his own soul'.[30] Suicide betokened spiritual despair; and unlike the murderer, the person who took his or her own life was liable to die without the chance of repentance and the benefits of grace. Suicide was also regarded as an act of spiritual impatience. Only God, it was argued, has the right to bring our lives to an end; as God's creatures and property, we must patiently abide his will.

The topic of suicide is debated with particular vigour in Europe from the late sixteenth century onwards, and the debate is deeply influenced by the opinions expressed by Augustine in *The City of God*. Lucretia is commonly adduced as an example not to be followed by Christians; her suicide is regarded as rash and mischievous. 'Lucrece's poniard made her neither chaste nor brave,' writes John Case severely in

1596. Robert Burton condemns Lucretia along with other classical heroes who took their own lives: 'these are false and pagan positions, profane Stoical paradoxes, wicked examples,' he writes; 'it boots not what heathen philosophers determine in this kind, they are impious, abominable, and upon a wrong ground.' John Sym, writing in 1637 the first book in English devoted entirely to the topic of suicide, dismisses Lucretia amongst other 'wofull examples' who killed themselves for worldly reasons of honour or fame. William Vaughan in *The Golden-groue* condemns Lucretia for having killed herself out of impatience, faint-heartedness, and fear of scandal. Augustine was too kind to Lucretia; if Lucretia allowed Tarquin to rape her, says Vaughan, then there is no doubt that she committed adultery. Vaughan takes an equally stern view of Pelagia and the virgin martyrs: 'Surely the constancie and faith of these virgins was to be commended,' he writes, 'but no doubt, in this fact they sinned grieuously.' John Donne in *Biathanatos* analyses the case of these women with particular interest, finding here an inconsistency in the Church's teaching on the question of suicide. He notes drily that the apologists for these women will go to some lengths to suggest that they did not really kill themselves at all; of the virgin and martyr Appollonia, for example, who, after torture, leapt into the fire, it is said that she was 'as good as thrown in. Or else that she was provoked to it by divine inspiration.'

The case of women who kill themselves to avoid or atone for rape continues to be a profoundly problematical one for writers on suicide in this period. Jeremy Taylor discusses the entire problem with sympathy and learning in 1660, looking with particular care at the death of Pelagia. '. . . the case is indeed very hard', he writes, 'and every one in this is apt not onely to excuse, but to magnifie the great and glorious minds of those who to preserve their honour despis'd their life'; yet finally, Taylor concludes, the actions of such women must also be condemned. J. Adams in 1700 considers the problem in relation to the death of Lucretia, which 'indeed may justly raise Compassion'; yet 'it does not follow that because *Lucretia's* Death was much Applauded therefore it was *Lawful* or is to be *imitated'*. Reluctant to condemn 'those who fall into mistakes only through *too severe* and *nice a sense of Honour'*, Adams finally reaches a compromise position: her death 'ought not to be imitated, but in just *the same Circumstances'*. If this view is taken, he says with optimistic confidence, few women will have just cause to kill themselves in emulation of Lucretia.[31]

IV

The changing attitude to Lucretia's suicide cannot be explained, however, solely in terms of the development of Christian arguments against suicide. For one thing, it must be remembered that many Christian ideas about suicide had their origin in pre-Christian thought. The notions that men are the possessions of the gods, and that they have no right to release their souls from the fleshly prisons of the body; that suicide may be seen as a mark not of courage but of cowardice; and that man is a sentinel who has no right to leave his post without the express orders of his commander, God, are commonplaces of Greek and Roman thought. All these notions are repeated by Christian writers, whose hostility to suicide is not, philosophically speaking, especially original.[32] Moreover, Christian views of suicide (like pre-Christian views) were by no means simple and unanimous. In neither the Old Testament nor the New is any direct prohibition of suicide to be found, and there has always been room for a legitimate diversity of opinion amongst Christians upon this subject, and for an acceptance of what Albert Bayet in his classic study of suicide has called *la morale nuancé*: a recogniton that suicide may be permissible (or, at the very least, less culpable) in certain given circumstances, though impermissible in others.[33]

The discomfort with Lucretia as a heroine seems rather to come from deeper causes; and in particular, from a sense that something was amiss with the *motives* for which she killed herself. The change of sensibility that allows Lucretia to be seen as a reprehensible, rather than a heroic, figure might be described, in terms made popular by E. R. Dodds, as a change from a shame culture to a guilt culture.[34] In the classical versions of the story, Lucretia makes it quite clear to the men that she feels no guilt over what has happened. Yet her conviction that she is innocent is ultimately of less consequence to her than her awareness of the demands of reputation. It is not enough for Lucretia to be innocent; she must also be seen to be innocent. Lucretia kills herself not out of a sense of guilt but out of a sense of shame; her death is intended to expunge dishonour. For Christians, much occupied with the notion of guilt, this kind of death was puzzling and distasteful. Christians search their consciences; Lucretia, on the other hand, thought primarily of her reputation, looking to the possible opinions of others. Lucretia prided herself too much on 'glory' and the opinion of men, writes Tyndale contemptuously. She gloried in her chastity, and when she had lost that, she despaired; 'and for the very pain and thought which she had, not that she had displeased God, but that she had lost her honour, slew herself'. This pride, says Tyndale, 'God more abhorreth than the whoredom of any whore'.[35]

Jean François Senault in 1644 contrasts the way in which Christians are primarily concerned with conscience, rather than 'glory':

This *Roman* lady, and consequently haughty, was more carefull of preserving her glory, than her Innocencie, she feared lest she might be thought guilty of some fault, if she should out-live the outrage that was done her; and thought she might be judged to be confederate with *Tarquin*, should she not take vengeance on herself: Christian Women, who have had the like misfortune, have not imitated her despaire, they have not punisht the faults of others in themselves; nor committed Homicide, to revenge a Rape: The witnesse of their conscience, was the glory of their Chastity; and it sufficed them that God who is the searcher of hearts, knew their Intentions; and shutting up all their vertue in their obedience, they went not about to violate Gods Laws, to save themselves from the calumnie of men.[36]

The Christian stress on conscience replaces the old Roman stress on honour. What is seen by other people is of less consequence than those inner thoughts and promptings, be they guilty or innocent, which are perceived by 'God who is the searcher of hearts'. Hence for an ancient Roman and a modern

Christian the act of rape may have an utterly different value and utterly different consequences. The revaluation of the death of Lucretia is seen by Christian writers as part of a much larger revaluation of the actions and the moral principles of the heroes and heroines of the ancient world. 'Of like pride', writes Tyndale sweepingly, 'are all the moral virtues of Aristotle, Plato, and Socrates, and all the doctrines of the philosophers, the very gods of our school-men.' 'Thus are all the vertues of the *Pagans* nothing but Pride,' writes Senault, 'their Justice; be it either slack, or severe, is interested: Their Continency is vain glorious, and their courage, hath in it more of despaire then of Fortitude.'[37]

Many Christian writers recalled the story of Lucretia precisely in order to challenge the Roman ethic of shame. John Prince, writing in 1709 on the subject of suicide, takes Lucretia as the crowning example of the way in which pagan heroes and heroines were motivated by false notions of honour and dishonour:

Most famous is the Story of *Lucretia*, a *Roman* Lady, who being ravish'd by *Tarquin* the younger, impatient of the Injury and Disgrace, slew herself openly. It was grown into a Proverb among the *Romans, Praestat emori, quam per dedecus vivere*

> Better far it is to die
> Than to live in Ignomy.

Whereas,'tis truly better to undergo all the Shame and Contempt in the World than for any to embrue their Hands in their own Blood.[38]

Others viewed the story less dogmatically, examining Lucretia's motives for suicide with an air of relatively dispassionate scientific enquiry, in a larger search for the psychological origins of the moral virtues. Bernard Mandeville, for example, curious to know what feelings could ever be strong enough to counter a person's natural horror of death, finds the explanation for Lucretia's suicide not in her love of virtue so much as in her greater horror of shame. 'The Courage then which is only useful to the Body Politick, and what is generally call'd true Valour, is artificial', he concludes, 'and consists *in a Superlative Horror against Shame, by* Flattery *infused into*

Men of exalted Pride.'[39] Behind this passage lie memories of Bayle, Esprit, and La Rochefoucauld; and behind these authors, as Aphra Behn points out in the preface to her translation of La Rochefoucauld in 1685, there may lie an older tradition of speculation. La Rochefoucauld is not the first to assert that the virtues, if closely scrutinized, turn out to be less fine than they may at first appear:

> ... if I did not fear to boast of too much Learning for my Sex, I could cite you many Authors, as well Fathers of the Church as great Saints, who were of Opinion that Self-love, Interest, and Pride, was the cause of the most Glorious Actions of the greatest Heroes of the World. Who applauded the Chastity of *Lucretia* (whom all the World now celebrates for a Vertuous Woman) till they made it a subject of private Revenge, and the occasion of the Liberty of *Rome*? Do you think it was virtue in *Junius Brutus* to Sacrifice his own Sons to set up a Commonwealth?[40]

Thus the entire moral basis of the ancient story of the rape of Lucretia and the establishment of the Roman Republic is progressively undermined. Lucretia's apparent virtue, along with that of Lucius Junius Brutus, is now seen to derive from instincts and motives which are far from admirable.

Other writers approached the story in a spirit of creative scepticism. For these writers, the notion that Lucretia killed herself out of a sense of shame is not enough. In order to make the story intelligible, they imagine that Lucretia must have killed herself out of a sense of guilt, and fantasize about possible causes and complications which may have driven her to her death. One common speculation was that Lucretia killed herself because she had not been able totally to suppress all feelings of pleasure when Tarquin raped her. Coluccio Salutati's Lucretia confesses that, despite everything, she could not prevent herself from feeling a furtive enjoyment in the rape; for this reason, if for no other, she must die.[41] Bandello's Lucretia admits that for all her high principles she is a woman of flesh and blood, and could not wholly control her physical responses when Tarquin made his advances. To pardon the adultery, she says, would be tacitly to acknowledge the pleasure of the act; therefore she must die. For Bandello's

Lucretia, the will and the body cannot easily be separated.[42] G. Rivers in 1639 wonders whether Lucretia could really have suppressed all her natural feelings during the rape. What other explanation could be found for her suicide? 'This revenge may argue chastitie before and after: but not in the nick of the act, which yeelding to some secret enticement, might staine her thought; then loathing her selfe for the act, held death a more satisfactory revenge then repentance.'[43] Jacques du Bosc, also writing in the 1630s, pushes this line of enquiry a little further. Was Lucretia really as chaste a lady as tradition would have us suppose?

All men know, how *Lucrèce* killed her selfe, by reason of *Tarquinius* his rape; she said as she was dying, she had two irrefragable witnesses of her innocence, her bloud before men and her spirit before the Gods. But I am almost of the opinion of a great Authour, who accuseth her for having been not alwayes so chast, as she would make us beleeve. And that if she had not been guilty, without doubt she had found more remedie in her Conscience, then in her death. They say, she resisted rather of a humour, then of vertue, and that having spent her time with other Gallants of lesse qualitie, then the Tyrant, she feared least all her other faults would be discovered in this, and that this feare made her resolve to go forth of the world, by her own hand, rather then to remaine there any long time, to see her reputation lost.[44]

The thinking of all these writers is dominated by Christian notions of conscience, and it is easier for them to hypothesize a secret guilt of this kind than to imagine other reasons that may have led Lucretia to take her own life. Lucretia's suicide, so far from being proof of her innocence, is now seen to be a tacit confession of her moral corruption.

V

Augustine's arguments in *The City of God* have a major impact upon the development of the story of the rape of Lucretia. Many later commentators are content merely to repeat his arguments in a spirit of dialectical triumph. Senault's remarks upon Lucretia in 1644, for example, are little more than a paraphrase of Augustine, whose arguments are taken to be irrefutable: 'But truely I find that Saint *Austine* hath so justly blamed her as that she is not justly to be defended; and that he hath made a *Dilemma*, to which the subtillest Philosophers cannot answer.'[45] Yet Augustine's 'dilemma' – as the word itself suggests – had an air of debater's cleverness about it, an element of provocation that often generated counter-argument and rebuttal; 'the subtillest Philosophers' were not silenced. The tradition of the virtuous Lucretia, protomartyr, continued to flourish alongside that of the Lucretia whose actions and motives (in Tyndale's words) 'God more abhorreth than the whoredom of any whore'. The moral issues of the story were commonly debated *pro* and *contra*. In the *Declamatio Lucretiae* written early in his life, the Italian humanist Coluccio Salutati sets out the arguments for and against Lucretia's suicide, finally allowing a victory to the defence: Lucretia is shown to have acted in accordance with the highest ideals of the society in which she lived. Though the *Declamatio Lucretiae* was very popular in Salutati's lifetime, in old age he may have viewed the verdict of the *Declamatio* in another light, for the work is excluded from the list of his writings drawn up in 1406, shortly before his death.[46] Yet Salutati's method of arguing both sides of the case lingered on. In Rivers' *The Heroinae* (1639), for example, the arguments *Pro Lucrecia* and *Contra Lucreciam* are set out at length, without any formal conclusion being reached. The 'dilemma' posed by Lucretia's actions was seen by some writers to be well-nigh insoluble. 'Though there have been severall ages since this accident hapned, and that it is almost as old, as ancient *Rome*,' writes Georges de Scudéry in 1642, 'It cannot yet be decided, if she did well in killing her self after her misfortune, or if she had not done better, to have let *Tarquin* kill her, and died innocent, though she had not been believed so.'[47] (The possibility of Lucretia's not having to die at all as a result of the rape seems never to have occurred to Scudéry, who entirely disregards the central, humane, tendency of Augustine's argument.)

It is not only in discursive works of a theological or semi-philosophical nature that the debate about Lucretia continues.

The problems are also explored and extended, often in a remarkably ingenious way, in the numerous dramatic, fictional, and poetic redactions of the story. In the following chapters we shall see what happens when the debate enters literature: how the Augustinian 'dilemma' proves to various writers either a creative stimulus or a creative stumbling block; how the moral difficulties of the story are 'solved', extended, or found intractable; and how, as a result of the pressures of the debate, the myth is imaginatively transformed.

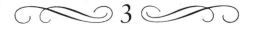

3

'A Theme for Disputation': Shakespeare's Lucrece

What goes wrong with Shakespeare's *The Rape of Lucrece*? Despite many local subtleties and felicities, the poem never quite adds up to a coherent whole, or to a totally compelling human drama. There is a sense – so rare in Shakespeare's work as to be doubly remarkable – that the central moral complexities of the story are in some ways curiously evaded, while the simpler outlying issues are decoratively elaborated. The poem repeatedly begins to analyse the nature of a moral predicament, only to break off abruptly, diverting us into an extended metaphor, lament, or topical digression. Like its two principal characters, the poem seems alternately to scrutinize and retreat from problems, to debate and to grow weary of debate. The issues are talked around, but seldom through. Yet there are frequent reminders of how complex these issues are:

> 'Let my good name, that senseless reputation,
> For Collatine's dear love be kept unspotted;
> If that be made a theme for disputation,
> The branches of another root are rotted,
> And undeserv'd reproach to him allotted
>   That is as clear from this attaint of mine
>   As I ere this was pure to Collatine.'
>
> (820–6)

' "*If that be made a theme for disputation . . .*" ': by Shakespeare's day, 'a theme for disputation' is precisely what the classical Lucretia's reputation had become, her conduct with Sextus Tarquinius and her decision to take her own life being matters that were sometimes formally debated *pro* and *contra*.[1] Casting apprehensively into the future, Shakespeare's Lucrece unwittingly forecasts the fate that was indeed to overtake her own 'good name'. Her words have something of the same ironically prophetic force as those of Troilus and Cressida when they exchange their vows ('True swains in love shall in the world to come/ Approve their truth by Troilus . . .' etc. III.ii.169 ff.), reminding us of the ways in which hopes and reputations are affected by the passage of time. Yet where Shakespeare's poem stands in relation to the familiar 'disputation' about the classical Lucretia, whether his own Lucrece is intended to be seen as a wholly admiring or as a partly critical portrait, are matters which are far from clear.

In one sense, perhaps, this open-endedness might be thought not to matter very much; it might even be said to be the poem's strength. The processes of a poem are not identical with the processes of logical argument, and it should not surprise us if Shakespeare does not approach the moral problems of the Lucretia story in the unremittingly logical manner of an Augustine. Shakespeare seems in fact to be less interested in arguing a particular case within the poem than in exploring the states of mind from which argumentation springs. More specifically, he dramatizes the difficulties which people have in pursuing their thoughts logically and consecutively while under the stress of suffering or sexual passion — stress that creates dilemmas which (ironically) particularly demand the elucidation of steady thought. Tarquin and Lucrece, both separately and together, try to argue through their predicaments, and are constantly frustrated. The questions that Tarquin puts to himself before the rape seem circular, incapable of resolution, scarcely even *questions* so much as signs of internal agitation:

> Thus, graceless, holds he disputation
> 'Tween frozen conscience and hot-burning will . . .
>
> (246–7)

Tarquin's 'disputation' is something less than disputation, a wretched worrying to and fro, ultimately short-circuited by a blind decision to act. 'I have debated, even in my soul', Tarquin announces to the hapless Lucrece (498), but the debate has in fact long since been abandoned: 'Then, childish fear avaunt! debating die!' (274). The debate has been between rational and sub-rational forces (represented by 'will', and the memory of Lucrece's sighs and graces: 'All orators are dumb when beauty pleadeth' (268)). After the rape, Lucrece also 'holds disputation', attempting forlornly to debate her way out of her dilemmas:

> So she, deep-drenched in a sea of care,
> Holds disputation with each thing she views,
> And to herself all sorrow doth compare;
> No object but her passion's strength renews,
> And as one shifts, another straight ensues.
>   Sometime her grief is dumb and hath no words;
>   Sometimes 'tis mad and too much talk affords.
>   (1100–6)

This disputation is (again) a state of anxiety, not a process of ratiocination. Lucrece is unable to think things through, unable also to cease from thought. Whether she is speechless, whether she is garrulous, language is inadequate to express her grief.

> 'Out, idle words, servants to shallow fools!
> Unprofitable sounds, weak arbitrators!
> Busy yourselves in skill-contending schools,
> Debate where leisure serves with dull debaters;
> To trembling clients be you mediators.
>   For me, I force not argument a straw,
>   Since that my case is past the help of law.'
>   (1016–22)

Yet though Lucrece dismisses 'idle words', it is to idle words that she constantly returns: talk is her main solace and occupation. Unlike the sorrowing Hecuba in the painting of fallen Troy ('so much grief and not a tongue' (1463)), unlike the raped and tongueless Lavinia in *Titus Andronicus*, Lucrece talks of her griefs, but her talk seems to get her nowhere.[2]

In Livy's and Ovid's versions of the Lucretia story, Shakespeare may well have noticed a recurring stress on the superiority of deeds to words. In Livy's narrative the initial argument amongst the men concerning the virtue of their wives is cut short by Collatinus, who tells his companions that there is no point in sitting about debating the issue when they can resolve their differences by the simple action of riding off to Rome: *Collatinus negat verbis opus esse*. Ovid develops this sentiment: *Non opus est verbis credite rebus ait*: 'No need of words! Trust deeds!' cries Collatinus, and the men take to their horses. One of the larger ironies of the story is of course the fact that the *deeds* which follow this confident cry are more various and more complex than the innocent Collatinus realizes: they are to include the rape and suicide of his own wife and the later expulsion of the Tarquins. Brutus in Livy's account urges the Romans to leave their idle lamentations (*inertium querellarum*) and act like men. The Romans respond by rising against the Tarquins and driving them from Rome, at last abandoning speech for action. In Shakespeare's poem, this climax is very subdued, as is the entire political dimension of the story.[3] The banishment of the Tarquins is mentioned briefly in the final stanza of the poem, almost as a narrative afterthought. Shakespeare does not give us a story of triumphant action. Whenever in Shakespeare's poem deeds seem preferable to words, it is only as the lesser of two evils. Tarquin decides to rape Lucrece, and Lucrece decides to take her own life, yet neither of these actions seems to have been proved to be logically or morally defensible; they are undertaken rather out of a kind of despair, because they seem the only effective way of ending the whole wearisome and seemingly interminable processes of debate:

> This helpless smoke of words doth me no right.
> The remedy indeed to do me good
> Is to let forth my foul defiled blood.
>
> (1027–9)

It is a typical irony in the poem that these words initiate in Lucrece's mind a further series of doubts about the wisdom of suicide and a further 'smoke of words' before she finally puts an end to her own life. Longing for the simplicity of action, Shakespeare's characters find themselves entangled in a web of words.

Shakespeare's achievement in dealing with the traditional story is to have opened up a new interior world of shifting doubts, hesitations, anxieties, anticipations, and griefs. No other version of the Lucretia story explores more minutely or with greater psychological insight the mental processes of the two major characters, their inconsistent waverings to and fro, before they bring themselves finally and reluctantly to action. Yet this subtlety is achieved at a certain cost. In so vividly dramatizing Tarquin's and Lucrece's moral uncertainties, Shakespeare introduces a fatal element of moral uncertainty into the poem itself. It is not simply a matter of Shakespeare allowing us to feel (as he does, say, with *Antony and Cleopatra*) that the characters' behaviour may in some way transcend or invalidate common standards of moral judgement, or that a purely adjudicative response to their actions is somehow beside the point. There is instead a deeper feeling of irresolution in the poem, a wavering between different criteria for judgement, a sense that Shakespeare, while sharing some of his contemporaries' doubts about the way in which Lucrece chose to act, is attempting – not altogether successfully – to retell Lucrece's story in a manner which is by and large approbatory. The poem veers from incipient criticism of Lucrece towards a muted celebration of her actions, yet the treatment of the story remains curiously problematical. For all the poem's delicacy of psychological insight, Shakespeare has not quite managed to achieve what elsewhere he so often achieves with such arresting effect: he does not take moral repossession of the older story, confidently charging it with new depth and intricacy of significance.

I

The post-Augustinian debate about the character of the classical Lucretia turned essentially upon one point. How was Lucretia to be judged: by the moral standards of ancient Rome, or by those of Christianity? The most thorough-going critics of Lucretia, such as William Tyndale, took a very severe line, condemning her as a woman who had sadly failed to live up to the standards of Christianity. 'She sought her own glory in her chastity, and not God's,' wrote Tyndale sternly, as if to imply that, if only she had made a decent effort, Lucretia ought to have been able to anticipate the wishes and precepts of the Christian God.[4] Others took a more tolerant and relativistic view of the matter, conceding that Lucretia did not behave in the manner to be expected of a modern Christian, but arguing none the less that she behaved courageously and unexceptionably according to the highest moral standards of her time. This was the attitude, for example, of Pierre Bayle, and many writers before him.[5] One of the difficulties of Shakespeare's poem is that it is never made clear whether we are to judge the actions of the characters by Roman or by Christian standards; nor is it even clear what kind of moral universe they inhabit. Christian terminology and Christian thinking constantly recur throughout the poem. There is talk of heaven and hell, of saints and sinners and angels and devils, of grace and gracelessness. 'The blackest sin is clear'd with absolution,' says Tarquin (354), as he finally decides to rape Lucrece, and both Tarquin and Lucrece express anxiety about the salvation of their immortal souls. It is tempting to say that such Christian references do not affect the coherence of the poem, but merely enlarge its suggestive power; that only a literal-minded reader would baulk at Shakespeare's 'timeless' fusion of Roman and Christian worlds. 'It is not a Roman thought', noted an early twentieth-century editor of the poem dutifully against a stanza in which Lucrece meditates the possible perdition of her soul, and the comment is swept aside as unimaginative quibbling by the recent Arden editor: 'It is indeed a Christian thought; but Shakespeare's whole procedure precludes historical accuracy, and we would rather have his Elizabethan interpretations of Roman character and thought than reconstructions by more scholarly minds.'[6] Yet the matter is not quite as simple as that. The Christian references in the poem are not casual anachronisms like the chiming clock in *Julius Caesar*, nor can they be said to amount to anything as systematic as 'Elizabethan interpretations of Roman character and thought'. What Shakespeare actually gives us is an alternation between

Roman and Christian viewpoints, which generates constant
uncertainty as to the way in which the poem is to be read.

Some of the difficulties can be seen in a passage such as the
following:

> He thence departs a heavy convertite,
> She there remains a hopeless castaway;
> He in his speed looks for the morning light;
> She prays she never may behold the day.
> 'For day,' quoth she 'Night's scapes doth open lay;
>   And my true eyes have never practis'd how
>   To cloak offences with a cunning brow.
>
> 'They think not but that every eye can see
> The same disgrace which they themselves behold;
> And therefore would they still in darkness be,
> To have their unseen sin remain untold;
> For they their guilt with weeping will unfold,
>   And grave, like water that doth eat in steel,
>   Upon my cheeks what helpless shame I feel.'
>
> (743–56)

Two conflicting ethics are in evidence. Picking up the distinction made in chapter two, we might say that Lucrece is thinking here (on the one hand) in terms of a shame culture. She
worries about 'disgrace' and 'helpless shame', about the
searching eyes and opinions of other people, where a Christian
might worry about the searching eye of God. What she dreads
is public dishonour, the possibility of the act becoming known;
hence she longs that the dawn will never come. This way of
thought takes her naturally in the direction of suicide. Yet the
passage invites us simultaneously to think of Lucrece's
dilemma in terms of a guilt culture. Tarquin is a 'convertite', a
penitent; Lucrece is a 'castaway', the common theological term
for a lost soul; she is vexed by thoughts of 'guilt' and of 'unseen
sin'. Lucrece's plight is 'hopeless' in the sense that she has the
misfortune to live half a millennium before the birth of Christ,
and can therefore think only of pagan solutions to her problem; yet the Christian terminology goes deeper than that,
imbuing Lucrece with a Christian sensibility (a sensibility
which will lead her in due course to doubt the wisdom of

suicide) and suggesting moreover her possible moral implication in what has occurred. Whether Lucrece is to be seen as merely dishonoured by the rape or as more deeply and spiritually affected is not simply a question for 'more scholarly minds': it is a central human question which needs to be answered if we are to understand the nature of Lucrece's distress and the inner logic of her suicide.

On this point, however, the poem wavers, as Lucrece herself wavers. For the classical Lucretia, suicide is not a matter for wavering or for debate; her decision is swift and sure. Though the suicide at first surprises and distresses her menfolk, its propriety is never questioned. For Shakespeare's Lucrece, the matter is otherwise. The story is no longer one of moral certainties, though critics often assume it is.[7] Lucrece seems unsure of the moral consequences both of rape and of suicide, hesitantly debating her way towards death. Once again, the simpler code of honour is complicated by newer, Christian, considerations:

'To kill myself,' quoth she 'alack what were it,
But with my body my poor soul's pollution?
They that lose half with greater patience bear it
Than they whose whole is swallowed in confusion.
That mother tries a merciless conclusion
  Who, having two sweet babes, when death takes one,
  Will slay the other and be nurse to none.

'My body or my soul, which was the dearer,
When the one pure, the other made divine?
Whose love of either to myself was nearer,
When both were kept for heaven and Collatine?
Ay me! the bark pill'd from the lofty pine,
  His leaves will wither and his sap decay;
  So must my soul, her bark being pill'd away.

'Her house is sack'd, her quiet interrupted,
Her mansion batter'd by the enemy,
Her sacred temple spotted, spoil'd, corrupted,
Grossly engirt with daring infamy;
Then let it not be call'd impiety
  If in this blemish'd fort I make some hole
  Through which I may convey this troubled soul.'

(1156–76)

'Then let it not be call'd impiety': Lucrece has an uneasy awareness of the way in which her suicide may be regarded from other cultural and religious viewpoints, seeming almost to anticipate Augustine's objection that a woman who kills herself after rape puts her immortal soul in jeopardy. The whole debate is quite un-Roman in the way it considers the relationship of souls and bodies. Yet the Augustinian point is no sooner glimpsed than dismissed by means of a curious analogy. The soul 'must' in any case decay now as a result of the assault upon the body, just as a pine tree must decay when the bark is peeled; hence, Lucrece argues, there is surely no harm in speeding it on its way. The logic is hardly compelling; and the view of the inevitable effect of Tarquin's act upon Lucrece's soul seems at odds with the view which Lucrece herself (echoing Livy's Lucretia) puts to the men later in the poem:

> 'Though my gross blood be stain'd with this abuse,
> Immaculate and spotless is my mind;
> That was not forc'd; that never was inclin'd
>   To accessary yieldings, but still pure
>   Doth in her poison'd closet yet endure.'
>
> (1655–9)

Does Tarquin's rape merely affect Lucrece's body, or do its consequences extend further, threatening the mind and soul? The analogy of the pine tree and that of the 'poison'd closet' point in opposing directions, the first suggesting that body and soul inevitably react together, the second that the body alone is affected.[8]

A third analogy gives yet another view of the matter. Lucrece is again contemplating suicide, and this time rejecting it as a vain solution to her problems:

> 'Poor helpless help, the treasure stol'n away,
> To burn the guiltless casket where it lay!'
>
> (1056–7)

The 'casket' is the body, which is 'guiltless' in the sense that it is ungilded, of small value, and in the further sense that it is innocent, without guilt. This time it is implied that the body is unaffected by what has happened; instead it is an inner 'treasure', something of infinitely greater value, that has vanished. Not only is this analogy at odds with the other two; it is also, morally speaking, less sophisticated. A thousand years before the time of Shakespeare, St. Augustine had argued that a woman's virtue 'is not a treasure which can be stolen without the mind's consent' in the act of rape. True virtue, he argued, is not like a material possession at all; it is a quality that resides in the will, withstanding physical accidents and disasters.[9] The poem's shifting analogies seem to reflect other shifts between Roman and Christian ways of thought, a basic indecisiveness over the story's central moral issues. How, if at all, is Lucrece affected morally by the rape? Is her suicide an act of authentic heroism, or just the result of muddled thinking? How is the idea of Lucrece's tragic loss ('the treasure stol'n away') to be reconciled with the idea that essentially she is untouched by the rape, that her chaste mind 'doth . . . yet endure'? Morally and metaphysically, the poem raises more questions than it manages to answer.

II

Shakespeare being Shakespeare, the questions are never dull. And it is typical of the unevenness of the poem that the simple notion of Lucrece's stolen 'treasure' should form part of a larger and much subtler fabric of ideas on the subject of ownership, possession, and theft. One of the central themes in *The Rape of Lucrece* is that of the precariousness of all forms of possession, material and immaterial: of beauty, virtue, happiness, fortune, love, and ultimately life itself. As in *Venus and Adonis*, there is a recurring sense that nothing perfect will last:

> . . . no perfection is so absolute
> That some impurity doth not pollute.
> (853–4)

The more perfect the possession, the more fragile its existence, the more vulnerable its state. Tarquin may wish to rape

Lucrece (Shakespeare suggests) precisely *because* she is so chaste, so invitingly, arousingly, perfect. And was not Collatine himself at fault, for having bragged so rashly of his wife's perfections?

> For he the night before, in Tarquin's tent,
> Unlock'd the treasure of his happy state –
> What priceless wealth the heavens had him lent
> In the possession of his beauteous mate;
> Reck'ning his fortune at such high-proud rate
>   That kings might be espoused to more fame,
>   But king nor peer to such a peerless dame.
>
> O happiness enjoy'd but of a few!
> And, if possess'd, as soon decayed and done
> As is the morning silver-melting dew
> Against the golden splendour of the sun!
> An expired date, cancell'd ere well begun:
>   Honour and beauty, in the owner's arms,
>   Are weakly fortress'd from a world of harms.
>
> Beauty itself doth of itself persuade
> The eyes of men without an orator;
> What needeth then apologies be made
> To set forth that which is so singular?
> Or why is Collatine the publisher
>   Of that rich jewel he should keep unknown
>   From thievish ears, because it is his own?
>   (15–35)

Shakespeare sets in train here a complex sequence of ideas on the subject of possession. The ultimate possessors of Lucrece's 'treasure', as the passage makes clear, are 'the heavens'; she is merely 'lent' to Collatine, who fails to realize the true value and the ultimate revocability of the gift. At the end of the poem Collatine and Lucretius are to contend childishly for the possession of the dead Lucrece and for the right to mourn her most:

> The one doth call her his, the other his,
> Yet neither may possess the claim they lay.
> The father says, 'She's mine.' 'O mine she is!'

Replies her husband. 'Do not take away
My sorrow's interest; let no mourner say
 He weeps for her, for she was only mine,
 And only must be wail'd by Collatine.'
(1793–9)

The squabble highlights the absurdity of Collatine's (and Lucretius') notions of 'possession'. Through his recklessness, Collatine loses his wife and 'the treasure of his happy state', and even as he laments his loss fails to understand what has happened and why. In one respect, Collatine's situation resembles that of Tarquin, who is after 'possession' of Lucrece in the narrower, sexual sense of that word, and who is similarly bewildered by loss. Tarquin is caught in the circular sequences of lust that Shakespeare describes again in Sonnet 129:

Mad in pursuit, and in possession so;
Had, having, and in quest to have, extreme;
A bliss in proof, and prov'd, a very woe....

For Tarquin, 'great treasure is the meed proposed' (132), yet he loses both what he expects to gain and what he already has. As he meditates the rape, the poem moves to some general moral reflections which anticipate a thought that is to return insistently in *Macbeth*:

Those that much covet are with gain so fond
That what they have not, that which they possess
They scatter and unloose it from their bond,
And so, by hoping more, they have but less....

So that in vent'ring ill we leave to be
The things we are for that which we expect;
And this ambitious foul infirmity,
. In having much, torments us with defect
Of that we have; so then we do neglect
 The thing we have and, all for want of wit,
 Make something nothing by augmenting it.
(134–7, 148–54)

The moral applies both to Tarquin and to Collatine. Remembering the traditional outcome of the story, we may also see that it applies, beyond the formal framework of the poem, to

Tarquin's father, Lucius Tarquinius Superbus, who (as the poem's Argument reminds us) had unlawfully 'possessed himself of the kingdom', only to lose it through his son's (and his own) rashness. That 'great treasure' on which Tarquin gambles is not merely Lucrece; it is also Rome.

But Tarquin has lost something more important than either Lucrece or Rome. The vital loss is not material but spiritual. *Quid victor gaudes? haec te victoria perdet*, wrote Ovid, playing upon a paradox that we noted in chapter one: that Tarquin's rape of Lucretia is, as it were, a reflexive act, finally more damaging to himself than to Lucretia. 'Why, victor, do you rejoice? This victory will ruin you.' Shakespeare intensifies this paradox by suggesting that Tarquin's most important loss (the ultimate perdition) is that of his soul:

> Ev'n in this thought through the dark night he stealeth,
> A captive victor that hath lost in gain;
> Bearing away the wound that nothing healeth,
> The scar that will despite of cure remain,
> Leaving his spoil perplex'd in greater pain.
>   She bears the load of lust he left behind,
>   And he the burden of a guilty mind.
>
> (729–35)

'A captive victor that hath lost in gain': even as he echoes Ovid, Shakespeare deepens the resonance of the Ovidian idea. The reflexiveness of Tarquin's action is further emphasized by another and more remarkable image. Shakespeare pictures Tarquin's soul as a 'princess' who has been assaulted and 'spotted' by Tarquin's own crime against Lucrece (715–28). The effect of the personification is striking. As one critic has suggested, it is almost as though, in a spiritual sense, Tarquin had *raped himself*.[10] Rape is seen not merely as a destructive, but also as a self-destructive, act.

The 'treasure' which Tarquin loses is ultimately his own soul. But what is the treasure which Lucrece loses? Here again one becomes aware of a disequilibrium in the poem.

> But she hath lost a dearer thing than life,
> And he hath won what he would lose again.
>
> (687–8)

1. Lorenzo Lotto, A Lady as *Lucretia*, c.1534.

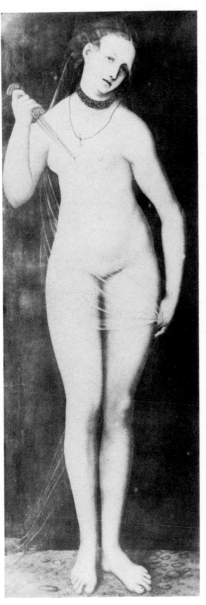

8. Cranach, *Lucretia and Judith*, after 1537.

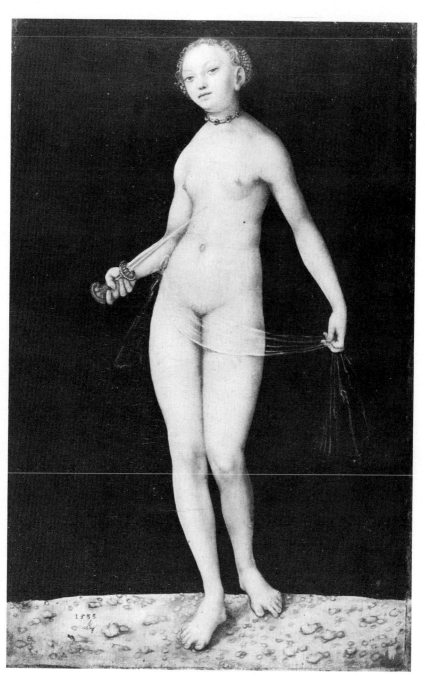

9. Cranach, *Lucretia*, 1533.

10. Botticelli, *The Tragedy of Lucretia*, *c*.1499. At left, Tarquin threatens Lucretia (beneath a relief of Judith and Holofernes); at right, Lucretia receives her husband and father (beneath a frieze of Horatius defending the bridge); centre, Brutus excites the Romans to vengeance (beneath a statue of David with the head of Goliath, and reliefs of Mucius Scaevola, Marcus Curtius, Achilles with the body of Hector, and a Roman triumph).

Despite the symmetry of these lines, Shakespeare appears to be invoking two quite different concepts of gain and loss, which in turn imply two quite different ethics. For what Lucrece seems essentially to have lost is her honour and good name, while what Tarquin has gained is a sense of guilt and probability of damnation. The qualitative differences between these two ethics are not always kept distinct in Shakespeare's poem. The difference between being dishonoured and being damned, a matter so scrupulously explored in a play such as *Measure for Measure*, is never vitally experienced in *The Rape of Lucrece*; nor is the notion of the 'fate worse than death' firmly challenged in human terms as it is in that play.

> *Isabella*   O were it but my life!
> I'd throw it down for your deliverance
> As frankly as a pin.
> *Claudio*   Thanks, dear Isabel.
> (*Measure for Measure*, III.i.105–7)

At once we feel the sting of a more urgent, more deeply dramatic, exchange. 'Thanks, dear Isabel': in the very curtness of Claudio's response (such hypothetical readiness for heroism is of little comfort to a man condemned to death) we glimpse a sensibility that apprehends in a fuller sense what it may mean to die, that views a little warily the notion that a woman's honour may be 'a dearer thing than life', that values life more richly than a pin.

III

Near the end of the poem, however, we hear a voice that speaks with another kind of curtness. As Collatine and Lucretius fretfully and proprietorially lament over the body of Lucrece, Brutus calls them sharply to order:

> 'Why Collatine, is woe the cure for woe?
> Do wounds help wounds, or grief help grievous deeds?
> Is it revenge to give thyself a blow,
> For his foul act by whom thy fair wife bleeds?

> Such childish humour from weak minds proceeds.
> Thy wretched wife mistook the matter so,
> To slay herself that should have slain her foe.'
>
> (1821–7)

The dead Lucrece is here rebuked almost as sharply as are Collatine and Lucretius. The final couplet of the stanza introduces yet another doubt as to the logic of Lucrece's suicide, though from quite another moral standpoint. Brutus' voice is that of brusque and savage worldly wisdom. Suicide, Brutus implies, is no answer to Lucrece's dilemma; the only answer would have been for her to have struck back at her assailant. Brutus' comment is never expanded, nor is it ever countered. It is simply allowed to hang in the air, registering, yet not resolving, one further doubt about Lucrece's conduct and about the legitimacy of the notion of 'a fate worse than death'.

'*Do wounds help wounds?*': Brutus's words also help to stimulate quite another kind of doubt. In the earliest versions of the Lucretia story, as we saw in chapter one, much play is made with the notion of knives and of wounding. Tarquin threatens Lucretia with a knife, and it is with a knife that Lucretia gives herself her fatal wound; on this knife Brutus and the other men swear solemnly to drive the Tarquins from Rome. As many of the painters were to perceive, the story seems to propose a sequence of dependent threats and wounds: one violent deed prompts another, one knife turns against another, Lucretia's death being the signal for revenge and for weapons to move against the Tarquins. Shakespeare's Lucrece refers to such a sequence when she suggests that it is Tarquin, and not she herself, who guides her dagger:

> She utters this: 'He, he, fair lords, 'tis he,
> That guides this hand to give this wound to me'
>
> (1721–2)

and again when she says, preparing to wound herself fatally, 'How Tarquin must be us'd, read it in me' (1195). But Shakespeare is interested in the notion of *wounding* in a wider and more complex sense. Wounds, the poem suggests, are not always literal and physical. Lucrece sees that Collatine has been wounded by the rape without so much as realizing it:

> 'O unseen shame! invisible disgrace!
> O unfelt sore! crest-wounding, private scar!
> Reproach is stamp'd in Collatinus' face,
> And Tarquin's eye may read the mot afar,
> How he in peace is wounded, not in war.
>
> (827–31)

Tarquin, too, is invisibly wounded:

> Bearing away the wound that nothing healeth,
> The scar that will despite of cure remain.
>
> (731–2)

After Lucrece's suicide, as Collatine and Lucretius compete with each other in grief, it is Brutus (Brutus, whom we have seen 'Burying in Lucrece' wound his folly's show' (1810)) who calls them to their senses: '*Do wounds help wounds?*' Brutus is of course summoning the men to their act of revenge. But the words he chooses are curious, seeming as they do to challenge the whole intricate series of retributive acts upon which the story is built. They may unwittingly remind us of what Shakespeare has shown us throughout the poem: that there are metaphorical and spiritual wounds that are deeper and more lasting than fleshly wounds, wounds 'that nothing healeth'; and that there are other ways of dealing with grief than through violent retribution and blood vengeance. Christian considerations are beginning to impinge upon the pagan story, new complications and ethical possibilities are briefly glimpsed. Yet the moment is soon gone, and the story is back on its familiar lines. Shakespeare, after all, was to respect the traditional shape of the story more than many other writers were to do, or possibly to find it artistically more intractable. Though Shakespeare's imagination seems repeatedly to have perceived the deficiencies of the moral premisses on which the older story was built, it is to these premisses and to the familiar narrative pattern of the story that he ultimately returns.

Early work though it is, *The Rape of Lucrece* is a poem of remarkable yet sporadic brilliance. The power of

Shakespeare's poetic intelligence is always in evidence; yet the intelligence is restless, unsettled. The poem gives a constant sense of problems perceived but not solved; of 'disputations' which are neither concluded, nor, on the other hand, finely poised in their inconclusiveness. It is as though Shakespeare has begun to Christianize the old story, begun to question in an Augustinian fashion the logic and wisdom of its central actions, only to shut off such questions, being finally content to allow the story to drift down its traditional narrative course. Yet the current of the story is disturbed. Behind the lengthy rhetorical laments of the poem, one senses some uncertainty in Shakespeare's handling in particular of the principal issue of the poem, that of the proper course of action for a 'dishonoured' woman to take; an issue to which he was to return with greater thoughtfulness in the work of his maturity.

4

'Another Lucretia':
Clarissa and the Dilemmas of Rape

Samuel Richardson's *Clarissa* is a novel about a woman who is abducted, drugged, and raped by a man with whom she is more than half in love; who afterwards resolutely declares that she will not marry her seducer, and that in all essential ways she is untouched and unchanged by what has happened to her; but who lapses none the less into an illness from which she eventually dies. Her death is avenged by a relative, who hunts down her seducer and kills him in a duel. It is not surprising that a novelist treating a subject of this kind should have been reminded of another, classic, story of a woman who dies as a result of a rape which she too declares has not affected her ultimate integrity, and whose death is similarly avenged by a relative, who brings about the downfall of the rapist and of his father, the last of the Roman kings. This story, the story of the rape of Lucretia, is frequently recalled throughout *Clarissa*, and in a manner which highlights some of the central problems with which Richardson struggled while writing the novel. The story of Lucretia cannot be called a 'source' for *Clarissa*, nor is it brought forward simply as a familiar analogue or archetype intended to give the novel historical or tragic resonance – though this may well be part of its total effect. It is recalled primarily for different reasons. It is intended to be seen as a story which is not merely like Clarissa's, but also in some crucial respects unlike it. It is intended also to be seen as a simple yet morally problematical story, from whose narrative and ethical design Richardson's own vast, meticulous, and complex novel significantly departs, and against which it may in some sense be measured.

The story of Lucretia was a popular and controversial one

around the time that Richardson wrote. Voltaire's tragedy of *Brutus*, first performed in Paris in 1730 and revived with success in 1742, had prompted a number of English imitations, including one in 1733 by William Bond (whose paper *The Plain Dealer* Richardson had probably printed in the 1720s) and another in 1734 by Richardson's friend William Duncombe.[1] These versions concentrate more upon the fortunes of Lucius Junius Brutus than of Lucretia. But the story of Lucretia herself was being more closely scrutinized (as we have seen) in numerous philosophical and religious writings of the time, and in particular in contemporary treatises on the subject of suicide.

Some idea of the vigour and complexity of the contemporary debate about the wisdom of Lucretia's suicide is afforded by Pierre Bayle's long article on Lucretia in his *Dictionnaire* of 1697, which appeared in an English translation in 1738. In a series of lengthy and pugnacious footnotes to this article, Bayle takes issue with the arguments of Saint Augustine and many of his modern followers. Bayle's contention is that Lucretia died in a manner which may be considered as exemplary, judged by the standards of her time and country: her actions 'should excite no other sensations but those of pity and admiration'. When it comes to the point, however, it is clear that Bayle is not entirely happy about Lucretia's suicide. In attempting to justify her actions, he moves defensively off into a discussion of other cases of rape, actual and hypothetical, which he believes may throw light on the point at issue:

It sometimes happened, in the infant ages, that very pious maidens, who had devoted themselves to a life of celibacy, for the service of God, were ravished. This happens but too often in the present age; and we are daily told the story of an Abbess, who with her Nuns had been debauched by a company of Irish soldiers in Piedmont, and who made her complaints to Monsieur de Catinat. Suppose a Nun should, on such an occasion, be seized with such a fit of grief as should bring upon her a mortal distemper. Suppose that the testimony of her conscience, strengthened by the most solid consolations a Divine can give, should not be able to soothe her melancholy. Let us suppose that she had contracted such a love for the purity both

of body and mind, that the bare idea of the most involuntary pollution, should throw her into a most insupportable sorrow, and she
should die of it, would not this be convincing proof of the highest
chastity? Would not her innocence and virtue be thereby set in a
more lovely light?[2]

The analogy is not very persuasive: there is an obvious distinction to be made between a voluntary and an involuntary death,
between stabbing oneself in the breast and dying of grief.
And this is precisely the distinction which Richardson is later
to explore in *Clarissa*. Unlike Lucretia, Clarissa does not coldly
and deliberately kill herself after she has been raped; instead
she dies of grief, in the manner of Bayle's nun, her death being
seemingly adduced in a similar way as a 'convincing proof of
the highest chastity', as an event which is tragic and yet at the
same time obscurely consoling and redemptive. Before turning
to see how Richardson develops these ideas in *Clarissa* (1747–
8), however, we may pause for a moment to notice how he
touches upon the story of Lucretia, and the problems related to
that story, in *Pamela* in 1740.

I

At one point in the earlier novel, Mr B. makes an attempt to
take the innocent Pamela on his knee. This is how she reacts:

O how I was terrify'd! I said, like as I had read in a Book a Night or
two before, Angels and Saints, and all the Host of Heaven, defend
me! And may I never survive one Moment, that fatal one in which I
shall forfeit my Innocence! Pretty Fool! said he, how will you forfeit
your Innocence, if you are obliged to yield to a Force you cannot
withstand? Be easy, said he; for let the worst happen that can, *you'll*
have the Merit and *I* the Blame; and it will be a good Subject for
Letters to your Father and Mother, and a Tale into the Bargain for
Mrs. *Jervis*.
    He by Force kissed my Neck and Lips, and said, Who ever blamed
Lucretia? All the Shame lay on the Ravisher only: And I am content
to take all the Blame upon me; as I have already borne too great a
Share for what I have deserved. May I, said I, *Lucretia* like, justify
myself with my Death, if I am us'd barbarously? O my good Girl!
said he, tauntingly, you are well read, I see; and we shall make out

between us, before we have done, a pretty Story in Romance, I
warrant ye.

He then put his Hand in my Bosom, and Indignation gave me
double Strength. . . . (i.31)[3]

For Pamela, to be raped by Mr B. would be a fate worse than
death; 'For to rob a Person of her Virtue', as she later says to
Mrs Jewkes, 'is worse than cutting her Throat' (i.145). Mr B.'s
light-hearted treatment of Pamela's fears, for all its (no doubt
reprehensible) cynicism and self-interest, actually touches
upon the very question which Augustine had asked about the
suicide of Lucretia: what is the logical point of such a death if
the blame is attributable entirely to the man? There is no
opportunity within the framework of this novel for such a
question to be properly pursued: 'a pretty Story in Romance'
Pamela and Mr B. do indeed finally make, but in a very
different sense from that which Pamela fears; the resolution of
their story is that of sentimental comedy, not tragedy: Mr B
does not rape Pamela but simply and meekly marries her.
Pamela never has to think by what means and in what manner
her life would cease the moment after rape; the question
remains entirely hypothetical.

Yet at one point in the novel Pamela is forced to think briefly
about the propriety of suicide. Preparing to escape from Mr
B.'s Lincolnshire estate, Pamela throws some of her clothes
into a pond in order to divert her pursuers; while they are
dragging the pond, she hopes to make her getaway. When she
comes to the garden gate, however, Pamela discovers that the
lock has been changed and her key will not open it. She tries to
climb the wall, but the bricks crumble away in her hand, and
she hurts herself in her fall. She looks in vain for a ladder.
Finally, Pamela sits down beside the pond and wonders
whether she should throw herself in. The thought is tempting.
How sorry they would all be! How clearly would it show them
that she valued her honour more dearly than her life!

And my Master, my angry Master, will then forget his Resentments,
and say, O this is the unhappy *Pamela*! that I have so causlesly
persecuted and destroy'd! Now do I see she preferr'd her Honesty to

her Life, will he say, and is no Hypocrite, nor Deceiver; but really was the innocent Creature she pretended to be! Then, thought I, will he perhaps shed a few Tears over the poor Corpse of his persecuted Servant. (i.234)

The temptation passes, and Pamela limps away to spend an uncomfortable night instead in the corner of the woodshed, where she is eventually discovered the following day. But the sight of Pamela's clothes in the pond has meanwhile aroused in Mr B precisely the feelings about which Pamela has fantasized the previous night. She has innocently staged, one might say, a mock suicide, which affects her persecutors in much the same way as her actual suicide might have done – the episode has a profound effect on Mr B. – while preserving herself entirely free of moral blame. Yet here, as so often elsewhere in *Pamela*, Richardson is skirting close to a moral issue which deserves to be more squarely confronted. If death is really to be preferred to dishonour, and if suicide is really a temptation to be shunned, what can a woman in extreme circumstances honourably do?

II

For Clarissa Harlowe, the temptation of suicide is almost continually present; and throughout this later novel Richardson explores the fine distinction which exists between the legitimate longing which a Christian may feel for death, and the illegitimate longing which he or she may have for suicide – 'the dreadfullest of all deaths', as Richardson calls it (vii.209).[4] Clarissa at times may seem, like Pamela, to have an almost romantic longing for death as a way out of present troubles. In her very first letter to Anna Howe, Clarissa speaks of her wish 'that it had pleased God to have taken me in my last fever, when I had every-body's love and good opinion' (i.5), and repeatedly in the letters that follow she plays, often a little wildly, with various prospects of death. 'I will die, rather than have that man,' she says early in the novel about Solmes, her unwelcome suitor; 'I had rather be buried alive, indeed I had, than have that man!' (ii.353, i.127). Rather than have Lovelace visit her family and cause further trouble, 'if there were no other way, I would most willingly be buried alive' (i.210). She would readily consent to accompany Solmes to the altar, she says, if she could be sure of being struck dead at that very spot before exchanging vows (i.307). With one part of her mind, Clarissa struggles for the freedom and integrity of her own personality, against the combined pressures of her family and her rival suitors; with another part of her mind, she longs extravagantly for extinction. 'I will undergo the cruellest death – I will even consent to enter the awful vault of my ancestors, and to have that bricked up upon me, rather than consent to be miserable for life' (ii.207). Clarissa imagines herself consenting dutifully to a death imposed upon her by God, by tyrannical relatives, or by blind natural forces; she hankers after catastrophe, after a fatal initiative taken by others. These fantasies are indulged not merely after Clarissa's rape, but from the very outset of the novel, and are an important part of Clarissa's character as we perceive it throughout the novel.

That they come perilously close to a wish for suicide, Clarissa is well aware. She stumbles even as she tries to articulate her wishes: 'I don't know what to do, not I – God forgive me, but I am very impatient! I wish – but I don't know what to wish, without a sin! Yet I wish it would please God to take me to his mercy! – I can meet with none here . . .' (ii.38). To Solmes she writes: 'could I, *without an unpardonable sin*, die when I *would*, I would sooner make death my choice, than take a step, which all the world, if not my own heart, will condemn me for taking' (ii.298).

It is with particularly mischievous intent that Clarissa's brother sends her a copy of the works of Francis Spira, the sixteenth-century Italian lawyer who, forced by the Papal legate to recant his newly won Lutheran beliefs, had killed himself in despair. 'My Brother's wit, I suppose. He thinks he does well to point out death and despair to me. I wish for the one, and every now-and-then am on the brink of the other' (iv.28). Clarissa is suspected of indulging this despair: her family fears that she may be taking drugs to make herself ill; and Sally, the woman who is set to watch her after she is abducted, considers that she is deliberately starving herself to death, and lectures her accordingly: 'Your Religion, I think, should teach you, that starving yourself is Self-murder' (vi.276).

More than once, Clarissa's situation in likened to that of Lucretia. Lovelace's friend Belford writes: 'But what I most apprehend is, that with her own hand, in resentment of the perpetrated outrage, she (like another Lucretia) will assert the purity of her heart: Or, if her piety preserve her from this violence, that wasting grief will soon put a period to her days' (iv.363). 'Another Lucretia'; in making this comparison, Belford adds a significant modification: Clarissa may perhaps kill herself violently as Lucretia did, yet it is also possible that she may die more religiously, as die she eventually does, through 'wasting grief'. Here and elsewhere in the novel Richardson is careful to show that Clarissa is caught in an infinitely more complex dilemma than was Lucretia. Clarissa desires death yet dreads suicide, lacks hope in life yet also lacks Lucretia's confidence in the propriety of ending life. 'A less complicated villainy cost a Tarquin – But I forget what I would say again,' says Clarissa after the rape (v.337), while Lovelace avers that he is sure that Clarissa will commit 'No Lucretia-like vengeance upon herself in her thought' (v.350). On yet another occasion, Lovelace writes that Clarissa will never commit suicide:

Her innate piety (as I have more than once observed) will not permit her to shorten her own life, either by violence or neglect. She has a mind too noble for that; and would have done it before now, had she designed any such thing: For to do it, like the Roman Matron [Lucretia], when the mischief is over, and it can serve no end . . . is what she has too much good sense to think of. (vii.13)

Despite such confidence, Lovelace is often alarmed by the possibility that Clarissa may do herself harm. When Clarissa's nose begins to bleed, Lovelace, seeing the blood, imagines that she must have stabbed herself (v.378). Like the scene in *Pamela* where Mr B. discovers Pamela's clothes in the pond, the episode works like a mock suicide, affecting the witness as a real suicide or suicide attempt might do while preserving the woman free of actual moral blame.

Yet Lovelace has some cause for his concern. At one point in the novel Clarissa goes so far as to invite Lovelace to kill her, or alternatively to give her the means to show him 'that my Honour is dearer to me than my Life' (iv.394). On another occasion, confronting Lovelace and the women who are assisting him, and finding herself with a weapon, she comes even closer to violence. Lovelace gives this account of the episode to his friend Belford:

To my astonishment, she held forth a penknife in her hand, the point to her own bosom, grasping resolutely the whole handle, so that there was no offering to take it from her.

'I offer not mischief to any-body but myself. You, Sir, and ye, women, are safe from every violence of mine. The LAW shall be all my resource: the LAW', and she spoke the word with emphasis, The LAW! that to such people carries natural terror with it, and now struck a panic into them. (vi.67–8)

This tableau of 'the Lady and the Penknife', as Lovelace is later to call it with studied casualness (vi.73), is reminiscent of several of the paintings and drawings of Lucretia's suicide by Lucas Cranach and others which we examined in chapter one. Like the artists, Richardson captures the moment at which the woman stands holding the dagger at her own breast, the moment at which, while apparently at her most vulnerable, most desperate, she is able to exercise a surprising and paradoxical power over her oppressor.[5]

This element of paradox, a central feature (as we have seen) of many versions of the story of Lucretia, lies also at the heart of Richardson's novel, which is also vitally concerned with the nature of power: power as it is exercised in particular within a family and in the relationship between the sexes. 'Who loves not power?' asks Clarissa casually near the outset of the novel (i.80), and it is the strategies of power which we see intricately deployed in the pages that follow. 'How soon may a young creature, who gives a man the least encouragement, be carried beyond her intentions, and out of her own power!' writes

Clarissa, as she gradually seems to surrender all power to Lovelace (ii.289). 'And is she not IN MY POWER?' writes Lovelace gloatingly to Belford (iii.31). One would say that Richardson was fascinated by the nature of this sort of power, were it not that this way of putting it might suggest misleading affinities with a writer such as Laclos, obscuring Richardson's real concern and apprehension over the way in which such power is commonly used. '*Men*, no more than *women*, know how to make a moderate use of power,' says Anna Howe at one point of the novel (iii.230); and later on Clarissa's cousin Morden is reported as saying, 'Both Sexes . . . too much love to have each other in their power: Yet he hardly ever knew man or woman who was very fond of power, make a right use of it' (vii.390). It would also obscure the subtlety with which Richardson explores the paradox of Clarissa's power: the power of the raped and dying woman.

   In the story of Lucretia, and especially in its pictorial versions, we noticed how power was symbolized by *knives*: the knife with which Tarquin threatens Lucretia, the knife with which Lucretia kills herself, and upon which Brutus and the other men swear to liberate Rome. The knives are symbolic and yet at the same time literal: power is seen in terms of actual weapons, of physical force and physical wounding.[6] In Richardson's novel power is conceived in very different terms: it is the gradual but massive accumulation of subtle psychological pressures which holds our interest throughout the vast length of the narrative: the oppressive and possessive wheedlings and blusterings of Clarissa's family, the theatricalities and insinuations of Lovelace, the polite importunities of Solmes and Hickman. Near the end of the novel, Clarissa's behaviour is contrasted with that of Calista in Nicholas Rowe's tragedy *The Fair Penitent*, who stabs herself in order to redeem her lost honour after the disclosure of her affair with Lothario (see plate eighteen). ('But, indeed, our Poets hardly know how to create a distress without horror, murder, and suicide,' says Belford, carefully distinguishing Clarissa's more scrupulous attitude: longing for death, but not hastening it through any deliberate act, vii.134–5.)[7]

In the scene of 'the Lady and the Penknife', Clarissa's knife does not enter her bosom: it does not have to. It is not simply a matter of Richardson disapproving of suicide; it is, more radically, that the knife does not represent the kind of power in which he or his character is interested. Clarissa exercises her real power through force of character; by virtue of a characteristic which Richardson calls, surely with full awareness of the word's multiple senses, her superior *penetration*. 'How then can she be so impenetrable?' Lovelace exclaims impatiently of Clarissa early in the novel (i.216); an ironical cry, it might seem, for a future rapist, who is, however, complaining of the fact that Clarissa, having penetrated his motives all too well, is impervious to his specious arguments. 'Penetration' and its cognates are words which recur over and again throughout *Clarissa*, denoting a quality not merely of intellectual and moral discernment but of pathetic sensibility as well.[8] It is a quality particularly associated with Clarissa, and is seen especially in the way she looks at people: 'we have the most watchful and most penetrating Lady in the world to deal with: A Lady worth deceiving! But whose eyes will pierce to the bottom of your shallow souls . . .'; 'She looked at me, as if she would look me thro': I thought I *felt* eye-beam, after eye-beam, penetrate my shivering reins'; 'that searching eye, darting into the very inmost cells of our frothy brains'; 'What heart but must have been penetrated?'; 'her penetration is *wonderful*' (iii.351, iv.289, 365, 394, v.355). Lovelace's wish is utterly to know and to possess and to rule Clarissa's personality; he will leave her no freedom, no independence of identity, no room for manoeuvre; he cannot rest until he knows what is in her letters. He also wishes, though in a much cruder sense, to 'penetrate' Clarissa, to subdue and possess her by means of an act of sexual domination. He discovers, however, that such physical penetration is in this sense quite trivial; to rape Clarissa is not to possess her. Richardson has in short moved the whole legend of rape now on to a subtler metaphorical or spiritual level. And it is one of the consequences of this shift that Clarissa does not need literally to stab herself in order to gain a victory over Lovelace. Clarissa counters Lovelace's act of rape not (like Lucretia) by another violent act upon her person, but by the tenacity and strength of her moral character.

Yet like Lucretia, Clarissa dies as a result of the rape; and her death is the ultimate answer to Lovelace, the act that finally breaks his power, just as Lucretia's suicide finally breaks the power of Tarquin. Why does Clarissa die? The problem distressed the earliest readers of the novel and is likely to puzzle many readers today. The precise cause of Clarissa's death is never explained. Margaret Doody, in a recent study of Richardson, conjectures that Clarissa dies of 'galloping consumption', but this is really no more than guesswork.[9] Richardson deliberately allows the exact nature of Clarissa's illness to remain obscure. Were it to be precisely identified as (say) galloping consumption or typhoid fever it might seem too casually related to the suffering which Clarissa has undergone, a random accident for which Lovelace need feel no personal responsibility. Instead, it emerges mysteriously, imprecisely, as something not quite diagnosable in physiological terms but not quite attributable to Clarissa's conscious and volitional self either.[10] For to speak, as another recent critic (Anthony Kearney) does, of Clarissa's 'deliberate' and 'determined act of dying' is to simplify the issue in another direction, and to place oneself in dubious alliance with Lovelace, who considers that Clarissa's illness, like the sham illness which he himself once staged in order to play upon Clarissa's affections, is quite consciously induced.[11] Women can make themselves sick at will, he believes, just as they can make themselves blush at will. If we see Clarissa's illness as even partly self-induced, a number of awkward questions are indeed likely to present themselves. 'Does this Lady do right to make herself ill, when she is *not* ill?' asks Lovelace indignantly (vi.15). Can Clarissa's death be justified in terms of moral necessity? And if so, how would such a justification be framed? If not, doesn't it follow that Clarissa must be held responsible, at least in part, for her own destruction, and that Lovelace's responsibility is correspondingly diminished?

These questions are ingeniously pursued near the end of the novel by Lovelace himself in conversation with Lord M. and

Lovelace's cousins the two Misses Montague; and it is not surprising that Lovelace at this point should turn, as Mr B. did with Pamela, to the story of the rape of Lucretia. Lovelace plays in his own swaggering, jocular, patronizing way the role of a new Augustine. '. . . what honour is lost', he asks, 'where the *will* is not violated, and the person cannot help it? . . . Both my Cousins were silent; and my Lord, because he could not answer me, cursed me; and I proceeded.'

But will you take upon you to say, supposing (as in the present case) a Rape (saving your presence, Cousin Charlotte, saving your presence, Cousin Patty); Is death the *natural* consequence of a Rape – Did you ever hear, my Lord, or did you, Ladies, that it was? – And if not the *natural* consequence, and a Lady will destroy herself, whether by a lingering death, as of grief; or by the dagger, as Lucretia did; Is there more than one fault the *man*'s? Is not the other *her*'s? Were it not so, let me tell you, my dears, chucking each of my blushing Cousins under the chin, we either have had no men so wicked as young Tarquin was, or no women so virtuous as Lucretia, in the space of – How many thousand years, my Lord? And so Lucretia is recorded as a single wonder!

You may believe I was cry'd out upon. (viii. 160–2)

The crucial phrase here is 'destroy herself'. Clarissa does not, in the simple sense of this phrase, destroy herself; she is instead destroyed, however reluctant Lovelace may be to face the fact. The question of voluntary and involuntary actions is so crucially important in the novel, however, that it is worth examining it a little more closely.

'I have never been faulty in my Will', Clarissa says near the end of the novel (viii.23). *Will* is a word of the greatest lexical complexity in the novel, ranging widely in its senses to include volition, consent, power of choice, intellectual sturdiness, wilfulness, and lust. 'How prompt a thing is *will*!' Clarissa writes to Anna Howe early in the novel (ii.161). Much of the novel is concerned with the opposition of different kinds of will: will in its different lexical senses, and opposing wills of people in conflict. The word operates throughout as a central, complex pun, drawing together many of the novel's diverse yet related moral preoccupations. Clarissa finds herself caught up in a struggle of opposing wills. '. . . surrender your whole will to the will of the honoured pair, to whom you owe your being', she is told (ii.36) – and recognizes that her mother ('A Wife who has no Will but his!' (ii.14)) has already surrendered *her* whole will to that of her husband. Clarissa complains that she is detained and coerced by her brother 'against my will': 'How strong is will!' is his contemptuous reply (ii.244–5). Lovelace plumes himself upon his 'own imperial will', devising ways of exerting his will against Clarissa's: 'I will see how *her* will works; and how *my* will leads me on' (iii.34, 32). Skilled in the strategies of power, Lovelace tests from time to time the effectiveness of a feigned surrender: 'All obedience, all resignation – No will but hers' (iv.266). Lovelace's abduction, imprisonment, and rape of Clarissa are acts which are knowingly and wilfully committed against her will. They derive from his conviction that he must overpower her will with his, and that sexual relationships, marital and extramarital, are based upon power and conquest: '*Women are born to be controul'd.* . . . A tyrant-husband makes a dutiful wife. And why do the Sex love Rakes, but because they know how to direct their uncertain wills, and manage them?' (iv.265).

'*I have never been faulty in my Will*': Clarissa means several things by this declaration. She means that she has never wantonly defied the authority of her family. She also means that she has never assented to Lovelace's rape and that his act has left her essentially untouched: 'it has not tainted my mind; it has not hurt my morals. . . . My will is unviolated' (vii.232). Anna Howe insists after the rape that Clarissa has 'a will wholly faultless', and even Lovelace, in an uneasy blend of chagrin and self-exculpation, concedes the same: 'It is true, that I have nothing to boast of as to her Will. *The very contrary*'; 'the *will*, the *consent*, is wanting'; 'Her will is unviolated' (v.319, 324, 381). Clarissa's assertion is not unlike the proud retort of the Lady in Milton's *Comus* to the threats of her seducer: 'Thou canst not touch the freedom of my mind'.[12] It may remind us, too, of Lucretia's declaration in Livy's narrative: 'my body only has been violated: my heart is innocent'. In Livy's narrative and in other early versions of the

Lucretia story, the question of will is complicated by the fact that Lucretia consciously chooses to be raped, rather than undergo posthumous disgrace. Certain late medieval narrators were sufficiently disconcerted by this aspect of the story to vary the narrative, and allow Lucretia to swoon at the critical moment rather than exercise her moral choice. In Chaucer's version of the story she lies 'in a swogh', as though 'ded', during the rape; in Gower's, she is 'ded oppressed'.[13] Clarissa is likewise raped while she is unconscious, having been heavily drugged by Lovelace. Her unconsciousness, like that of Chaucer's and Gower's Lucrece, is offered to the reader as a kind of guarantee that during the act itself her conscious will cannot in any way have been actively engaged. Like the swoon of Chaucer's and Gower's Lucrece, Clarissa's unconsciousness is also presented as a kind of death, prefiguring the final death. In her final testament, Clarissa acknowledges that Lovelace may 'insist upon viewing *her dead*, whom he ONCE before saw in a manner dead' (viii.107). Only drugs and death can totally relax the firm volitional control with which Clarissa attempts to direct her actions and to mitigate the effect of actions done to her by others.

'*I have never been faulty in my Will*': Clarissa also means – and this meaning is of crucial importance in the novel – that she is not wilfully inducing her own death. Writing to Anna after the rape, she explains more fully her thoughts on this matter; the 'penknife' incident is still on her mind:

> But now my dear, for *your* satisfaction let me say, that altho' I wish not for life, yet would I not, like a poor coward, desert my post when I can maintain it, and when it is my *duty* to maintain it.
>
> More than once, indeed, was I urged by thoughts so sinful: But then it was in the height of my distress: And once, particularly, I have reason to believe, I saved myself by my *desperation* from the most shocking personal insults; from a repetition, as far as I know, of his vileness; the base women (with so much reason dreaded by me) present, to intimidate *me*, if not to assist *him*! – O my dear, you know not what I suffered on that occasion! – Nor do I what I *escaped* at the time, if the wicked man had approached me to execute the horrid purposes of his vile heart.

As I am of opinion, that it would have manifested more of Revenge and Despair, than of Principle, had I committed a violence upon myself, when the villainy was *perpetrated*; so I should think it equally criminal, were I now *wilfully* to neglect myself; were I *purposely* to run into the arms of death (*as that man supposes I shall do*) when I might avoid it. (vi.411)

Clarissa insists that she will not 'wilfully' neglect herself, that she will do everything necessary to prolong her life until the time that God calls her away; she will eat, she will drink, as appetite serves; she will take what her physicians prescribe for her.

In short, I will do every-thing I can do, to convince all my friends, who hereafter may think it worth their while to enquire after my last behaviour, that I possessed my soul with tolerable patience; and endeavoured to bear with a lot of my own drawing: For thus, in humble imitation of the sublimest Exemplar, I often say: – Lord, it is thy will; and it shall be mine. (vi.412)

'Lord, it is thy will': unlike Lucretia, Clarissa does not coolly and deliberately *will* her death in order to cancel dishonour or satisfy social expectations, atone for possible guilt or trigger retribution against the man who has wronged her.[14] Instead, she piously surrenders her will to that of heaven: 'The will of Providence be resigned to in the rest: As *that* leads, let me patiently, and unrepiningly, follow! — I shall not live always! – May but my *closing* scene be happy!' (ii.264)

Yet the issue is more complex that that, for Clarissa's behaviour cannot be analysed merely in terms of the pieties she utters. The causes of Clarissa's death lie deep in the subconscious parts of her being. In dying, she declares that she surrenders her own will to that of God. But it would be possible also to say that Clarissa loses the will to live. Like the raped nun whose case Pierre Bayle discusses in relation to the story of Lucretia, Clarissa dies of grief; a grief compounded of many factors. Grief at the stubbornness of her family, at the way in which her own best-intentioned actions have vexed them, and in which certain of their prophecies about her may seem, to a careless eye, to have been fulfilled; grief at the way in which

they have given her no true freedom, shown her no trust, left
her in an ultimate sense with nowhere to go. Grief at the way in
which Lovelace, like many of her own family, has also tried to
crush the freedom of her personality, resorting at the last –
from vindictiveness, resentment, exasperation, megalomania,
love, calculation, and panic – to an act that ignores her as a
person, treating her contemptuously as an inert body upon a
bed; grief at the way in which her guarded love for Lovelace
and her hopes to redeem him were so disastrously misplaced.
We have already noticed the way in which, from the earliest
letters in the novel, Clarissa betrays a constant longing for
death as a means of release from the problems that face her.
With the conscious part of her mind Clarissa rejects the temptation to bring about her own death; but other, deeper parts of
her being draw her none the less steadily towards death. The
impulses towards self-destruction, as Freud has made us
aware, may take many forms, unconscious as well as conscious; Clarissa's death, while not a morally culpable act, may
be seen as an example of what Freud calls 'semi-intentional
annihilation': the subconscious welcoming of a threat to life
which might, in other circumstances, be thrown off.[15]
Richardson's achievement is to show us how different parts of
Clarissa's personality are moving simultaneously in different
directions. He leaves us in no doubt that, in terms of conscious
intention, her conduct is technically blameless, both in relation
to Lovelace's advances and to her own death. Yet Richardson
also allows us to see how powerfully the attractions both of
Lovelace and of death (her new lover, as Lovelace aptly puts it)
affect her. In the matter of the rape, as in the matter of her
death, Clarissa's conscious will is clear. But at a deeper level
Clarissa may seem to drift towards the destinies she consciously rejects.

   Human will can be exerted not merely by the living but also
by the dead: and the wishes of the dead are traditionally
expressed in a document that we call, significantly, a *will*. Such
wills play a dominant part in Richardson's novel, which opens
with a detailed account of the will of Clarissa's recently
deceased grandfather, and closes with an equally detailed

account of the will of Clarissa herself. At least eight other wills are spoken of in the course of the novel, which Richardson originally intended to call *The Lady's Legacy*.[16] 'Wills are sacred things, child,' says Anna to Clarissa (i.182), and such wills are indeed seen at times as possessing an almost religious authority and force. Clarissa and her mother visit a dying woman who superstitiously believes that the making of her will is likely to precipitate her death, and that the burning of a will may be restorative of health. The early part of the novel dramatizes the conflict between Clarissa's grandfather's will and the opposing wills of the rest of the family; Clarissa is told 'that your Father's *living* Will shall controul your Grandfather's *dead* one' (i.337). This conflict between the will of the living and the will of the dead remains of great interest in the later parts of the novel. Through the means of her will, Clarissa continues to affect and influence others after her death. The written document she draws up and calls her 'will' is a full and final expression of a personal will that, throughout the closing stages of her brief lifetime, has been thwarted, constricted, and brutally violated.

In the story of the rape of Lucretia, an opportunity is given to Lucretia in a curiously similar way to reassert at the moment of her death her personal will, to say what her deepest wishes are. In Shakespeare's *The Rape of Lucrece*, Lucrece sends a letter after she is raped to summon her husband Collatine, and describes this as her *will*, which Collatine must 'oversee' and execute. (Shakespeare's poem, like Richardson's novel, plays on the various senses of this word; Tarquin has been figured as an agent and victim of will: 'But Will is deaf and hears no heedful friends' (l. 495).) In this and other versions of the story, Lucrètia's will is of course that her death be revenged. This 'will' is expressed not merely in Lucretia's letters to her husband and father but also in the speech she makes before she kills herself. This is the traditional turning-point of the story, the moment at which the balance of power reverses and Tarquin's fate is sealed. Many of the narrators make much of this moment; here is Nathaniel Lee's Lucrece, for example, in his tragedy of *Lucius Junius Brutus*:

All that I ask you now is to revenge me;
Revenge me, father; husband, O revenge me.
Revenge me, Brutus, you his sons revenge me,
Herminius, Mutius; thou Horatius too,
And thou Valerius; all, revenge me all,
Revenge the honor of the ravished Lucrece . . . [*Stabs herself*]
Revenge me; O revenge, revenge, revenge. [*Dies*]

(I.403–9, 418).

In Ovid's account, and versions of the story deriving from it, Lucretia's spirit continues to hover over the Romans, urging them on to their great task of vengeance. Clarissa, on the other hand, insists in her will that no vengence be taken on the man who has raped and destroyed her, bidding her executor, Belford, that 'he will (as he has repeatedly promised) studiously endeavour to promote peace with, and suppress resentments in, every one; so as that all farther mischiefs may be prevented, as well *from* as *to* his friend' (viii. 118–19). Though the memory of Clarissa and her dying injunctions have a powerful effect upon other characters in the novel, her wishes in this particular matter are not complied with. Lovelace is sought out and killed in Europe by Clarissa's cousin Morden, who – like Lucius Junius Brutus in the Lucretia story – stands significantly just outside the immediate family group, which in both stories bears some responsibility for the original crime. In both stories the act of rape brings about the death of the woman, which in turn brings about the downfall of the rapist. There is, perhaps, a slight air of having it both ways in the conclusion of Richardson's novel. Yet Clarissa's dying request for amnesty stands in significant contrast to Lucretia's dying request for vengeance, marking yet another change of sensibility, a new hesitation over the value and propriety of revenge, a sense that true power may express itself in other ways than in blood feuds. And once again it is the contour of the old legend that enables us to see the extent of this change in sensibility.

Richardson is not interested in those aspects of the story of Lucretia that evidently attracted such writers as Lee, Bond, and Duncombe. He shows little interest, for example, in the political dimension of the story. His novel has no explicit political significance, concentrating rather upon the intricacies of family life and individual psychology. Lovelace tries to minimize the gravity of what he has done by stressing the fact that the rape at least has no serious political consequence: 'the man, however a Tarquin, as some may think me in this action, is not a Tarquin in power, so that no *national point* can be made of it' (vii.13). The plea is desperate. Richardson allows us to see that Lovelace's act is no less grave for having been committed against a private person of no political importance, that tragedy may occur in a private household despite the fact that it has no impact on the destinies of nations. In this respect Richardson has affinities with a dramatist such as George Lillo or Sir Richard Steele, who had argued in *The Tatler* (no. 172) that tragedy is not merely about 'the history of princes, and persons who act in high spheres' but may also concern itself with 'such adventures as befall persons not elevated above the common level'. Ironically, Lovelace's attempt to minimize the importance of this act goes counter to his normal tendency towards self-aggrandizement. Throughout the novel, Lovelace 'Romanizes' the style both of his letters and of his actions, comparing himself freely with heroes from the classical past: with Caesar, Alexander, Hannibal, Hector, Brutus, Aeneas, Tarquin. Richardson's own scepticism about the kind of 'heroism' associated with those names is always clearly implied.[17] Like Milton in *Paradise Lost*, like Steele in *The Christian Hero*, Richardson is looking rather for models of better and more Christian fortitude. In a letter to William Duncombe's daughter-in-law Susanna Highmore in 1750, Richardson makes this point quite explicitly:

As for the old Romans, they were abominable fellows, thieves, robbers, plunderers: love of their country they were not satisfied with. They would not allow any other nation to love theirs. From robbery to robbery they proceeded, till they had enlarged their den so as to take in the greatest part of the then known world. The Turks, not more mean in their beginnings than they: and from their beginnings, to this day, a much better people. Yet from these banditti are our university-men, and dramatic-writers, to borrow their heroes. –

Shrink you not, Madam, at the crimes of their Tarquins, their Decemviri, their Mariuses, their Syllas, their Pompeys, their Caesars – almost all their Caesars?[18]

Clarissa Harlowe's fortitude, on the other hand, may represent a new kind of heroism: a Christian heroism, more finely attuned to the new moral pressures of the time. '. . . it is plain to me', writes Belford, 'the Sinner is the real Coward, and the Saint the true Hero' (vi.424).

For Richardson, the story of the rape of Lucretia is what one might call an uncomfortable myth, a myth whose moral implications leave much to be desired. Yet Richardson's discomfort, unlike Shakespeare's, results in a powerful new conception of a different kind of story which can be told about another kind of heroine, another kind of rape, and another range of moral dilemmas and moral possibilities. It is in this sense that Clarissa Harlowe can be called 'another Lucretia'.

III

And powerful the novel certainly is: a work of great psychological subtlety and imaginative force, which is at the same time strikingly 'modern' (one is tempted to say) in many of its moral attitudes and implications. Yet certain aspects of *Clarissa* may none the less seem to a modern reader to be as problematical in their own way as aspects of the story of Lucretia may well have seemed to Richardson himself. To put this another way, one might say that while Richardson was acutely aware of one morally questionable aspect of the Lucretia story (Lucretia's suicide), he has failed to challenge other aspects of the story which today may seem to be equally objectionable. In particular, Richardson may seem too easily to accept the notion that also governs the story of Lucretia: that rape is a 'fate worse than death' and a fate that in some sense necessitates death. A morally fastidious woman, Richardson implies, may quite literally die as a result of rape. Not merely that: the fact that she does die is in a sense the *proof* of her moral fastidiousness, and of her total and absolute rejection of the sexual act to which she has been subjected. Clarissa is in this respect like Lucretia, who in Livy's narrative offers her death as evidence of her chastity: *animus insons, mors testis erit*, 'my heart is innocent: death will be my witness'. She is also like the (imaginary) raped nun whose case Pierre Bayle discusses, and whose death he offers as 'convincing proof of the highest chastity'.

The assumptions underlying *Clarissa* are, therefore, not so different from those underlying the story of the rape of Lucretia as one might at first think. In both stories, rape is seen as a lethal act, and death as an event which redeems possible dishonour. Both these assumptions are a little curious. There is, of course, an all too familiar sense in which rape can be a lethal act, when accompanied by physical brutality; but Lovelace's rape of the heavily sedated Clarissa is clearly not an act of this kind. (So very unforceful does Lovelace seem, indeed, at the climactic moment of the novel that one critic has even queried whether the rape is actually carried out.[19]) Clarissa dies not from the physical violence of the rape but from the trauma of its larger implications and complications. The psychological causes of this trauma are minutely and sympathetically traced in the novel. Yet there is an extremism about the whole proposition that seems perilous, and ultimately perhaps faintly dehumanizing. Lovelace's question is apt to linger in the reader's mind: 'Is death the *natural* consequence of a Rape?' Clarissa's death is not, of course, presented as though it *were* a 'natural', predictable, and commonplace event; the unexpectedness of her death is in a sense the point. Nor for that matter is Clarissa presented as a 'natural', predictable, and commonplace person, but rather as a woman of exceptional sensibility, whose physical delicacy serves as a fine index of the delicacy of her soul. It is precisely in this area, however – in the assumption that sensibility manifests itself in outward, physical ways such as pallor and frailty, and that the shock of rape must be registered in Clarissa by ill health, decline, and death ('convincing proof of the highest chastity') – that the novel seems weakest, skirting dangerously close to cultural and fictional stereotype. Rape puts an end to a woman's life: 'In all those English books your goodness has procured for me, I find that it is the leading idea,' says one of the characters in Robert Bage's novel *Mount Henneth* (1781):

Women who have suffered it, must die, or be immured for ever. Ever after they are totally useless to all the purposes of society. It is the foundation of an hundred fabulous things called novels, which are said to paint exactly the reigning manners and opinions. All crimes but this may be expiated. No author has yet been so bold as to permit a lady to live and marry, and be a woman after this stain.[20]

There is no compelling reason in physiology or logic for the notion that delicacy of spirit is reflected in delicacy of health. There is no reason why a highly sensitive woman may not also be physically robust and tenacious of life. There is no reason why death after rape should 'prove' or enhance a woman's chastity, any more than failure to die after rape should 'prove', or raise the slightest suspicion of, her lack of chastity. Why then should such a bizarre notion ever develop?

Here it is necessary to be a little speculative. One of the central problems about rape has always been that of difficulty of proof. How can it be known for certain that a sexual act was rape, and not something else? That the apparent victim did not in fact entice, collude, enjoy, and only afterwards protest, reject, and indict? If rape is an act committed against the will, it obviously rests with the woman herself to say what her will was; a will that may legitimately change one way or another during the course of the act, or be divided against itself.[21] Other people can as a rule only deduce and conjecture, in much the same manner in which people down the centuries have tended to conjecture about the 'real' facts of the story of the rape of Lucretia. The particular edge and anger of current feminist discussions of rape derives from a conviction that much official (and popular) conjecture about rape tends all too readily towards scepticism and facetiousness, that the word of the woman herself is often too lightly set aside, that nothing short of the most spectacular injuries or (better still) death will be taken as 'proof' that a rape has indeed been committed. 'Failure to have died, or even looked like dying, for the sake of protecting her virtue heightens speculation that the victim contributed to the crime by not preventing it. . . . Victims are supposed to prefer death to rape.'[22] Thus there are two, somewhat contradictory, reasons why the death of a rape victim may seem darkly satisfying. First, there is the sense that moral 'ruin' may just as well be accompanied by physical ruin; that a raped woman has no future, having been in some way irreparably damaged by the act and consequently become, as Bage puts it, 'totally useless to all the purposes of society'. And secondly, there if the conflicting notion that the death 'proves' (a little late in the day, to be sure) that the woman was not so irretrievably ruined after all, for she can scarcely have colluded in an act which brings about her own death. The tension set up between these two contradictory impulses of relief and regret, rejection and acceptance, gives rise to feelings of the sentimentally tragic kind, and to the sort of pietism that led to the canonization of Maria Goretti.

The notion of sexual 'ruin' which underlies such thinking derives essentially from the fear of pregnancy and the known stigmas attaching both to unmarried motherhood and to bastardy. In *Clarissa*, this central issue is touched upon only with hesitation and reluctance. Clarissa's mother fretfully wonders whether Clarissa may be pregnant; such a fate, if proved true, 'would perpetuate her stain' (iv.51). Richardson never reveals if Clarissa is indeed pregnant, though her illness seems to be in some way obscurely connected with this possibility. With Clarissa's death, however, all doubts, speculations, and possible 'stain' are at once erased; the situation is (in once sense) saved, as it is in the older story by the suicide of Lucretia.

For all its subtlety and thoughtfulness, *Clarissa* is not entirely free of simpler ways of thinking about sexual issues. In admiring the way in which Richardson rejects certain cultural assumptions about rape, it is important to notice that he is still in the bondage of others which are equally curious and equally open to challenge. He is less radical in these matters than novelists who are in other respects greatly inferior to him, such as Bage and Thomas Holcroft. Holcroft's *Anna St. Ives* (1794) is clearly influenced by *Clarissa*, but when Anna St. Ives defies her would-be rapist Coke Clifton, the similarities with Richardson's novel are less important than the differences of tone and emphasis:

'Why, man, what would you do? Is murder your intent? – While I have life I fear you not! – And think you that brutality can taint the dead? Nay, think you that, were you endowed with the superior force which the vain name of man supposes, and could accomplish the basest purpose of your heart, I would falsely take guilt to myself; or imagine I had received the smallest blemish, from impurity which never reached my mind? That I would lament, or shun the world, or walk in open day oppressed by shame I did not merit? No! – For you perhaps I might weep, but for myself I would not shed a tear! Not a tear! – You cannot injure me. . . .'[23]

Like Lucretia, Clarissa (and Milton's Lady), Anna declares that her mind cannot be touched by rape; unlike Lucretia and Clarissa, however, Anna pursues more logically and vigorously the consequences of that declaration, seeing no need to feel personal shame, guilt, sorrow, or the necessity to die on account of an act for which she is not personally responsible. Despite the hectoring, exclamatory tone of the passage, it is evident that Holcroft is questioning in a more fundamental way than Richardson the entire mythology of rape, the 'fate worse than death'.

Or again, to take a novelist of powers more nearly comparable to Richardson's, one thinks of Thomas Hardy and *Tess of the d'Urbervilles*. Throughout *Tess*, Hardy returns in a variety of ways to the central question which we have been following: why should a woman be thought to be dishonoured by a sexual act for which she is not herself responsible? Hardy's presentation of Tess after her fall as 'a pure woman', 'a spiritual Lucretia', is not entirely free from confusion, as more than one critic has pointed out: Hardy's reticence makes it impossible to know whether Tess is initially raped or seduced, and as Mary Jacobus remarks, 'To invoke purity in connection with a career that includes not simply seduction, but collapse into kept woman and murderess, taxes the linguistic resources of the most permissive conventional moralist.'[24] Yet Hardy is more consistently vigilant than Richardson about the stereotypes of seduction, betrayal, and dishonour. Though Tess is in her own way quite as obsessed by death as Clarissa is – feeling the bone along her eye socket and sensing the skull beneath the skin, thinking of the unknown date in the calendar that will be the day of her death, sleeping on the tomb of her ancestors in Kingsbere church ('Why am I on the wrong side of this door!') – Tess does not succumb to death after she has been seduced. 'Let the truth be told – women do as a rule live through such humiliations, and regain their spirits, and again look about them with an interested eye. While there's life there's hope is a conviction not so entirely unknown to the "betrayed" as some amiable theorists would have us believe' (p. 133).

One of the achievements of the early half of the novel is the way that Hardy shows Tess, despite her calamities, renewing her life and energies, charting 'the invincible instinct towards self-delight', 'The irresistible, universal, automatic tendency to find sweet pleasure somewhere, which pervades all life . . .' (pp. 128, 132). 'Dead! dead! dead!' murmurs Angel Clare in the sleep-walking scene after he has heard the news of Tess's past (p. 272), but the woman he carries in his arms is as full of vitality as the milkmaids he carried one Sunday morning across a flooded road. Tess does not die on account of any 'dishonour' that Alec d'Urberville has done to her, but for quite other reasons, for love of Angel Clare. Like Richardson, Hardy focuses upon the importance of *will*. Angel 'asked himself why he had not judged Tess constructively rather than biographically, by the will rather than by the deed?' (p. 393). 'The beauty or ugliness of a character', he realizes, 'lay not only in its achievements, but in its aims and impulses; its true history lay, not among things done, but among things willed' (p. 363). The realization comes to Angel only with difficulty, after much pain. For Angel, advanced and emancipated as he seems, is surprisingly enmeshed in traditional ways of thinking about sexual dishonour. Hardy tests these ways of thinking more searchingly than Richardson in his time was able to do, seeing them as potentially more destructive than the initial seduction itself.[25]

Seen in the light of subsequent developments in fiction and

in ways of thinking about sexual behaviour, Clarissa Harlowe's death may ultimately seem something of an evasion of the real dilemmas of rape, as Lucretia's death no doubt seemed an evasion to Richardson himself. Richardson's novel deserves to be judged in the same way in which he judged the story of Lucretia: not simply by 'the standards of its day' (however these are to be discovered) but by standards which we ourselves judge, in our day, to be fully credible, defensible, and humane. Judged by such standards, *Clarissa* must be reckoned a work of great narrative, imaginative, and moral power. Yet the implied priorities of the novel are no longer easy to accept, nor is its dark and at times luxuriant dallying with the beauties of death. Modern readers of the novel may find it hard to be persuaded that the sufferings which Clarissa undergoes are more terrible than death itself.

5

Joking About Rape:
The Myth Inverted

Saint Augustine's condemnation of Lucretia's suicide in *The City of God* has a curious effect on the development of the old story. One might expect that Augustine's comments would do something to dampen interest in the story or inhibit its growth. Yet the effect is entirely the contrary: the very difficulties which Augustine discovers in the story seem to act as a creative stimulant, prompting writers to speculate further about the way in which the events as traditionally reported might 'really' have occurred, and to refashion and extend the story in a variety of ways. Some of these refashionings take very large liberties. Sometimes they seem virtually to turn the story inside out, reversing its traditional narrative outlines and moral assumptions in an attempt to make the story more comprehensible or acceptable to readers of another age. One way of making the story comprehensible and acceptable is to joke about it. And the many jokes about the story of Lucretia – parodies, epigrams, quips, comic rewritings – can sometimes tell us as much about the growing discomfort with the story as do the more serious rewritings and more serious works of analysis and argumentation. These jokes form, indeed, a significance aspect of the story's post-Augustinian reception and transformation.

I

The serious and the comic rewritings of the story often have something in common. Perhaps the most obvious and central feature of the traditional story is the presentation of Lucretia as a scrupulously faithful wife, single-mindedly devoted to her

husband Collatinus. In certain redactions of the story, both
serious and humorous, it is precisely this feature that is called
into question. In one of the most popular and influential
versions of the story, Madeleine de Scudéry's enormous
romance *Clélie* (1654–60), Lucretia displays indifference,
even hostility, towards her husband, a man of quite unremark-
able and unheroic qualities. Scudéry's Lucretia is in love with
another and altogether more dashing figure: Lucius Junius
Brutus – a variation of the traditional plot that gives rise to
some surprising narrative developments and necessitates a
radical adjustment of conventional ideas about Brutus'
character as well as about Lucretia's.[1] Other writers give
Lucretia other lovers. A. V. Arnault, in his tragedy *Lucrèce, ou
Rome libre* (1792), imagines his heroine to feel a lingering
fondness for her rapist, Sextus Tarquinius, a former suitor
whose earlier attentions to her had been discouraged by her
father on the grounds that he belonged to the hated family of
Tarquins. The rape occurs during an affectionate reunion that
gets somewhat out of hand. Rousseau's unfinished play, *La
Mort de Lucrèce* (first published in 1792 and possibly known
to Arnault), conceives the situation in similar terms: Tarquin is
a former suitor who has once been betrothed to Lucretia, and
still has a hold on her affections; Collatinus is a contemptible
figure, ambitious for royal favour and willing to entertain
Tarquin's friendship and encourage his attentions to Lucretia
in order to advance his own position at court; Brutus alone is
capable of observing the way in which this inflammatory situation gradually builds up.

Scudéry, Arnault, and Rousseau each try in their different
ways to transform Lucretia from a severe Roman matron into
a Woman of Sensibility, poised on the brink of adultery,
endowing her with a disposition and a predicament intended
to make her appear more interesting and understandable to
readers of their times. Their portraits are nevertheless basically
admiring. Lucretia in all three versions is seen as a passionate,
but highly principled, woman; the strength of her principles is
indeed the more to be admired (it is implied) because of the
strength of her passions. 'It is not her insensibility that has

given Lucretia eternal fame, but her chastity,' the preface to the 1824 edition of Arnault's play roundly declares; and each of these versions gives prominence to Lucretia's struggle between her natural feelings and her sense of wifely loyalty. To romanticize the story in this way, however, is also to take certain artistic risks. Arnault's and Rousseau's versions of the story are curiously close to those sceptical interpretations of writers such as Jacques du Bosc, who asked whether Lucretia might not have encouraged Tarquin or secretly rather have enjoyed the rape, killing herself afterwards out of a sense of guilt or because her true feelings for Tarquin had been publicly revealed.[2]

Rousseau, at least, was well aware of some of the risks inherent in treating the story in this way, and possibly failed to complete his play when he felt the risks to be insurmountable. He had began to think about the play as early as 1754 while in Geneva. 'I planned a prose tragedy on no less a subject than Lucretia,' he writes in the *Confessions*, 'with which I had some hope of overcoming derison, even though I ventured to bring that unfortunate woman back to the stage when she had become an impossible subject for the French theatre.'[3] This testimony as to popular attitudes to the story at the time is revealing. Jacques Sherer, the leading authority on Rousseau's drama, declares that Lucretia's story appeared so shocking or absurd to French audiences in the eighteenth century that no serious dramatic version of the story ever reached the stage.[4] This is not quite the case. But it is certainly true, as Sherer points out, that the story had become a popular subject for parody at this time, and Rousseau's remarks confirm the impression that French audiences may have been predisposed to regard the story light-heartedly. Jean-Jacques Bel's *Le Nouveau Tarquin* (1732), a little musical skit half in verse, half in prose, gives some indication of the characteristic style and approach of these parodies. Bel's Tarquin has been in love with Lucretia for six years; though she is unmarried and rather fancies him, she keeps holding him at bay. When finally he takes on the form of a god and enjoys her favours in the Temple of Vesta, however, she doesn't seem altogether displeased. An elaborate legal case ensues, presided over by Brutus; the lawyers argue learnedly over the nature of the 'rape', Tarquin finally escaping punishment, and Lucretia – lustily singing – remaining very much alive.[5] The existence of such pieces as this may well have given Rousseau reason to doubt whether the story could be treated seriously in the theatre of his day. It is perhaps the more remarkable, however, that Rousseau, like Bel, should have chosen to imagine Lucretia as a woman secretly rather fond of the man who raped her, boldly entering into a sensitive area of the story that the parodists were often ready to exploit.

It was not merely in eighteenth-century France that the parodists attacked the story at precisely this point, presenting Lucretia as a woman less fond of her husband than of Tarquin or some other man. Most of the many parodies found in different countries at different times take exactly this line of approach. An extreme example is Noel Langley's modern novel *Cage Me a Peacock* (1935), whose heroine Lucrece (or Althea) is a highly promiscuous young woman who has had affairs at some time or another with most of the Senators of Rome; Sextus Tarquinius is her first husband, whom she abandons for many years, and who finally catches up with her to claim at long last his conjugal rights. Thus the 'rape' occurs. Sextus threatens to take Lucrece back to Spain with him, and it is *this* fate (not any sexual assault) which she reckons to be worse than death. In the end – a better fate – she is sent off to Spain with Collatinus' young brother. Parodies of so open and rumbustious a kind, though often amusing enough in their own way, are perhaps less interesting in what they tell us about the story than are parodies which are mixed with more serious intent – and parodies which occur, so to speak, by accident.

In this latter category must be placed a number of English dramatic versions of the story, such as Thomas Heywood's *The Rape of Lucrece* (published 1608), a tragedy which slithers disconcertingly between high rhetorical lament and low facetiousness. After Lucrece is raped, Valerius, Horatius Cocles, and a Clown sing a bawdy catch merrily reflecting on the event. Heywood's intermittent humour reveals the stresses and strains which he evidently felt to inhere in the original story, and seems designed to relieve tension, allowing audiences a hearty response to those parts of the story which may have seemed to them implausible, titillating, or overwrought. Heywood does not openly parody the story, but he moves near the brink, opening up the comic possibilities.[6] Other overtly serious English plays on the same subject often show a similar sporadic facetiousness. Sometimes it is the epilogues to these plays which offer the principal outlets for humorous release. William Hunt's tragedy *The Fall of Tarquin* (1713) concludes with an epilogue spoken by the actress who has played the part of Tarquin's mother Tullia: she tells the audience frankly that she would have preferred to play the part of Lucretia and struggle valiantly with the rapist – not to repel him, but 'least he shou'd depart'.[7] Thomas Southerne's *The Fatal Marriage* (1694), while having nothing directly to do with the Lucretia story, nevertheless clearly alludes to that story in its incongruously light-hearted epilogue. Isabella, the heroine of the piece, has run mad and killed herself. The actress Mrs Verbruggen steps forward.

> Now tell me, when you saw the Lady dye,
> Were you not puzled for a Reason why? . . .
> We Women are so Whimsical in Dying.
> Some pine away for loss of ogling Fellows:
> Nay, some have dy'd for Love, as Stories tell us.
> Some, say our Histories, though long ago,
> For having undergone a Rape, or so,
> Plung'd the fell Dagger, without more ado.
> But time has laugh'd those follies out of fashion;
> And sure they'l never gain the approbation
> Of Ladies, who consult their Reputation.
> For if a Rape must be esteem'd a Curse,
> Grim Death, and Publication make it worse.
> Should the opinion of the World be try'd,
> They'l scarce give Judgment on the Plaintiff's side.
> For all must own, 'tis most egregious Nonsense,
> To dye for being pleas'd, with a safe Conscience. . . .[8]

Such epilogues as these retrospectively qualify the dramatic experience which the audience has just been through, shifting the mood more comfortably from tragedy back to comedy. They function in much the same manner as the parodies so popular in the French theatre of Rousseau's time, querying the notions of high heroic sacrifice and of the 'fate worse than death' upon which the Lucretia story traditionally turns: 'time has laugh'd those follies out of fashion'. Artistically speaking, such humour is often ruinous, finally demolishing whatever pretensions to seriousness the tragedies may originally have had. Yet the fact that the story should so often provoke a response of this sort even from those who are attempting to treat it seriously is in itself revealing; and the nature of this response – half flippant, half shrewd – is worth examining more closely.

The impulses behind such humour are perhaps revealed more clearly in this passage from another epilogue, this time from a comedy, Henry Fielding's *Rape upon Rape* (1730). It is spoken once again by an actress:

> 'Twas a strange doctrine that Lucretia taught,
> Who on herself revenged her lover's fault!
> Heathenish wretch! the pious Christian wife,
> Though ravish'd, still contents herself with life:
> So zealous from self-murder we refrain,
> We live, though sure of ravishing again.[9]

There are two somewhat contradictory elements in this bantering; the joke is at once serious and frivolous. The premiss is Augustinian, recalling arguments in *The City of God* which Fielding is scarcely wishing to deride; unlike his great contemporary Samuel Richardson, Fielding is not especially taken by the notion of women dying, voluntarily or involuntarily, as a result of rape. Yet these humane ideas are given a droll and knowing inflection: 'We live, though sure of ravishing again.' To the speaker, this prospect does not appear totally unwelcome. Such knowingness is characteristic of many jokes about rape; a knowingness that insinuates that the act is not always what it seems. In Fielding's *Jonathan Wild*, the lecherous Fireblood meets and takes an instant fancy to the

equally lecherous Laetitia, and moves at once into the attack.
He 'in a few minutes ravished this fair creature, or at least
would have ravished her, if she had not, by a timely com-
pliance, prevented him'.[10] Unlike jokes about other crimes –
murder, theft, incest, arson – jokes about rape have a special
quality: they characteristically imply that the crime may not in
fact exist; that it is a legal and social fiction, which will dissolve
before the gaze of humour and the universal sexual appetite.
Rape is what it is because of an attitude of mind, because a
woman withholds her consent from the act which is performed. When that attitude of mind changes – as it may do, the
jokes insist, in the twinkling of an eye – the same act is no
longer rape, and criminality and suffering are at once converted into mutual pleasure. Behind the words that are conventionally used, behind the fiction, a different truth (it is
implied) is to be found. In Vanbrugh's comedy *The Relapse,*
Berinthia is carried bodily off into a closet by Loveless,
exclaiming as she goes – but exclaiming, we are told, '*Very
softly*' – 'Help, help, I'm ravish'd, ruin'd, undone. O Lord, I
shall never be able to bear it.'[11] Like Bel's Lucretia and
Fielding's Laetitia, Berinthia happily consents to the act
against which she nominally protests. Such jokes about rape
play upon a presumed disparity between a woman's words and
her actual desires. Implicitly the jokes deny the existence of real
suffering, real resistance, real rape; *così fan tutte* is their
unvaried theme. Where they also register an Augustine-like
point against the 'strange doctrine' which dictated that
Lucretia should take her own life, however, these very simple
jokes begin to acquire a possible complexity. In Fielding's case,
at least – as reference to the larger contexts of *Rape upon Rape*
and *Jonathan Wild* would reveal – the predictable facetiousness is mingled with a more searching and compassionate
understanding.

II

'What did you make of Lucretia?' wrote Pietro Aretino in a
letter to a friend; 'Was she not mad to follow the promptings

of honour? It would have been a clever thing to have had her fun with Master Tarquin, and have lived.'[12] Aretino's moral outlook was scarcely that of Saint Augustine, yet like Augustine he had his doubts about the wisdom of a moral code built upon the idea of 'honour', and like Augustine he saw little point in the idea of a woman taking her own life after a mischance of the kind which Lucretia suffered. Like certain Augustinian commentators, though in a spirit of some mischievousness, Aretino begins through his questions to open up the possibility of another version of the story, a version in which Lucretia might frankly have enjoyed the sexual opportunity that was offered to her, and subsequently remained discreetly silent about the whole affair. Like most of the parodists, he assumes that Lucretia must secretly have been attracted to Tarquin. It was a fellow countryman of Aretino's, however – Niccolò Machiavelli – who produced what is probably the best-known comic version of the story along these lines: *Mandragola*.

In *Mandragola*, Machiavelli plays not merely with the traditional story of the rape of Lucretia but also with Saint Augustine's commentary upon that story. The plot of the play runs briefly as follows. Callimaco has returned to his native Florence in search of one Donna Lucrezia, whose beauty he has heard praised in Paris by one of her kinsmen, during an argument as to where the more beautiful women are to be found, in Italy or France. The argument recalls the argument about wives which precipitates events in the classical story of Lucretia, and Callimaco is here cast as a kind of comic Tarquin. Callimaco sees, and, Tarquin-like, at once falls in love with Lucrezia, who is as beautiful as her reputation suggests, but who also has a reputation for extreme chastity. Callimaco's only hope seems to lie in the fact that Lucrezia's husband Messer Nicia is as stupid as his wife is beautiful and chaste, and is obsessed by the need to produce a child. Ligurio, parasite and matchmaker, advises Callimaco to pose as a doctor and to recommend to Messer Nicia a cure for his wife's apparent barrenness. She should drink a potion made from the root of the mandrake (*mandragola*), which will be sure to make her pregnant. The only difficulty is that the first man who sleeps with her after she has taken the drug will die within a week. It will therefore be necessary (Ligurio urges Callimaco to say) to find some dispensable male to perform this slight service, kidnapping, for example, a stranger from off the streets and pressing him into action.

There is a further problem: the virtuous Lucrezia will have to be persuaded that the scheme is a good one. The task of persuasion is left to Lucrezia's confessor, the friar Timoteo, a man of dubious morals. Timoteo decides to attack Lucrezia through her very goodness, and to argue that the truly virtuous course of action would be for her to comply with her husband's wish that she bear him a child. This is how part of his argument proceeds:

In matters of conscience, you must accept this general truth, that where there is a prospect of certain good and uncertain evil, we should never let the good slip for fear of the bad. Here you have a certain benefit – that you will conceive, and create a new soul to praise God. The uncertain evil is that the man who lies with you, after you take the potion, may die – but in fact they don't always die and some do survive. But since the point is uncertain, it is better that your husband should not take the risk. As for there being anything sinful in the act itself, that's all nonsense. It's the will that sins, not the body. If you were to offend your husband, that would be a sin; but in this case you are doing what he wants. If you took pleasure in the act, that would be a sin; but you hate the thought of it. Besides, we must always look to the intention in these things; and your intention is to fill a place in heaven and make your husband happy.[13]

Through Timoteo's speech, Machiavelli skilfully parodies two familiar arguments connected with the Lucretia story. Timoteo's insistence that 'It's the will that sins, not the body' (*perché la voluntà è quella che pecca, non el corpo*) subtly recalls the arguments which, in Livy's account, the husband, father, and friends of the classical Lucretia put to her after she has been raped, attempting to persuade her that there is no need for her to feel guilty about an act in which her mind and will have not been involved: 'it was the mind that sinned, not the body', they tell her; 'without intention there could never be guilt; (*mentem peccare, non corpus, et unde consilium afuerit, culpam abesse*). Timoteo grossly perverts this subtle argument by presenting it in order to persuade Lucrezia that it is perfectly in order for her to take a man other than her husband. Timoteo's other argument, that it is better to choose a certain good rather than try to avoid an uncertain evil, has been compared by one scholar with Machiavelli's own arguments in the *Discourses* and *The Prince* regarding political ends and means.[14] What appears not to have been noticed is that Machiavelli is also here parodying the arguments of Augustine. In the sections of *The City of God* immediately following that in which he discusses Lucretia's suicide, Augustine asks whether there is any justification for the notion that it is wise to kill oneself in order to avoid being raped. No, he replies, for there is in any case no guilt which a woman need feel if she has been raped: the fault is not hers. But what if she finds that, despite herself, she is enjoying it; would that not be a sin, and would it not be better for her to have killed herself than sin in such a way? No, says Augustine, for that instance is altogether hypothetical, and in the event the woman may not feel that way at all: there is no point in committing a certain evil, self-murder, in order to avoid an uncertain evil, the remote possibility of enjoying being raped. The certain good of preserving one's life is not to be renounced out of fear of an uncertain evil, the possibility of adultery.[15]

Donna Lucrezia succumbs to Timoteo's cleverly debased versions of these arguments, and agrees to take the potion and spend the night with the man whom her husband chooses for her, though she fears she will not survive the experience. Through a series of predictable but ingenious contrivances, Callimaco, in disguise, manages to get himself kidnapped and thrust into Lucrezia's bed by her eager husband Messer Nicia. To Ligurio, Nicia expresses his regrets about 'that poor young fellow – to think he's going to die so soon, and that last night's going to cost him so dear!' (*Di quel povero giovane, ch' egli abbi a morire sí presto, e che questa notte gli abbi a costare sí cara.*) His words ironically and unconsciously echo Ovid's lament over Collatinus:

Quid victor gaudes? haec te victoria perdet.
Heu quantum regnis nox stetit una tuis.

Why, Victor, do you rejoice? This victory will ruin you.
Alas, how dearly a single night cost your kingdom.

In this comically inside-out version of the story of the rape of
Lucretia, however, there is no death to be feared; all that will
eventuate from this night is Lucrezia's wished-for pregnancy.
In the original story, fear of pregnancy is one of the reasons
why Lucretia kills herself: she sees her 'blood', the family
line, as threatened by Tarquin's rape. But in the context of
Machiavelli's comedy, Donna Lucrezia's pregnancy, however
curiously it is achieved, is seen as a happy outcome, the end for
which both Lucrezia and Messer Nicia in their different ways
have striven. The chaste Donna Lucrezia is not raped. She finds,
to her pleasure and surprise, that she enjoys the company of
her young lover Callimaco, and tells him (as does Messer
Nicia, innocently and cheerfully handling him the key to his
house) that he should feel free to come back any time.
Callimaco promises he will. The company retire into church to
give thanks for their various blessings.

Machiavelli's comedy is a deft and witty commentary upon
the traditional story of the rape of Lucretia. Behind the farcical
events of the play there is a discernible attitude to life: cynical,
opportunistic, valuing intelligence more highly than morality,
humorously celebrating the power of those who know how to
manipulate the outward forms of religion, honour, and respec-
tability while privately securing the pleasures they really crave.
The analogues with Machiavelli's political philosophy are
plain to see. Yet in attempting to demythologize the story of
Lucretia, Machiavelli is himself dependent upon other common myths and assumptions about sexual behaviour. One of
these assumptions is that moral innocence is little more than
moral ignorance. Donna Lucrezia's chastity is simply a form of
worldly inexperience; once she knows what is afoot, she is
keen to have Callimaco call on her as often as he can. Another
is that there is really no such thing as rape; that women are

likely to enjoy what is offered, despite their formal pro-
testations to the contrary. 'I wish that you might some day be /
Tricked just as she was, with as little pain,' says the Prologue,
and that, morally speaking, is where the matter rests.[16]

The point may be made another way, by contrast with the
work of a greater dramatist than Machiavelli, Ben Jonson.
Jonson's *Volpone* awakens some curious memories of the
Lucretia story, and part of its plot also in some respects
resembles that of *Mandragola*. Jonson's Corvino, anxious to
ingratiate himself with the apparently dying Volpone and inherit his fabled wealth, agrees to try to persuade his own wife
Celia to go to bed with Volpone. Volpone, he believes, is too
near to death to harm his wife in any way, and as the encounter
will take place in strict secrecy, there will be (what is more
important) no harm to his reputation as a husband. Volpone,
of course, is more vigorous and more scheming than the naïve
Corvino imagines, and has his own designs upon Celia. As in
Mandragola, we are presented with the sight of a husband
eager to persuade his young and virtuous wife to sleep with
another man in order to bring some benefit to himself – in
Mandragola, so that Nicia may have a child; in *Volpone*, so
that Corvino may inherit Volpone's wealth. In each case, the
man who is to substitute for the husband is in fact lecherous
and self-interested. In *Volpone*, Corvino threatens his wife
with an extreme punishment if she refuses to comply with his
wish that she go to bed with Volpone; and his threat bizarrely
recalls, and exceeds, the threat which Tarquin made to the
reluctant Lucretia:

> (Death) I will buy some slave,
> Whom I will kill, and binde thee to him, alive;
> And at my windore, hang you forth; devising
> Some monstrous crime, which I, in capitall letters,
> Will eate into thy flesh, with *aqua-fortis*,
> And burning cor'sives, on this stubborne brest.
>
> (III.vii.100–5)

The classical memory here allows us briefly to identify Corvino
with the rapist Tarquin, and by this momentary identification
to recognize the full monstrosity of the present situation: that

here it is a husband who threatens his own wife with even fiercer menaces than those of Tarquin and with an even more preposterous sexual proposition. The extremity of these threats is comic in its way, but at the same time appalling. Both here and in the later scene in which Volpone attempts to rape Celia, we are allowed to feel, behind and despite the surface comedy, the presence of real violence, appetite, and aggression. We are also allowed to feel, as in Machiavelli's comedy we are not, the presence (however frail) of some real moral resistance to these forces. Unlike Donna Lucrezia, Celia is not simply a comic version (or inversion) of the classical Lucretia, a figure of innocent fun, ready to fall in with the seducer's proposition once she realizes what he is offering her. For Machiavelli, Donna Lucrezia's 'goodness' is mere naïveté, the quality which makes her most vulnerable; later, it becomes the screen behind which she and Callimaco can privately act as they please. Jonson's Celia is not a powerful figure, but her goodness, for all its fragility, is patently genuine; like the classical Lucretia, Celia does actually prefer death to sexual dishonour. Though Jonson is in his own way as darkly pessimistic a writer as Machiavelli, his comedy does not ride along, as *Mandragola* does, upon easy assumptions about sexual behaviour, nor does it attempt to dissolve through humour the actual facts of suffering and of rape, nor to deny the possibility of some moral resistance existing somewhere in a world of almost ubiquitous evil and self-interest. It is for this reason (amongst others) that Jonson's comedy may seem a more complex and more telling achievement than Machiavelli's, a more subtle, if more distant, transformation of the myth.[17]

III

Pushkin's verse parody of the Lucretia story, *Count Nulin* (December 1825), is set in yet another key. Pushkin himself described the genesis of this poem:

Re-reading *Lucrece*, a rather weak poem of Shakespeare's, I thought: what if it had occurred to Lucrece to slap Tarquin's face? Maybe it would have cooled his boldness and he would have been obliged to withdraw, covered in confusion. Lucrece would not have stabbed herself, Publicola would not have been enraged, Brutus would not have driven out the kings, and the world and its history would have been different.

And so we owe the republic, the consuls, the dictators, the Catos, the Caesars, to a seduction similar to one which took place recently in our neighbourhood, in the Novorzhev district. . . .

History does repeat itself strangely.[18]

Like Pascal speculating on the ways in which the history of the world might have been different had Cleopatra's nose been a trifle longer, Pushkin is intrigued by the way in which small facts and events may have great historical consequences. A friend of Pushkin's had been accused of seducing the daughter of a local parish priest; was it an equally trifling and common-place event which brought about the downfall of the Roman kings? Pushkin transposes the Lucretia story into a little drama of Russian provincial life. His Lucretia is Natalia Pavlovna, a Russian lady who lives in the country, reads novels, and longs for some change in her unvaried routine. While her husband is away hunting, a passing carriage overturns, and she offers hospitality to its occupant, Count Nulin, while it is being repaired. The Count is a fashionable nonentity who neverthe-less brings with him some of the glamour of metropolitan life. As they retire for the night, Natalia presses his hand encourag-ingly, leaving the Count in a state of excited perplexity. After agonizing for some time in his bedroom, Nulin decides to respond to this evident invitation, and tiptoes to Natalia's bedroom. Out of sudden panic, Natalia unexpectedly slaps Count Nulin; her dog begins to bark, her nurse wakes up, and the Count retreats in confusion. Next day, the embarrassed couple begin tentatively to repair the situation, when Natalia's husband returns unannounced, and is surprised when the Count refuses his invitation to stay for dinner. After Nulin's departure, Natalia tells her husband what has happened the previous night, and he angrily vows to send his dogs after the Count. But when the story reaches the ears of their young neighbouring landlord, his reaction is very different: he laughs in delight.

And laughter, Pushkin implies, is the proper reaction to a story of this kind. Both in Shakespeare's poem and in the classical story, Pushkin found an element of extravagance and absurdity. 'I was struck by the idea of parodying both history and Shakespeare,' he wrote; 'I could not resist the double temptation . . .'[19] His parody suggests that sexual misdemeanours are seldom quite as simple, as one-sided, and as fraught with tragic significance as the myth would have us think, and that chastity is, moreover, sometimes preserved by accident as much as by design. The encounter between Natalia Pavlovna and Count Nulin arouses a sense of expectation, nervousness, misunderstanding, inefficiency, and embarrassment in both parties in roughly equal measure. Yet none of this really matters, for nothing really happens. Pushkin's story is a comedy of non-events. Like Pope's *The Rape of Lock*, it reminds us of an older, graver, story of sexual assault in order to establish a sense of comic perspective and general good humour, gently showing us that the events of the present story are of somewhat less consequence than the flustered participants are able to believe; that they are indeed scarcely 'events' at all.[20]

In Jean Giraudoux's version of the Lucretia story, *Pour Lucrèce* (1953), there is (once again) no rape and indeed no physical encounter at all, but the implications and results of this non-encounter are very different from those in *Count Nulin*.[21] Giraudoux's play is set in Aix-en-Provence in 1868. The character corresponding to Lucretia is Lucile Blanchard, a woman of strict and uncompromising morals who is married to the local prosecutor. Her downfall is contrived by a woman named Paola, after Lucile, by studiously ignoring her one day in a café, indirectly reveals to Paola's husband Armand that Paola has been having an affair behind his back. Paola takes her revenge on Lucile by surreptitiously slipping a sleeping potion into her drink, and having her conveyed while unconscious to the the house of one Barbette, a brothel-keeper. Acting on Paola's instructions, Barbette arranges matters so that when Lucile wakes up she imagines she has been raped during her sleep – by Paola's own lover, Marcellus, a well-

known and disreputable philanderer. Deeply upset by this
apparent discovery, Lucile – unlike the classical Lucretia –
nevertheless decides that there is no point in killing herself on
account of an act for which she is not responsible. The guilt,
she believes, lies elsewhere – and so should the punishment.
She therefore goes to Marcellus and demands that he kill
himself. Marcellus has been told of the trick that has been
played on Lucile, and his interest in her has been aroused.
Keeping up the deception, he tells her maliciously that while
she was drugged she responded eagerly to his advances, and
suggests that in so doing she revealed her true nature and her
true desires; her puritanism, he tells her, is just so much play-
acting. He agrees, however, to kill himself, but on one condition: that Lucile will make love to him again; this time while
fully awake, and of her own free will.

Lucile is extricated from this situation by the arrival of
Paola's husband Armand, who challenges Marcellus to a duel
– in which, eventually, Marcellus is killed. Meanwhile, however, another and more complex situation develops. Lucile
returns home to her priggish husband Lionel, and, without
telling him what has occurred, begins to test his views on the
question of marital fidelity. Lionel, she discovers, holds
extreme views on this matter: if he ever learns that his wife has
been so much as touched by another man, he says, even against
her will or while unconscious, he will have nothing more to do
with her. This revelation shatters Lucile more deeply than the
original revelation of her apparent rape; and at this point she
decides to kill herself, and quietly goes out and takes a lethal
dose of poison. Before it takes effect, Paola and Barbette arrive
to tell Lucile the truth: that she was never raped, never so much
as seen by a man while at Barbette's house. In one sense, her
suicide is absurd. Yet in another sense, Lucile feels that it is the
only fitting response to what has happened, to her new-found
knowledge of what her husband, and the world, are really like.

In Paola and Lucile, Giraudoux contrasts two ways of life.
Paola is spontaneous, physically alive, quick to show her affections and jealousies, holding no abstract or absolute standards
of morality, ready if need be to lie and compromise and wound

in order to gain what she wants. Lucile is an absolutist; puri-
tanical, yet at the same time heroic – even saintly – in her
aspirations. Imperfection has no place in her world; she will
kill herself sooner than live with compromise. The contrast
between the two women, Giraudoux suggests, is in effect a
contrast between comic and tragic attitudes to life; and it is
significant that Paola should mock Lucile for her tragic pretensions and try to persuade her that the events which have
occurred make her life a mere comedy, a melodrama, a farce.
The sympathies of Giraudoux's own play move for a time
between these two ways of life and these two modes of
experience before shifting towards Lucile and the tragic style
she chooses to adopt. In rewriting the Lucretia story,
Giraudoux does not parody it, nor does he turn it in any simple
way from tragedy to comedy. Instead, he allows us to see the
comic potentialities of the story, the possible absurdity of
Lucile's acts and aspirations, the way in which events might
easily have gone otherwise.

   How far Giraudoux is successful in his attempt to bring the
play to a tragic conclusion is another question; Paola's
remarks about melodrama have an uneasy relevance to the
play as a whole, with its succession of sensational events. A
more central weakness is Giraudoux's tendency to lapse into a
kind of pious sentimentalism, as in this last speech of
Barbette's, purporting to explain why Lucile should die:

It's true you were ravished. But not by Marcellus. You could have got
over that, fifty women have got over that; you knew yourself you
could. But what struck you down was being made aware of man's
stupidity, and coarseness, and wickedness, too much all of a sudden.
And if you're as tender a creature as you, you die of it.

The notion of Lucile's dying because she at last sees the true
nastiness of the world seems scarcely preferable to the notion
which Lucile explicitly rejects – that of dying, like Lucretia, in
order to purge the apparent dishonour of rape. Once again, the
notions of physical and spiritual delicacy are comfortably
elided, and death imagined as a saintly solution to the hard
dilemmas of rape: 'And if you're as tender a creature as you,

you die of it.' *Pour Lucrèce* has moved a long way from the original story of the rape of Lucretia, and its moral emphases are significantly different. Yet Giraudoux is still entranced by one central feature of that story: its sanctification of death.

The tragic versions of the myth tend to present Lucretia as a saint; the comic versions, as a whore. The two views, equally dehumanizing in their different ways, are not so radically opposed as might at first appear. Both are products of male thinking; both present women according to popular stereotype. A veneration and a contempt for women are often closely allied, opposite sides of the same coin. The parodies and inversions of the Lucretia story examined in this chapter are all to some extent critical in design, highlighting absurdities and difficulties in the traditional story with greater or lesser degrees of wit. Yet parody is a complex art, and seldom so totally subversive as it may at first appear. The Lucretia myth and counter-myth are to some extent mutually reinforcing; the parodies often play along with the story's central assumptions, even as they turn its narrative features inside-out. Joking about the myth may be one way of criticizing it; yet it may also be covertly sustaining.[22]

II

LUCIUS JUNIUS BRUTUS

vis et Tarquinios reges, animamque superbam
ultoris Bruti fascisque videre receptos?
consulis imperium hic primus saevasque securis
accipiet, natosque pater nova bella moventis
ad poenam pulchra pro libertate vocabit,
infelix, utcumque ferent ea facta minores:
vincet amor patriae laudumque immensa cupido.

Virgil, Aeneid, vi. 817–23

Next view the *Tarquin* Kings: Th'avenging Sword
Of *Brutus*, justly drawn, and *Rome* restor'd.
He first renews the Rods, and Axe severe;
And gives the Consuls Royal Robes to wear.
His Sons, who seek the Tyrant to sustain,
And long for Arbitrary Lords again,
With Ignominy scourg'd, in open sight,
He dooms to Death deserv'd; asserting Publick Right.
Unhappy Man, to break the Pious Laws
Of Nature, pleading in his Children's Cause!
Howe're the doubtful Fact is understood,
'Tis Love of Honour, and his Country's good:
The Consul, not the Father, sheds the Blood.

Dryden's translation, 1697[1]

6

The Shaping of the Myth (2):
Rape and Revolution

We have already noticed some of the ways in which the story of
the rape of Lucretia changes when seen from different cultural
and narrative perspectives, certain features of the story taking
on at times a new depth or prominence, other features at times
receding or disappearing altogether from view. Such changes
of perspective may be observed, in a quite literal sense, in the
many drawings and paintings relating to this story. Many of
the Renaissance painters who treated Lucretia's suicide chose
to depict Lucretia – as we noticed in chapter one – as a solitary
and often naked figure, emphasizing her tragic isolation and
her centrality in the story. Cranach's and Veronese's Lucretias,
for example, stand alone and self-absorbed, caught in a moment of private grief. The social context of the suicide – so
prominent in the classical accounts, which stress the fact that
Lucretia killed herself ceremoniously before witnesses specially summoned for the occasion – is allowed to recede. But
the suicide can also be seen in other ways, from other angles of
vision. In Gavin Hamilton's large canvas of *The Oath of
Brutus* (plate twelve, early 1760s), Lucretia is no longer a
solitary figure, nor is she even dominant in the composition.[2]
The dominant role has passed instead to Brutus, who stands
centrally in the group, urging his fellow countrymen to their
great oath of vengeance. It is Brutus who generates what
energy the painting has, forcefully indicating to his companions with a gesture of his arm the task that now awaits them.
The subsiding Lucretia clings to his tunic, seeming to place her
trust in him and draw her remaining strength from him. By
moving the story forward a fraction in time, Hamilton catches
the moment at which life in Lucretia is almost spent, and in

Brutus newly aroused. Jacques-Antoine Beaufort's *Brutus* (plate nineteen; 1771), probably composed with a knowledge of Hamilton's painting, catches a moment fractionally later still in time, subtly shifting the perspective once again.[3] Lucretia, now dead, lies in a more removed position to the left of the painting, behind the men whose oath is here unambiguously the central focus of attention. Dressed in their plumed helmets and mailed tunics, Brutus and his companions are ready for action; no time is wasted upon lamentation. We have moved from the woman's world to the world of men. Brutus, not Lucretia, holds the centre of the stage.

In this chapter and the next, our attention will likewise move from the part played by Lucretia in the story to the part played by Brutus. To shift perspective in this way will be to shift at first from the private to the public aspect of the story, from the role of the suffering woman to that of the active man, from dilemmas of a primarily personal and primarily ethical nature to dilemmas relating to the exercise of public office. As Lucretia and her problems move to the background, the political dimension of the story comes into new prominence. The story takes on a different aspect, emerging as a powerful myth of revolution.

I

Those interested in the political implications of the story often saw Brutus, rather than Lucretia, as the central and compelling figure in these events. Machiavelli, for example, regarded the story of Lucretia's rape rather light-heartedly, but found the political problems facing Brutus to be of absorbing interest. The rape in itself (Machiavelli thought) was scarcely important, being merely the final event that triggered a revolution which had other and more serious causes. If Lucretia had not been raped, some other pretext for action would have been found. The reason for the expulsion of Tarquinius Superbus, wrote Machiavelli,

was not that his son, Sextus, had ravished Lucretia, but that he had violated the laws of the kingdom and ruled tyrannically. . . . Hence, if the Lucretia incident had not occurred, something else would have happened and would have led to the same result. Whereas, if Tarquin had behaved like the other kings, when his son, Sextus, committed his crime, Brutus and Collatinus would have appealed to Tarquin to avenge it, and not to the Roman people.[4]

Sir Thomas Elyot, taking his cue from Plutarch, saw the situation in a similar light, focusing primarily on the political lessons to be learnt from the story:

The pride of Tarquine, the last kyng of Romanes, was more occasion of his exile than the rauysshynge of Lucrecia by his sonne Aruncius, for the malice that the people by his pride had longe gathered, finding valiaunt capitaynes, Brutus, Colatinus, Lucretius, and other nobles of the citie, at the last braste out and takynge occasion of the rauisshement, all though the kynge were thereto not partie, they utterly expulsed hym for euer out of the citie. These be the frutes of pride, and that men do cal stately countenance.[5]

Two centuries later, Montesquieu, considering the way in which great events may be prompted by trivial ones, referred deprecatingly to Lucretia and Virginia as 'two little women of Rome' whose celebrated chastity was no more than 'a foolish little vanity'. For Montesquieu, too, 'the death of Lucretia was merely the occasion of the revolution which occurred; for a proud, enterprising, bold people, confined within walls, must necessarily shake off the yoke, or soften their ways.'[6]

Those who concentrated primarily upon Lucretia's part in the story tended (as we have seen) to interpret her dilemmas in the light of certain general moral and theological preoccupations of the day. Those who concentrated primarily upon the role of Brutus and the political significance of the story often made more precise connections with contemporary political events and ideas, allegorizing the story to a greater or lesser degree. Not surprisingly, this process of allegorization is particularly vigorous during periods of political revolution or unrest. The story is reanimated and reshaped by present events, taking on in time cumulative accretions of meaning from the various historical contexts in which it is told and retold. Lucius Junius Brutus is often invoked as a model for present generations to emulate. But the process also works the other way about: for the shadowy character of the first consul of Rome is sometimes conceived in terms of other, contemporary political figures, the past being imaginatively re-created in terms of the present.

This process begins very early. Indeed the earliest surviving major accounts of the story are marked by the pressure of recent political events, and in the character of Lucius Junius Brutus it is possible to glimpse the outlines of other more recent and more familiar political figures.[7] It is important to recall that at the time when these accounts were written, there was more than one Brutus who might be regarded as the saviour and liberator of his country. D. Junius Brutus Albinus and Marcus Junius Brutus, the assassins of Julius Caesar, claimed descent from the first consul Lucius Junius Brutus, enemy of the Tarquins, and their actions were often compared. The notion of lineal descent presented some difficulties – for one thing, Lucius Junius Brutus appears to have had no surviving descendants; for another, he was a patrician, whereas the later bearers of the name Junius Brutus were plebeian – but it seems to have been carefully cultivated for political reasons by earlier generations of the family, who were probably also responsible for elaborating the story of their alleged ancestor's life.[8] The parallel between these earlier and later champions of Roman liberty was noted and pressed home by Cicero on many occasions. From Cicero we learn that a family tree was in existence, establishing the line of descent; and that a bust of Lucius Junius Brutus was displayed in the house of M. and D. Junius Brutus.[9] After the death of Caesar, Marcus Junius Brutus (or Caepio Brutus, as he was known by then) issued coins carefully inscribed LEIBERTAS and L. BRUTUS. PRIM. COS.: 'Liberty'; 'Lucius Brutus, First Consul'. In Shakespeare's *Julius Caesar*, Brutus is reminded on more than one occasion of the actions of his great forebear:

> Shall Rome stand under one man's awe? What, Rome?
> My ancestors did from the streets of Rome
> The Tarquin drive, when he was call'd a king.
>
> (II.i.52–4)

The parallel was not Shakespeare's invention: it was a commonplace of the late Republic.

The parallel worked in two ways. The assassination of Caesar might be seen as an event reminiscent of the expulsion of the Tarquins; or, looked at the other way about, the expulsion of the Tarquins might be seen as a historical anticipation of the assassination of Caesar, and narrated accordingly. Several of the first century BC accounts of the story of Lucretia, Brutus, and the fall of the Tarquins are coloured with memories of the recent event of the death of Caesar. This association is not exploited methodically, but it is brought to our minds by means of a number of occasional descriptive touches. Ovid's account of the death of Lucretia, for example, recalls in a curious way Suetonius' account of the death of Caesar, whose last thought, like Lucretia's, was to wrap his garments modestly about him as he fell.[10] Livy's description of Lucius Junius Brutus brandishing aloft the bloody knife taken from Lucretia's side and swearing to liberate Rome may recall Cicero's description of Marcus Junius Brutus after the death of Caesar holding his knife aloft, calling on Cicero by name, and congratulating him upon the recovery of lost liberty.[11] Lucius Junius Brutus' oration to the Roman people over the body of Lucretia, developed with particular detail in the narratives of Livy and Dionysius of Halicarnassus, is reminiscent of the oration of Marcus Junius Brutus after the death of Caesar, and he employs, as R. M. Ogilvie has remarked, 'the political vocabulary of the late Republic'.[12]

Thus even in the earliest tellings of the story there is an occasional doubleness of vision: while we are told of the political events of the sixth century BC and the founding of the Republic, we are simultaneously able to glimpse those of the first century and the Republic's later days. The story is subtly arranged in order to recall, if only fleetingly, the events of recent history; just as accounts of these events had themselves at moments been subtly arranged to recall the original story. The process is circular and incremental. A political myth is being fashioned; an archetypal and instructive story, against which later historical events may be measured, and to which in turn they may contribute.

II

The many recollections, analyses, and retellings of the story in Europe after the Renaissance extend this myth in a variety of ways. Often the story is retold in terms of contemporary politics. Heinrich Bullinger's play *Lucretia* (1533), for example, reflects the current political situation in Switzerland after the guilds had seized power: Brutus, drawing up the new democratic constitution of Rome, would have reminded the play's audiences of Bullinger's friend Zwingli, who had been similarly occupied in Zurich.[13] Just a few years earlier, Machiavelli in his *Discourses* had analysed with particular interest the constitutional arrangements of the early Roman Republic, admiringly contrasting the 'mixed' form of government introduced by Brutus (in which powers are divided between a head of state, an aristocracy, and the people) with the 'pure' form of government represented by an absolute monarchy such as Tarquin's. Later writers often looked at the story with Machiavelli's analysis in mind, noting particular correspondences with political institutions in their own times.

During the Revolutionary period in France, the story of Brutus and the fall of the Tarquin kings achieved immense popularity. Brutus was hailed as a hero from the ancient past whose moral and political ideals were precisely suited to the needs of the present hour; as the father of revolution, not merely in his own country but wherever people are oppressed. Towns in France were named after him (Montfort-le-Brutus, Brutus-le-Magnanime), as were suburbs, streets, and citizens; the town of Ris changes its patron from Saint Blaise to Brutus, and a *Fête de Brutus* was held in the Cathedral at Nevers.[14] Political pamphlets were issued in the name of Brutus.[15] Images of Brutus appeared on buttons and badges, porcelain and playing cards, and in paintings exhibited in the salons; while in the theatre his life and actions were further celebrated. Voltaire's tragedy *Brutus*, originally presented in 1730 without arousing much public excitement, was revived by the Comédie Française to tumultous scenes on 17 November 1790, being seen to have an immediate relevance to the present political moment. Royalists in the audience at the Théâtre National applauded lines favourable to the Tarquins, while Republicans applauded lines apparently favourable to their own political ideals (a reception reminiscent of that of Addison's *Cato* in England earlier in the century). At the second performance on 19 November, busts of Brutus and Voltaire were placed reverentially on either side of the stage. Voltaire had not written the play with a contemporary political situation specifically in mind; his admiration for Brutus may probably indeed be traced back to his early training with the Jesuits, who, in order to counter Jansenist pessimism, advocated the study of the lives of great men and women of the past as recounted by Livy, Plutarch, and Lucan. Like Jacques-Louis David's *Lictors Returning to Brutus the Bodies of his Sons* – with which, as Robert L. Herbert has shown in an important study, its fortunes were intimately involved – Voltaire's tragedy was largely politicized by subsequent events, becoming, despite itself, a fable for the times. It enjoyed great popularity up until 1794, when theatrical censorship was reintroduced in France, and the play's ending had to be rewritten.[16]

In 1789, Vittorio Alfieri, living in Paris in political exile from his native Italy, published his two linked plays *Bruto Primo* and *Bruto Secundo*, dedicating the first of these plays to George Washington: 'The name of the deliverer of America alone can stand in the title-page of the tragedy of the deliverer of Rome,' he wrote. *Bruto Primo* had been written in 1786 in conscious opposition to the *Brutus* of Voltaire, whom Alfieri saw as a social turncoat. The play is a sustained attempt to analyse the nature of political liberty; Alfieri implicitly invites his readers to look beyond the play, and to consider the ways in which liberty has been achieved or thwarted in recent times in Italy, France, and America.[17] A. V. Arnault's *Lucrèce*, first performed at the Théâtre Française on 4 May 1789, is a more cautious allegory for the times, intended as a warning both to supporters of the *ancien régime* and also to those whose unreflective love of liberty seemed to Arnault to lead in the direction of political anarchy. The play's political message is confused by the fact that it is Collatinus – who on other matters has been shown to be somewhat naïve – who is allowed to voice the play's doubts about the wisdom of the Revolution. Not surprisingly, the play failed to satisfy political extremists on either side, and performances were finally interrupted in August 1792 by more exciting revolutionary events occurring in the real world outside the theatre.[18]

The popularity of the story of Lucius Junius Brutus in France is linked in a close way with periods of political unrest. After 1794, official government disapproval made it difficult for writer and artists to treat the story, which nevertheless re-emerges when the political wheel turns again. The history of François Andrieux's tragedy *Lucius Junius Brutus* shows how closely the fortunes of the story were bound to political events. Andrieux's play had its first full-scale public performance on 13 September 1830, and many who saw it at that time assumed it to be a rapidly constructed piece intended to reflect upon the political happenings of July of that year. The genesis of the play was in fact far more distant and more complex. Andrieux had begun working on it as early as the spring of 1794, and in the following year had sent an early draft to the Théâtre de la République. By the time he had completed a satisfactory acting version, however, no government was prepared to tolerate a public performance of the play. An approach to the Minister for the Interior as late as 1828 brought the regretful reply that, despite the undoubted literary merits of the piece, the subject was quite unacceptable at the present time; and not until July 1830 was permission finally granted. In one sense Andrieux's play was occasioned by, and relevant to, the events of 1830; yet Andrieux drew also upon his knowledge of earlier revolutionary events in France, and of earlier ways in which the Brutus story had been applied to contemporary political situations.[19]

It is significant that the story should reappear again in France during the 1840s. Lamartine's friend and pupil François Ponsard wrote a tragedy of *Lucrèce* which was first performed in Paris on 22 April 1843, and translated into English in 1848, and which contained (as the anonymous translator remarked) 'the germ of many ideas which have lately sprung up, and which have so triumphantly developed themselves in France'. While ostensibly treating of events in ancient Rome, Ponsard glances also at recent developments in France, allowing Brutus to invoke the familiar political catch-cries of the Revolution:

> To renovate her soul, and make Rome grand,
> The flag of Liberty must take its stand!
> And, with that holy standard once unfurl'd,
> We'll rouse, to Freedom's call, the slumb'ring world,
> And the rallying cry to Liberty!
> Shall be Equality, Fraternity!
> This second ardor shall replace the first,
> Rome into splendour and existence burst!

And Brutus outlines in a little detail the constitutional arrangements for the new Republic: the Greek states will be Rome's model; there will be two consuls, just as in Lacedemon there are two kings ruling equally, sharing power and checking each other. Obviously such details as these were of more than mere antiquarian interest. The story of Brutus could be seen to provide a model for modern political behaviour, and modern constitutional reform.[20]

III

In England, the story of Lucius Junius Brutus was also seen to have continuing political implications, and precisely on this account often aroused hostility and suspicion. Devoted English Royalists found it difficult to recount with complete serenity this great republican myth, being haunted by the suspicion that they might be thought to be endorsing, either in a specific or a general sense, its revolutionary sentiments. Often they went to some pains to convey their disapproval of its apparent message and the orthodoxy of their own political loyalties. William Fulbecke, for example, retelling the story at the beginning of the seventeenth century, made it quite clear that he considered the expulsion of the Tarquins a political blunder on the part of the Roman people, who thereby 'changed gold for

brasse, and loathing one king suffered manie tyrants, scourg-
ing their follie with their fall, and curing a festred sore with a
poisoned plaister'.[21] When in 1637 Henry Cary published his
Romulus and Tarquin, a translation from the Italian of Vir-
gilio Malvezzi, he carefully dedicated the work to Charles I,
stressing – prudently, at this uncomfortable political moment
– the great differences between a ruler like Charles I and a ruler
like Tarquinius Superbus:

if contraries doe best appeare, when most directly opposed; how can
CHARLES *the Gratious* be better drawn to the Life, than by the
description of TARQUIN *the Proud*? How can the unparallel'd,
CHARLES *the Chaste,* bee better portraited, than by the deciphering
of TARQUIN *the foule Ravisher*?[22]

And lest his loyalty be doubted, Cary in the following year
buttressed the second edition of his translation with a number
of poems by well-known Royalists (Suckling, Davenant,
Carew, Townshend, and others) professing their admiration
for his work.
    During the political upheavals that followed only a few
years later, however, the parallel between the exiled Stuarts
and the exiled Tarquins became too obvious to resist.
Marchamont Nedham exploits the analogy extensively
throughout the early numbers of *Mercurius Politicus* in 1650,
and Milton invokes it more briefly in his political writings.[23]
Even Richard Lovelace, a good Royalist, could wryly play with
the parallel in his 'Mock-Song', in which the future Charles II is
seen as the banished Tarquin and Cromwell as the new Brutus:

> He that *Tarquin* was styl'd,
> Our white Land's exil'd,
>   Yea undefil'd,
> Not a Court *Ape*'s left to confute us:
>   Then let your Voyces rise high,
>   As your Colours did fly,
>   And flour'shing cry,
> Long live the brave *Oliver-Brutus*.[24]

Others worked out the historical equation in different terms.
Jonathan Swift – who, like Rousseau, regarded the elder

Brutus as a man of exceptional moral integrity – was disinclined to identify Cromwell with such an exemplary figure. Swift likened Cromwell instead to Servius Tullius ('a stranger, and of mean Extraction, was chosen Protector of the Kingdom, by the *People*, without the Consent of the Senate'), comparing Charles I with Tarquinius Priscus and James II with Tarquinius Superbus.[25]

To invoke such parallels was sometimes a risky business. On 11 December 1680, Nathaniel Lee's tragedy *Lucius Junius Brutus* was banned by the Lord Chamberlain on account of what were alleged to be 'very Scandalous Expressions and Reflections upon the Government'.[26] Lee's play (as will be shown in more detail in the next chapter) is in fact far from being the straightforwardly hostile political piece that this phrase might suggest, but its general political tendencies are clear enough. The followers of Tarquin talk arrogantly of rule by divine right, while Brutus discourses like a true Whig of the 'Laws, rules, and bounds, prescribed for raging kings' in a style unlikely to commend itself to Charles II. The counter-revolutionary conspiracy in Lee's play was likely, moreover, to remind audiences of the Popish Plot scare of 1678, and Vinditius, the 'busy slave' who uncovers the conspiracy, of the Popish Plot informer Titus Oates; while a scene in the fourth act of the play in which the conspiring Fecialian priests make human sacrifices was probably also intended as a further anti-Catholic satire, parodying the mass.

Subsequent English dramatists who treated the story of Brutus were cautious to avoid laying themselves open to the charges of historical parallelism that had been levelled at Lee's play. In 1703, Charles Gildon rewrote Lee's play, preserving more than half of the original lines but moving the setting from ancient Rome to Renaissance Florence, making Cosimo de Medici, rather than Brutus, the hero of the piece. Gildon loyally dedicated his play, *The Patriot*, to Queen Anne, assuring her that no adverse reflection was intended upon her reign; a point reinforced by John Dennis's prologue:

> *Our Characters and* Lee's *are still the same,*
> *Tho* Brutus *we have chang'd for* Cosmo's *Name;*

> *For Anti-Regal Principles we must*
> *Have else display'd; which would be now unjust.*[27]

Other eighteenth-century English dramatists who turned to the story betrayed a similar lingering nervousness about possible political misinterpretation, setting their works about with similar defensive and effusive dedications to people in high places. William Hunt's *The Fall of Tarquin: or, the Distressed Lovers* (1713) – a historically haphazard piece which owes something to Lee's play and to Madeleine de Scudéry's *Clélie* – is protected by a prologue announcing that the author is not a Republican, that 'his love of Monarchy is known', and that 'his Pointed Sting,/ Aims at the *Tyrant*, never at the *King*', and paying tribute to Queen Anne. 'My Intention in publishing', writes Hunt, '. . . is very remote from reflecting upon that glorious Constitution with which Providence has bless'd us, and the Loyalty of my Heart flatters me with the Hopes that *Tarquin* will be read without an ill-natur'd Application.'[28] William Bond's *The Tuscan Treaty; or, Tarquin's Overthrow* (1733) is significantly dedicated to Robert Walpole's old enemy Sarah Churchill, Dowager Duchess of Marlborough. The play itself concerns the double-handed role played by Tarquin's powerful and scheming 'Prime Minister', Quintus, in the dealings between the banished Tarquin and Lars Porsenna; at a time when George II was dominated by Walpole, the political point must have been plain.[29] William Duncombe's *Junius Brutus* (1735), an adaptation of Voltaire's *Brutus* intended to celebrate William III and the constitutional principles of the 1688 Revolution, was thought at the time to reflect upon the Walpole government – 'the furthest thing in the world from my thoughts', protested Duncombe.[30] The players refused to speak Duncombe's prologue in praise of the Prince of Orange, and made various other excisions. Duncombe's dedication of the published version of the play to a member of the House of Lords stresses the legitimacy and public-spiritedness of his undertaking, in a strenuous attempt to deflect adverse interpretation.

In the nineteenth century, the Brutus story continued to be

a difficult one for English dramatists to handle without giving political offence. When J. H. Payne's *Brutus; or the Fall of Tarquin* was performed in London in 1818, Sir William Scott, judge of the High Court of Admiralty and brother of Lord Eldon, the Lord Chancellor, was reported as saying that the play was unconstitutional and ought to be suppressed. When Payne wrote to Scott protesting that he had never conceived that he 'had introduced a single sentence which could give offence to the constituted authorities of the state', Scott was forced to confess that he had neither seen nor read the piece, but had ventured none the less to remark to his brother that the play 'did contain passages calculated to produce democratic impressions'.[31]

IV

'Democratic impressions' are indeed not easily to be avoided in any retelling of the story of Lucretia, Brutus, and the Tarquin kings: the political implications of the narrative are powerful and seemingly ineradicable. It is the more remarkable, then, that the most familiar of all English versions of the story – Shakespeare's – should deal with the political aspects of the story in the way it does. In chapter three it was argued that Shakespeare in *The Rape of Lucrece* was not altogether successful in coping with the complex moral problems which had developed in the traditional story of Lucretia's rape and suicide. Shakespeare's treatment of the political problems inherent in the story is, on the other hand, remarkably adroit; and in concluding this account of the political fortunes of the story it is worth briefly examining Shakespeare's tactics in the poem. At first sight these may appear to be mere tactics of avoidance: the poem appears to have virtually no political dimension, concentrating instead upon questions of individual psychology and private moral choice. As has already been noted, there is a curious foreshortening, almost a throw-away quality, in the final stanza of the poem in which we are curtly told that the consequence of the rape of Lucrece was the banishment of the Tarquin kings. Like William Fulbecke and others, Shakespeare cannot have wished to be thought to be questioning, even in a very indirect way, the system of monarchical government under which he lived and to which he owed allegiance. Yet Shakespeare makes the poem politically impeccable not merely through his reticence at certain points of the narrative, but also through subtler and more positive means, managing not merely to neutralize but actually to reverse the story's traditional significance.

The Rape of Lucrece, like *Measure for Measure*, is much concerned with the idea of *government*, in both the moral and political senses of that term. Through the skilful use of analogy and metaphor, Shakespeare constantly brings together in our minds the ideas of private and public governance, prompting us to see these ideas as necessarily and intimately related. People should be able to govern their instincts (it is implied) in the same way that kings should be able to govern the state: 'For kings like gods should govern everything', as Lucrece (the 'dear governess' of her own feelings) loyally avers (602, 443). The sentiment is entirely orthodox: kings, like gods, *should* indeed govern everything, and Lucrece is distressed that this son of a king seems quite unable to govern even himself. Hence she reminds him of his duties:

> 'Thou art' quoth she 'a sea, a sovereign king;
> And, lo, there falls into thy boundless flood
> Black lust, dishonour, shame, misgoverning,
> Who seek to stain the ocean of thy blood.'

(652–5)

The traditional comparison of kingship with the sea is obviously flattering to kingship: a Republican would scarcely compare kings with mighty oceans, rolling inevitably, boundlessly, and eternally on. Lucrece's use of this familiar figure decisively counters any incipient radicalism at this point in the poem. Such orthodoxy is a feature of the poem as a whole. Metaphors of mutiny, insurrection, and revolt are constantly used throughout the poem to suggest sexual and spiritual disorder. Commonplace as they are, their presence is surprising in a story about a great and justified rebellion, about the need to put down bad kings; a story which traditionally asserts the

11. Engraving from J. L. Gottfrid's *Historischer Chronik*, 1674. -

12. Gavin Hamilton, *The Oath of Brutus*, early 1760s.

13. G. B. Tiepolo, *Tarquin and Lucretia*, c.1745–50.

14. Artemisia Gentileschi, *Tarquin and Lucretia*, c.1645–50.

superiority of republican over monarchical rule. Two brief
passages will serve to illustrate Shakespeare's characteristic
methods in the poem. Firstly, here is Lucrece appealing to
Tarquin to return to his true self and remember that he is a
king:

> I sue for exil'd majesty's repeal;
> Let him return and flatt'ring thoughts retire ...
> > (640–1)

The words inevitably remind us of the fact that the story
climaxes with the banishment of the Tarquins, who are soon
indeed to be in a literal sense 'exil'd majesty'. Lucrece implies
that Tarquin has already, as it were, exiled himself; and like a
good Royalist she begs him to come back. And secondly, a
narrative passage, in which Tarquin gazes at the sleeping
Lucrece:

> Her breasts, like ivory globes circled with blue,
> A pair of maiden worlds unconquered,
> Save of their lord, no bearing yoke they knew,
> And him by oath they truly honoured.
> These worlds in Tarquin new ambition bred,
> > Who like a foul usurper went about
> > From this fair throne to heave the owner out.
> > > (407–13)

The worst thing that Shakespeare can find to say about Tarquin is that he is like a man who deposes a king. There is, of
course, an obvious irony here, for Shakespeare is again implying that Tarquin is in effect deposing himself. But it is worth
noticing, behind and despite this irony, what basic respect for
kingship is implied, and how heinous the very notion of rebellion is made to appear. Shakespeare's royalism is the stronger
for being inexplicit and unapologetic, rooted firmly as it is in
the imagery and metaphorical language of the poem.

V

Few other writers were as successful as Shakespeare in the art
of discreet political counter-attack. As we have observed, the

story slowly establishes itself over the centuries as a powerful Republican myth, successive versions of the story tending to be read (whether through authorial intention or inadvertence) in terms of contemporary politics. Brutus is seen not merely as the first consul of Republican Rome, but also as the man who killed Caesar or Charles I, or helped to bring Switzerland or America out of political oppression. Whether Brutus is judged to be politically heroic or foolhardy depends (again) upon the angle of vision: very different views of the man will be seen from the left and from the right. But it is also possible to shift perspective in quite another way, and to judge Brutus not simply in political terms, but as human being. This will be the perspective of the following chapter; and with this change we move back once more from the public to the personal areas of the traditional story.

7

The Questioning of the Myth (2):
The Judgement of Brutus

So little is actually known about Lucius Junius Brutus that historians still cannot finally agree as to whether or not such a man ever existed. Yet over the centuries a largely or wholly imaginary 'character' of Brutus is slowly created by historians, artists, philosophers, and writers of fiction. The truth about the real Brutus is hidden in the distance of time. The imaginary Brutus is also hidden, yet in quite another way. He is conceived of as a man who *hides himself*: as a man expert in political self-camouflage and stoical self-control, a man whose inner feelings and motives are ultimately inaccessible, mysterious. Dextrous in the actor's art, he calmly plays his chosen roles. When his father and brother are killed by Tarquin, Brutus prudently feigns stupidity, 'Covering discretion with a coat of folly', as Shakespeare puts it.[1] Journeying to Delphi with the sons of Tarquin, he carries a wooden staff whose golden interior is hidden from all eyes but his own: an emblem, the earliest narrators say, of Brutus himself, whose true nature lay concealed.[2] Brutus at Lucretia's death sheds no tear, utters no word of sorrow, reveals no personal feeling, but sharply urges his lamenting companions forward to revenge. Many commentators over the centuries wondered what actually drove Brutus on throughout all these events. Was it grief for his kinsmen or for Lucretia? Was it fear, anger, vindictiveness? Was it a cool and judicious awareness of the needs, pressures, and possibilities of the historical moment? Machiavelli assumed it was the last, analysing Brutus' skills of dissimulation in a section of the *Discourses* approvingly headed 'That it is a very Good Notion at Times to pretend to be a Fool'.[3] But how is such cool judiciousness in turn to be judged: as evidence of political altruism or of political opportunism and self-interest? At every stage of enquiry, more questions present themselves. Alongside Brutus' positive, heroic reputation another and more dubious reputation develops. The process is curiously similar to that which is undergone by the character of Lucretia. In each case a heroic myth is at first carefully developed, then sceptically queried; in each case a double reputation grows up, a myth and counter-myth. In each case attempts at character rehabilitation are made through the creation of new versions of the story, calculated to deflect criticism. Both characters in the course of time are thus imaginatively transformed, their transformations in each case revealing something of the changing moral sensibilities of the ages in which they occur.

I

The most controversial of all Brutus' actions occurred after the death of Lucretia and the establishment of the new Republic. The crucial episode, recounted with significantly different emphases by the earliest narrators, runs briefly like this. After the Tarquins had been banished from Rome, they sent envoys to the Senate, asking that their property be restored to them. After lengthy debate, the Senate agreed to this request. But the envoys had another reason for their visit to Rome. Taking advantage of their extended stay in the city, they talked with a number of young and disaffected noblemen, persuading them of the need to restore the Tarquins to power in Rome. Finally, it was agreed amongst this group to admit the Tarquins to the city under cover of darkness. Amongst the conspirators were Brutus' own sons, Titus and Tiberius; his wife's brothers, the two Vitellii, Marcus and Manius; and the Aquilii, Lucius and Marcus, sons of Collatinus' sister. The plot was discovered by a slave, Vindicius; arrests were made, incriminating letters found, and the conspirators brought before Brutus himself for judgement. 'It was a memorable scene,' says Livy grimly,

for the consular office imposed upon a father the duty of exacting the supreme penalty from his sons, so that he who, of all men, should have been spared the sight of their suffering, was the one whom fate ordained to enforce it. The condemned criminals were bound to the stake; all were young men of the best blood in Rome, but only the consul's sons drew the eyes of the spectators; the others, for all the interest they aroused, might have come from the gutter. There was pity for their punishment, and greater pity for the crime which had brought it upon them; in every heart was a sort of incredulous sorrow for such treachery at such a time: that these young men, in the very year when Rome was liberated – and by their father's hand – when the newly-created consulship had fallen first to a member of their own family, should have brought themselves to betray the entire population of Rome, high and low alike, and all her gods, to a man who had once been a haughty tyrant and now, from his place of exile, was planning her destruction!

The consuls took their seats on the tribunal; the lictors were ordered to carry out the sentence. The prisoners were stripped, flogged, and beheaded. Throughout the pitiful scene all eyes were on the father's face, where a father's anguish was plain to see.[4]

Livy's account of the scene is basically sympathetic. Brutus is placed in a situation of intolerable conflict, and the depth of his suffering is evident: 'a father's anguish' is indeed the focus of the scene, drawing all eyes more powerfully than the execution itself. Brutus in this account behaves heroically, yet his humanity is still in evidence; as father of the principal victims, his feelings run more strongly and turbulently than those of the other onlookers.

But the episode could also be pictured in quite another way. The account of the Greek rhetorician Dionysius of Halicarnassus twenty or so years later, for example, is already marked by a sense of moral and cultural distance. To the Romans, Dionysius remarks, the behaviour of Brutus may seem praiseworthy, but to a civilized Greek it must appear merely barbaric and cruel. And Dionysius' narrative, while conceding Brutus' great strength of purpose, plays upon this cruelty. He chooses to imagine Brutus at the execution as totally impassive, the only man present who displays no feelings at all. His sons are in tears, the citizens of Rome lament and plead with him to exercise mercy, yet Brutus moves implacably and with calm deliberation to the execution of justice.

But the most extraordinary and the most astonishing part of his behaviour was that he did not once avert his gaze nor shed a tear, and while all the rest who were present at this sad spectacle wept, he was the only person who was observed not to lament the fate of his sons, nor to pity himself for the desolation that was coming upon his house, nor to betray any other signs of weakness, but without a tear, without a groan, without once shifting his gaze, he bore his calamity with a stout heart. So strong of will was he, so steadfast in carrying out the sentence, and so completely the master of all the passions that disturb the reason.[5]

Plutarch, the third major narrator of these events, finds Brutus' behaviour more deeply perplexing, and wavers for a time between condemnation and praise. Plutarch's narration is more restrained than that of Dionysius. The only tears now are shed by the impulsive Collatinus; the others turn silently away from a sight which Brutus alone has the courage to witness.

This was such an acte, as men cannot sufficiently prayse, nor reprove enough. For either it was his excellent vertue, that made his minde so quiet, or els the greatnes of his miserie that tooke away the feeling of his sorowe: whereof neither the one nor the other was any small matter, but passing the common nature of man, that hath in it both divinenes, and sometime beastly brutishnes. But it is better the judgment of men should commend his fame, then that the affection of men by their judgements should diminishe his vertue. For the Romaines holde opinion, it was not so great an acte done of Romulus first to build Rome: as it was for Brutus to recover Rome, and the best libertie thereof, and to renewe the auncient government of the same.[6]

Nowhere in the early accounts is the moral ambiguity of Brutus' conduct more clearly and delicately stated than here. Plutarch is exercised by a problem about the nature of heroic action that is also to worry eighteenth-century writers. Is it truly heroic to behave as Brutus does, Plutarch wonders? If we are to commend as virtuous someone who keeps his feelings *almost* totally under control — Demosthenes, say, who resumed his public duties after a few days' grief for the death of his daughter – why should we not commend as supremely virtuous a man like Brutus, who appears to have kept his feelings under supreme and total control? Plutarch recoils for a time from the starkness of such logic. Brutus, according to popular legend, earned his name on account of his feigned stupidity; an ironic name, of course, for Brutus was not in fact stupid at all. But is there perhaps a sense in which that name was properly deserved? May there not have been 'beastly brutishness' as well as divinity in Brutus' ability to subdue all human feelings at this time?[7]

But Plutarch's doubts are only lightly registered, and in the end he is prepared to fall in with the common Roman verdict on Brutus. Like Dionysius, he contrasts Brutus' severity advantageously with Collatinus' more understandable but less admirable readiness to give way to emotion. Collatinus expresses, where Brutus suppresses, his natural feelings. It is Collatinus who breaks down at the death of Lucretia, Brutus who coldly urges revenge; Collatinus who humanely argues for the restitution of the Tarquin's property, Brutus his fellow consul who argues against; Collatinus who pleads that his own nephews, the Aquilii, be forgiven for their part in the conspiracy, Brutus who condemns the Aquilii to death, as he had condemned his own sons; and it is consequently Collatinus, not Brutus, who comes to lose his consulship, disabled for office not merely through his kinship with the banished Tarquins but by his propensity for prompt and unreflective displays of feeling. Heroism appears to demand after all the capacity to keep one's feelings firmly suppressed. But what is the cost, in human terms, of such suppression? Plutarch's account does not fully resolve this question.

Nor is this the only problem that the story presents. In being called upon to judge his sons, Brutus is confronted with a classic choice that stands at the centre of many a tragic drama from antiquity to the present day: the choice between a loyalty to one's own family and a loyalty to the state, between the demands of paternity and those of patriotism. Brutus' condemnation of his sons establishes him finally and beyond doubt as *pater patriae*, father of his country, not merely in the sense that he is the true founder and progenitor of the Roman Republic but in the further sense that, when faced with this choice of loyalties, he forsakes his own family for the larger family of the state. But Brutus' unwavering sense of priorities, his ruthless placing of public duty before private affections, might arouse doubts as well as admiration. How wise, how heroic, how humane is it to kill one's children in the name of patriotism? The issue is not easy. Even Virgil seems to hesitate in his verdict, writing of the elder Brutus in lines in which, as Augustine was to say, praise is mingled with 'a shudder of compassion':

> *infelix, utcumque ferent ea facta minores:*
> *vincet amor patriae laudumque immensa cupido.*

Unhappy he, however posterity extol that deed! Yet love of country shall prevail, and boundless passion for renown.[8]

The wisdom or otherwise of Brutus' judgement was sometimes discussed in relation to the judgement of another and even more implacable Roman father, Manlius Torquatus, who condemned his son to death for having fought, and beaten, one of the enemy without having first obtained his father's permission.[9] The episode also furthers the association between Brutus and his alleged descendant Marcus Junius Brutus, the assassin of Julius Caesar, whom Dante was to put in the lowest circle of hell, along with Cassius and Judas, for killing his rightful ruler in the name of patriotism.[10] It was a persistent tradition, moreover, that in murdering Caesar, Brutus had committed an even graver crime than tyrannicide, for it was sometimes alleged that Brutus was Caesar's illegitimate son.[11] The younger Brutus' sacrifice of his own father for the sake of his country thus seemed a mirror image of the elder Brutus' sacrifice of his own sons for the same cause. For Voltaire, these symmetrical episodes were to provide the linking motifs in his related tragedies, *Brutus* and *La Mort de César*. Around the figures of the elder and the younger Brutus, a double tradition thus grows up. Seen in one light, both men were heroes, liberators of their country. Seen in another light, their actions might appear morally dubious. Coluccio Salutati in 1400 justified Dante's placing of Marcus Brutus in the lowest circle of hell by stressing the unforgivableness of parricide: Brutus had murdered the father of his country and his natural father as well, thus putting himself on a par with Judas, who 'had for a price betrayed the son of the eternal God, father and creator of all things'.[12]

Salutati was less certain what to think about the elder Brutus. Early in his life, Salutati praised Lucius Junius Brutus, along with Manlius Torquatus, as models of virtuous justice. But later in life Salutati came to doubt the wisdom of his own earlier judgements, and to wonder if it was really possible to give unqualified praise to pagan heroes such as the two Brutuses, Lucretia, and Cato. As Hans Baron points out, 'such inconsistency and retraction are indicative not only of Salutati's personality, but of the general character of pre-Quattrocento Humanism'.[13] Petrarch was troubled by similar doubts and waverings, swinging from an early admiration of Cato, Lucius Junius Brutus, and Marcus Junius Brutus to a later grave mistrust, finally coming to share Augustine's view of the deficiency of Roman heroic ideals. On the day of his coronation, Petrarch had contentedly taken as his motto Virgil's words about the elder Brutus: *vincent amor patriae laudumque immensa cupido*; the same passion, Petrarch felt, had driven him on, too, to write his *Africa*. But what shade of praise or condemnation did Virgil's words in fact bear? Both Petrarch and Salutati later searched this line with care. 'Do you really believe', wrote Salutati in 1396, 'that Brutus . . . at the moment when he gave the order to have his sons beheaded for their plot to restore the monarchy, simply obeyed rigid justice enthusiastically, but did not rather remember, along with the salvation of his country, the glory that comes from praise in this world?'[14]

'Glory' is the problem here, as it was for those who sifted the motives of Lucretia. The process of questioning in each case is strikingly similar. Over the centuries (the reasoning seems to run), both Lucretia and Brutus have been glorified for their actions; thus it must be suspected that a lust for worldly glory was the 'real' motive for those actions. A Christian does good in private, careless of popular judgement, knowing that God can perceive the secrets of the heart. Pagan heroes do their fine

deeds in public, thirsting for glory, wanting to be seen to be
great in their own time and in times to come. To judge them
aright, we must look into their hearts (as God looks into ours),
searching for ultimate motives; and this the Christian inter-
preter confidently and inventively does, untroubled by the
intervening aeons of time and even by the question of the
historical authenticity of those whose spiritual characters he
dissects. So vivid is the myth of Brutus and Lucretia that they
seem to enjoy a real and continuing existence, the hidden
dimensions of which may freely be explored and denounced.

There were others, however, who looked at the story of
Brutus and were not troubled by doubts. Machiavelli, always
more interested in deeds than in motives, expressed his admiration of Brutus' unwavering firmness in condemning his sons.
'When Liberty has been newly acquired,' he wrote in the
heading to another of his *Discourses*, 'it is necessary in order to
maintain it to "kill the Sons of Brutus".' 'He who establishes a
tyranny and does not kill "Brutus",' Machiavelli goes on, 'and
he who establishes a democratic regime and does not kill "the
sons of Brutus" will not last long.'[15]

While later writers did not always express themselves quite
so bluntly on this matter, the continuing veneration for Brutus
as a political figure is based on a tacit acceptance of
Machiavelli's dictum. Brutus is respected as a man who knew
not merely how to seize power but how to keep it; who set
political considerations constantly above personal ones. Yet
alongside this positive reputation there is an uneasy awareness
that all is not well; that the story, to be wholly acceptable,
needs to be subtly adjusted.

II

It is a curious fact that the story of Brutus should have been so
popular in England and France during the late seventeenth and
eighteenth centuries, at a time when the virtues of *sensibility*
were so strongly commended from pulpit and page. If the
highest human qualities were reckoned to be warmth and
generosity, tenderness, spontaneity, subordination of the

demands of prudence to those of benevolence, what kind of a model for emulation was presented by the apparently stoical, tough, prudential figure of Lucius Junius Brutus? The interpretations and transformations of Brutus during this period are of special interest. There were two main ways in which the story of Brutus might be accommodated to the tastes of the age. One way, vigorously pursuing the lead of Dionysius of Halicarnassus, was to turn Brutus into a disagreeably insensitive figure, exaggerating by way of contrast the emotions which everyone else must have felt at the condemnation of his sons. This is the tactic employed, for instance, by Nathan Hooke in his *Roman History* in 1738. Hooke's Brutus delivers his judgement against a sentimental groundswell of Roman tears, sighs, murmurs, tremblings, and pleadings. Brutus calmly announces that he is delivering his sons to the lictors for punishment. 'At these words the whole assembly shrieked; the universal consternation was inexpressible; distress shewed itself in every face, and the mournful looks of the people pleaded for pity: but neither these intercessions, nor the bitter lamentings of the young men, who called upon their father by the most endearing names, could soften the inflexible judge.'[16] Robert Jephson in his *Roman Portraits* (1794) takes a similar line, presenting Brutus as a monster of impassivity:

> Unmov'd he sat; while tears and groans confess'd
> The heaving pangs of every other breast.
> O heart of triple brass! can love of fame
> Extinguish nature, to exalt a name?
> Serenely could thine eye a sight behold,
> Which chills the stranger's vital tide, when told?
> What praise, alas! can fortitude receive,
> Which none would imitate, nor all believe?
> Take then, inhuman! thy ambition's lot;
> Thy pride's remember'd, and their crime forgot.[17]

To follow this approach to its logical limit is to see the demonstrative Collatinus rather than the repressed Brutus as the true hero of the story. In Hugh Downman's tragedy of *Lucius Junius Brutus* (1779), Collatinus, like a proper eighteenth-century Man of Feeling, retires from the camp at Ardea to deplore and weep over the unpleasantnesses of war. By means such as these the peripheries of the story are sentimentalized, while the original hero of the story may be judged severely as a hard-hearted seeker after worldly glory.

But it was also possible to rework the story in another, more radical way, by transforming Brutus into a covert Man of Feeling. This bold and ingenious feat was first achieved by Madeleine de Scudéry in her immensely long, digressive, inventive, and popular romance, *Clélie,* published in France in thirty books between 1654 and 1660 and translated into English (as *Clelia*) between 1659 and 1677. *Clélie* is a rewriting of the entire story of the rise and fall of the Tarquin kings, filled out with many imaginary adventures, side-plots, and debates, often of an amorous nature. The life of Lucius Junius Brutus is described from birth to death, his story being likewise enlivened by many surprising adventures. Brutus flees from Rome with his mother after the murder of his father and brother, and takes up residence in Metapont, where he is taught by Pythagoras' daughter, overcomes in a fight the famous Milo of Crotona, and feigns stupidity in order to woo a woman named Chrysis. Pleased with the success of this ploy, Brutus returns to Rome, keeping up the pretence of folly for reasons of political safety. In Rome he falls in love with Collatinus' wife, Lucretia. The guise of folly is again convenient, and Brutus and Lucretia enjoy a clandestine, passionate, and chaste affair, finally terminated in a melodramatic nocturnal scene in Lucretia's garden at Collatia.

Scudéry entirely reverses the traditional emphases in the story of Lucretia and Brutus. Lucretia is no longer a model of marital devotion, or Brutus one of stern emotional repression. Collatinus, traditionally an impulsive man, is shown to be shallow and tepid in his feelings. Brutus' passion for Lucretia is the central driving force of the story, the fact that is intended to make all its events intelligible. It is this passion which fires Brutus in his zeal for revenge against the Tarquins; political considerations are altogether secondary:

in this emergency he minded not the Liberty of *Rome*, but in order to revenge the death of the innocent *Lucretia*, and made use of the

Interest of his Country, which was so dear to him, only to satisfie his Passion. Nor did he then think of revenging the death of his Father and Brother, and so much was his mind taken up with this sad accident, that *Lucretia* was the only cause of this great and dangerous attempt.[18]

Even after the establishment of the Republic, Brutus cares less for politics than for Lucretia: he would sooner be able to live with her under the Tarquins, we are told, than have established the Republic at the cost of her life. By rearranging the story in this way, Scudéry ingeniously 'solves' many of its traditional difficulties. Brutus cannot now be said to be an unfeeling Stoic, nor a crafty political opportunist, nor a thirster after glory, nor a man who values private affections less dearly than patriotism, nor even a person with particularly contentious political opinions. He is simply a man in love: this single fact explains and justifies all.

   Clélie might well be subtitled 'The Secrets of the Heart', for it is this private, inner world of feeling Madeleine de Scudéry is forever exploring. The secrets she reveals invariably turn out to be amorous secrets, rather than (say) secrets of political ambition. Her Brutus is by nature gallant, mild, obliging, but is changed by the shock of Lucretia's death and 'all his life after affected a certain austere vertue, wherein there seemed to be something of cruelty, to those who were not informed of the secret of his heart . . .'[19] Brutus' sons have their own secrets of the heart. They join the Tarquinian conspiracy not for political reasons but because, like Brutus, they are in love: with Ocrisia and Teraminta, two women who have been brought up with the Tarquins, and whose lives (they say) are in danger if Titus and Tiberius do not join the conspiracy. When Brutus learns of his son's involvement in the plot, he looks about for ways of saving them. Teraminta comes privately, in male disguise, to visit Brutus and inform him of the reason for his sons' actions, pleading for their release.

So that *Brutus* already yielding to that tenderness of soul he was much guilty of, felt his grief increasing upon him. He therefore spoke with much mildness to *Teraminta*, and told her he was resolved to do for his Sons, how guilty soever they be, whatever honour the interest of Rome, and the indeprecability of the people would permit.[20]

But the Roman mob begin to clamour for the death of Titus and Tiberius, and Brutus, moved as he is by 'paternal tenderness', fears also for the safety of Teraminta, and is at last forced to carry through his sentence. Once again, Scudéry achieves her 'solution' to the traditional problem of Brutus' severity by the simple expedient of reversing the familiar narrative pattern: instead of an implacable Brutus, unswayed by a lamenting public, she gives us a lamenting Brutus, swayed by an implacable public.

Lavishly and absurdly sentimental though Scudéry's romance is, it is important to see that she is rewriting the traditional story in an attempt to counter precisely the objections which had been urged against the character of Brutus by more learned and thoughtful commentators over many centuries. It had been asked what really lay behind Brutus' stoical mask, what the psychological origins of his actions really were, what motives, what secrets of the heart, really drove him on. Madeleine de Scudéry provided, at great length and with great ingenuity, some very convenient answers. Moral criticism of the story appears once again to stimulate rather than inhibit the creative imagination, prompting new elaborations and variations on an old theme.

Clélie has a major influence on the development of the story of Brutus and Lucretia in the late seventeenth century and throughout the eighteenth and nineteenth centuries. Alongside the character of the cold-hearted Brutus, brutal Stoic, there flourishes the contrary character of the warm-hearted Brutus, crypto-sentimentalist. Though few writers go so far as to present Brutus as Lucretia's lover, as Scudéry did, most of them attempt to modify the legendary severity of his character and, like Scudéry, to explore the private, hidden parts of his nature. Cathérine Bernard, defending herself against the charge of having 'softened' the title-character in her tragedy *Brutus* (Paris, 1691), points out that the classical historians depict Brutus in public, as he talks in the Senate or with the people of

Rome, while she herself shows him in private situations where he can give expession to 'the most secret impulses of his heart'. If Brutus is shown as an insensitive man, she argues, then his condemnation of his sons can scarcely be reckoned to be an act either of virtue or heroism.[21] Sensibility is for Bernard a necessary ingredient in heroic, as in tragic, action. Her Brutus condemns his sons only after a struggle between his natural *tendresse* and his sense of *austère devoir,* urged on by a pitiless Senate. Yet even duty, Bernard explains, was an emotional affair for the ancient Romans, who felt great love for their country and suffered greatly when, like Brutus' sons, they betrayed it. Brutus' sons in this tragedy, needless to say, betray their country only because of another, stronger love: both are infatuated with Aquilie (daughter of the conspirator Aquilius), for whom they both feel *tendresse extrème.* Like Scudéry, Bernard has moved the story away from the political and back into the private realm.

> O tyrannique amour! O funeste journée!
> A quel prix, liberté, nous estes-vous donné?
>
> O tyrannic love! O fatal day!
> At what price, liberty, are you given us?

are the concluding lines of the play. It is love, and not merely political rule, that is tyrannical now; and the value of liberty is carefully weighed against that of other, human, losses. Machiavelli's coldly practical way of regarding the story ('When Liberty has been newly acquired it is Necessary in Order to maintain it to "Kill the Sons of Brutus"') has been importantly modified.

Voltaire (*Brutus*, 1730) refashions the story in a somewhat similar manner – on the advice, as he tells us in his *Discours sur la tragédie,* of Bolingbroke and other English friends.[22] In the *Discours,* Voltaire describes how he has attempted to temper Brutus' traditional austerity by portraying him also as a loving father, how he has emphasized the tenderness and innocence of Tarquin's daughter Tullie, and tried to show her lover, Titus, as a man with great, but conflicting, passions. Voltaire seems a trifle uneasy about the way he has interlaced a love plot throughout a play ostensibly in praise of the sterner Roman virtues. Like Bernard, he attempts to resolve the contradiction by exploring the inner, private world of Brutus as well as the outer, public, world. In private, Brutus weeps tears over his guilty son; in public, he unflinchingly condemns him to death. He is at once a Stoic and a sentimentalist, a man of iron and a man of tears. While in England, Voltaire had been deeply impressed and influenced by Addison's tragedy of *Cato* (1713). There is an uneasy air of emotional disequilibrium about Voltaire's play as there is about Addison's, a certain sense of having it both ways, attempting simultaneously to celebrate the opposing virtues of emotional expressiveness and restraint. We might describe this tendency as heroic schizophrenia.

Almost all the dramatists who handled the story of Brutus in the eighteenth and nineteenth centuries attempted to exploit its sentimental potential, modifying its traditional and harsher aspects. Often they were explicit about their intentions. In Italy, Antonio Conti in the preface to his *Giunio Bruto* (1743) carefully analysed the evolution of the story from classical times and explained why he found it necessary to 'sweeten' the character of Brutus.[23] In England, most plays on this theme were heavily weighted in the direction of pathos. When Duncombe's adaptation of Voltaire's tragedy was performed at Drury Lane in 1734, 'there was scarcely a dry eye in the boxes during the last scene between Brutus and Titus'.[24] Richard Cumberland's *The Sybil, or the Elder Brutus* (never performed, published posthumously in 1813) presents a fragile Brutus, racked with sensibility:

> Limbs, bear me up
> Against this shock of nature, to support
> The dreadful office, which the Gods impose
> On me their trembling minister, whose heart
> They should have cas'd in marble; and made dead
> To human feelings, ere they bade me meet
> A spectacle, that harrows up the soul
> With terror and dismay.[25]

J. H. Payne's version of 1818 degenerates into even deeper melodrama. The play ends with Titus being led off to execution, and Brutus signalling his grief to the audience in hectic pantomime:

(He rises and waves his hand, convulsed with agitation, then drops in his seat, and shrouds his face with his toga. Three sounds of the trumpet are heard instantly. All the characters assume attitudes of deep misery. Brutus starts up wildly, descends to the front in extreme agitation, looks out on the side by which Titus departed, for an instant, then, with an hysterical burst, exclaims)

Justice is satisfied, and Rome is free!

(Brutus falls. The characters group around him.)[26]

In most dramatic versions of the Brutus story from the late seventeenth century onwards, sentiment is also heightened by means of love plots, as Andrieux scornfully points out in the preface to his tragedy *Lucius Junius Brutus* in 1830.[27] Yet Andrieux's own play is not so very different from its predecessors: Brutus' sons in this version are seduced into the conspiracy not by their love for Tarquin's daughters but by their love for his other son, Arons. Like many another dramatist before him, Andrieux does his best to squeeze passion from this story of an apparently passionless man. The conflict, he tells us (borrowing a remark by Alfieri) is that between the noblest of all human feelings, patriotism, and the strongest and tenderest of human feelings, paternal love. Like many another Brutus before him, Andrieux's Brutus weeps tears in private, speaking tenderly to his family about his sensibility and the secrets of his heart, while in public he acts with unyielding rigour. Half Man of Feeling, half Stoic, he attempts uneasily in his divided character to reconcile the contrary heroic aspirations of the age.

III

Most of the plays so far discussed, interesting though they may be as evidence of changing ways of looking at the character of Brutus, are notably lacking in subtlety and genuine literary distinction. One English tragedy on this theme, however, achieves a different order of success, and repays rather closer scrutiny: and that is Nathaniel Lee's *Lucius Junius Brutus: Father of His Country*. The first and most striking feature of Lee's play, as G. Wilson Knight has observed, is its moral openness.[28] Lee is not out merely to sanctify or merely to vilify Brutus, whose actions as presented in the play seem partly admirable, partly appalling. Lee raises precisely the doubts that occurred to Plutarch: doubts about the humanity of Brutus and about the quality of his alleged heroism. To a nervous government in 1680, *Lucius Junius Brutus* seemed a play scandalously critical of the established powers. But it is important to notice that the Republican Brutus is not presented altogether sympathetically in the play. For one thing, he is not always strictly truthful. Speaking to the Roman people in the Forum over the body of Lucrece, he declares that 'th' inspiring gods' have miraculously restored his powers of reason (II.140); yet we know that his madness has always been a pretence, and that the change in his behaviour now is a matter of willed and conscious choice. Condemning his son Titus to death later in the play, Brutus blandly passes responsibility for the act once again to the gods:

> Methinks I see the very hand of Jove
> Moving the dreadful wheels of this affair
> That whirl thee, like a machine, to thy fate.
> It seems as if the gods had preordained it . . .
>
> (IV.509–12)

'. . . *seems* as if', but actually the decision is Brutus' own. Like the skilled politician he is, Brutus is never at a loss in knowing how to plead necessity and how to employ the language of religion.

The play also invites us to consider whether Brutus, sworn enemy of tyrants, is not himself something of a tyrant. Brutus commits many of the atrocities he deplores in the Tarquins. In his call to the citizens of Rome, Brutus asks whether they wish to tolerate Tarquinian rule and see

> The city filled with rapes, adulteries,
> The Tiber choked with bodies, all the shores
> And neighbouring rocks besmeared with Roman blood?
>
> (II.219–21)

Blood is a prominent idea and image in the play; yet it is Brutus, quite as much as Tarquin, who is responsible for its shedding. His son Titus pictures Brutus as a doctor sent by the gods to cure the sickness of Rome by letting blood (II.434–47). Much of that blood is to be Titus' own. In the final act of the play he appears 'writ all o'er with blood' (V.i.35) after his flogging; his wife Teraminta, likewise smeared with blood, rails against Brutus as an 'inhuman, barbarous, bloody father', a 'god of blood' (V.i.52, 103). Whether Brutus is a man directed by the gods or by his own inhumanity, whether he is himself a kind of vengeful god, is allowed to remain in doubt. To his son Tiberius the issue is plain:

> Enjoy the bloody conquest of thy pride,
> Thou more tyrannical than any Tarquin,
> Thou fiercer sire of these unhappy sons
> Than impious Saturn or the gorged Thyestes.
> (V.i.115–18)

Tarquin and Brutus, monarch and revolutionary, may indeed seem curiously to resemble each other, each seeking harshly to exert his will over others and exact the shedding of blood.

The earliest narrators of the story of the fall of the Tarquin kings frequently mention blood. Lucretia fears that her blood has been tainted by Tarquin's rape, and sheds her own blood as a consequence and recompense; Brutus plucks the knife from Lucretia's side and swears by her blood – 'none more chaste until a tyrant wronged her' – to expel the Tarquins from Rome. Lee picks up and multiplies the suggestiveness of this notion in his tragedy. Blood of the most literal kind is often seen: Brutus draws from Lucrece's side the dagger 'All stained and reeking with her sacred blood' (I.433). The Fecialian priests – in a scene which Lee skilfully works up from a couple of unrelated hints in two of his sources – offer to the conspirators goblets of the blood of 'two very busy commonwealth's men' whom they have ceremoniously sacrificed in the royalist cause, 'That Rome may blush and traitors bleed'.[29] Titus is stabbed by his friend Valerius, while his brother Tiberius is beheaded by the common executioner. Lee also

conceives of the emotions in terms of the movement of blood.
Brutus speaks of his 'blood-shot anger' as he thinks of
Tarquin, while 'The flushing blood that mounted in his face'
reveals Sextus' passion for Lucrece. Speaking of the raped
Lucretia, Brutus significantly invokes a physiological analogy:

> As in the body, on some great surprise,
> The heart still calls from the discolored face,
> From every part the life and spirits down,
> So Lucrece comes to Rome and summons all her blood.
>
> (I.99–102)

Lucrece is pictured as the heart, the source and pulse of
sensibility. Shock, Lee suggests, prompts the heart to
summon vital reinforcements, draining the face of its natural
colour. Yet the 'blood' which Lucrece summons now to Rome
is of course her family, kindred by blood. Lee's word-play
alerts us to the crucial connections that exist in the play
between the notion of feeling, the notion of the family, and
the notion of sacrifice. The rape of Lucrece by 'the lustful,
bloody Sextus' is an offence not merely against Lucrece,
tainting her 'with the blood of Tarquin'; it is also an offence
against Sextus' kinsman Collatinus, 'his own blood', and will
lead in turn to the issue of blood.

Lee highlights the fact that the tragic events of the play
occur between people who are related to each other, who
share blood. The conspiracy, as he presents it, is essentially a
family affair:

> There's scarce one man of this conspiracy
> But is some way related, if not nearly,
> To Junius Brutus.
>
> (V.i.26–8)

Many of the conspirators are associated not merely with
Brutus but also with Tarquin:

> For these of all the youth of quality
> Are most inclined to Tarquin and his race
> By blood and humour.
>
> (III.i.130–2)

'Blood' here is kinship, but it is also high spirits; the conspirators are 'the young hot blood of Rome' (III.i.107), young 'bloods' recognizable through their Roman garb as Restoration bucks. Family ties and natural inclinations here move together. But at the centre of the play these things are at odds: Titus must choose between his loyalty to his father and to Rome, on the one hand, and his affection for Teraminta, who is 'the blood of Tarquin', on the other. '. . . thy blood I fear/ More than thy spirit, which is truly Roman,' says Brutus to his son: his 'blood' is his sexual feeling. Yet in another sense, Brutus and Titus share the same blood; and Lee subtly suggests that in sacrificing his sons, Brutus is also in a way sacrificing himself. 'I'll tear him from me though the blood should follow' (III.i.137), says Brutus when he learns of Tiberius' involvement in the conspiracy. Tiberius sees his father as a cormorant who 'preys upon his entrails, tears his bowels/ With thirst of blood and hunger fetched from hell' (V.i.120–1); Teraminta accuses him of cutting limbs from his own body (V.ii.119); Brutus sees himself as a man eviscerated by the gods:

> Hast thou, O gods, this night emboweled me?
> Ransacked thy Brutus' veins, thy fellow consul,
> And found two villains lurking in my blood?
> (IV.224–6)

Brutus himself is destroyed, and in several ways: for to be 'emboweled' is to be deprived of children, and also to be deprived of natural feelings of pity and compassion.[30] Treachery may arise in the family, but also out of one's own feelings: either way, 'blood' is not to be trusted.

The ramification of meanings here indicates a complexity of thought absent from most of the other dramatic versions of the story of Brutus and his sons. Like Scudéry and her followers, Lee is acutely interested in the nature and operation of the feelings, yet he does not sentimentalize the character of Brutus. His play instead leaves many questions open. Is Brutus an agent or a victim? Do the gods torment or aid him? Does he control his own destiny while having the language of religion on his lips? Does he triumph or is he destroyed? Is he a liberator or merely another and more subtle form of tyrant? The political sympathies of the play, as the Lord Chamberlain observed, run generally towards the ideals of Brutus and the new Republic. Yet it is not the play's political ideals (in any simple sense) that remain most vividly in the mind after reading this tragedy. Lee allows us rather to see the cost, in human terms, that such ideals impose, and to feel a genuine hesitation about the wisdom of the man who attempts so single-mindedly to live by them.

IV

In shifting attention from Lucretia to Brutus at the outset of chapter six, we shifted at first from the private and domestic area of the story to the public and political area, from the woman's world to the man's. Those who questioned the exemplary nature of Brutus' character, however, were often in effect questioning the wisdom of splitting up areas of human behaviour in this fashion; the wisdom of trying to separate, for example, private feelings from public actions, the world of women from the world of men. And from the time of Madeleine de Scudéry onwards, the story of Brutus and his sons ceases to be a story simply about men: women come to play an increasingly important role in the action. Scudéry invented the characters of Ocrisia and Teraminta, the two noble slaves of Tarquin with whom Brutus' sons are in love. Later writers converted these slaves into Tarquin's daughters (legitimate or illegitimate), sometimes introducing other women into the plot: Brutus' wife (who in Lee's play makes a forceful fifth act entrance in the company of other 'mothers of sad Rome,/ Sisters and daughters') and the daughter or daughters of the conspirator Aquilius. In the romantic world of *Clélie*, the women, though prominent in the story, are more absorbed in introspection and affairs of the heart than in public action. In later versions, their role is more positive. Often they plead with Brutus for the lives of his sons; sometimes they elect to die with them. The presence of

women in all cases modifies in an important way the orienta-
tion of the original story.

That story, as we have already seen, is essentially about the
need to behave like *men*. The earliest narrators imply that
Rome has in some way become effeminate under the rule of
the Tarquins, and that paradoxically it requires a woman to
teach the men of Rome how to achieve true manliness. '. . .
when you, who were given a woman's nature, have shown the
resolution of a brave man', says Brutus in Dionysius of Halicarnassus' account, 'shall we, who were born men, show
ourselves inferior to women in courage?'[31] In the classical
accounts, it takes Lucius Junius Brutus to bully and cajole the
Roman men in this way, to urge Collatinus and Lucretius to
stop weeping impotently over the body of Lucretia, and the
men of Rome to prefer action to lamentation; they must prove
themselves men. It is a token of Brutus' own manliness that he
is ready to suppress his own weeping and natural feelings,
and, dry-eyed, condemn his sons to death after he discovers
their involvement in the Tarquinian conspiracy.

Virtue, as the etymology of the word reminds us, was originally thought of as conduct worthy of a man, *vir*. The most
celebrated acts of Roman virtue tended to be acts of extraordinary self-control, self-mutilation, or self-destruction:
Mucius Scaevola placing his hand fearlessly on the altar of hot
coals after his capture by Lars Porsenna to show how in-
different to pain he and his fellow Romans are; Regulus
voluntarily returning to the Carthaginians to keep his honour
as a hostage, to undergo a fearful death in a spiked barrel. An
essential ingredient in manly virtue seems, for the Romans, to
have been the ability to subdue one's natural feelings of pain,
loss, bereavement, fear of death. Women who behaved in this
manner might also be recognized at times as *virtuous*, almost
like men. Marcus Junius Brutus' wife Portia proves herself
virtuous and worthy of political trust by wounding herself
deeply in the thigh, averring that she is unlike the rest of her
sex: 'I confesse, that a womans wit commonly is too weake to
keepe a secret safely: but yet, Brutus, good educacion, and
the companie of vertuous men, have some power to reforme

the defect of nature. And for my selfe, I have this benefit moreover: that I am the daughter of Cato, and wife of Brutus.'[32] Women – so the assumption seems to run – tend normally to express rather than suppress their feelings, talking freely, weeping freely, readily showing many of their fears and affections. Such expressiveness is 'natural' to women and therefore tolerable in its way, though apt to be something of a nuisance: it is indeed one reason (so it is implied) why women are generally unfit to hold public office or to be entrusted with the secrets of state.

These stereotypes are still to be found in the seventeenth- and eighteenth-century versions of the story of Lucretia and Brutus, but in a significantly modified form. The notion of 'virtue' is now often regarded in a somewhat more complex way, 'womanly' qualities of expressiveness and tenderness often being more highly esteemed than in the earliest versions of the story. In Lee's *Lucius Junius Brutus* it seems to be implied that virtue may lie in a blend of 'male' toughness and 'female' sensibility, extremes of either quality – the firmness of Brutus, Collatinus' readiness with 'women's drops' – being viewed with equal suspicion. Brutus struggles to suppress his 'tenderness' lest 'A woman's tear come o'er my resolution' (I.239). Titus, striving to emulate his father, sheds no 'woman's tear' at his flogging (V.i.46), and tries to 'muster all the tyrant-man about me' in parting from Teraminta (II.363). In a play concerned with political liberty, the phrase *'tyrant-man'* tells its own tale, subtly connecting in our minds the ideas of political and emotional repression. The protests of Teraminta and Brutus' wife Sempronia are powerfully registered in Lee's play, reminding us that there is more than one perspective from which these legendary deeds of male virtue may be regarded.

V

'Perspective' returns us to painting, where the new sensibilities are also to be felt. Jacques-Louis David's *Lictors Returning to Brutus the Bodies of his Sons* (plate twenty)

depicts Brutus not in the Senate or witnessing the execution of
his sons, but in the privacy of his house after the execution is
over. Privacy, or near-privacy: for it would be more accurate
to say that Brutus is depicted here at that critical time and
place at which private and public worlds meet. At the left the
lictors, representatives of the state, move past carrying the
bodies of Brutus' sons, as though along a public thoroughfare.
Under the ominously darkened figure of Rome, Brutus sits
tensely and in shadow, his eyes staring blankly away from the
procession entering the house. On the right of the painting,
bathed in quite another light and behaving in quite another
manner, are the women of the household: Brutus' wife and
daughters and (turning her face aside and shrouding it in a
fold of her garments) a female servant. David invents these
daughters, just as Scudéry invents Ocrisia and Teraminta, to
lend pathos to an otherwise harsh event; the story is now as
much a story of women as of men. Brutus struggles to contain
feelings which the women openly and spontaneously express
with eloquent freedom and sinuosity of movement. The
mother's outstretched arm and open hand contrast obviously
with Brutus's still-clenched fist. The women's sewing, the task
of the previous moment, lies abandoned on the table, while
Brutus cannot let go of the immediate past, clutching still the
letter which has established his sons' involvement in the conspiracy. The mother's looks, like her movements, are directed
instinctively towards the bodies of her sons; she meets the
lictor's steady and answering gaze. Brutus' looks are
resolutely averted. When David's painting was first exhibited
in Paris at the Salon in September 1789, it was criticized on the
grounds that it was really two paintings rather than one.[33] It
would be more accurate to say that within a single composition David is depicting the tragic separation of two worlds: the
public and the private worlds, the worlds of men and of
women, of duty and of love, of calculation and spontaneity.
The worlds are divided as though by an invisible wall. The
women's gestures can touch nothing, alter nothing, that the
men have already decreed and done. Yet in another sense the
two worlds complement and affect each other. The women

seem to express a grief that Brutus also shares, to authenticate in a sense Brutus' humanity; the two halves of the painting are related as well as contrasted.

In Gavin Hamilton's and Jacques-Antoine Beaufort's paintings of the oath of Brutus, Brutus himself buoyantly dominates the compositions. In David's canvas, the now chastened and sombre Brutus occupies a shadowy corner of the painting, seeming to ponder the relationships which the viewer's eye also inevitably traces as he looks from right to left, from background to foreground, from left to right, in an attempt to harmonize the painting's separate and unresolved worlds. Sitting apart in semi-darkness, Brutus is still in some sense a 'hidden' man. His eyes stare sightlessly and uncommunicatively ahead of him with the same gaze with which (as Dionysius tells us) he confronted the execution of his sons. He is not, as Lee's Brutus may be, a monster, a god of blood. Yet the silent presence of the women invites us none the less to judge his predicament – to judge the judgement of Brutus – and to feel its emotional weight. The perspective on the story has changed again.

III

AN EPILOGUE – AND AN ANALOGUE

Venerisque hic unicus usus,
Progenies; urbi pater est urbique maritus,
Iustitiae cultor, rigidi servator honesti,
In commune bonus; nullosque Catonis in actus
Subrepsit partemque tulit sibi nata voluptas.

Lucan, *De Bello Civili,* ii. 387–91

He sought no end of marriage, but increase,
Nor wish'd a pleasure, but his country's peace:
That took up all the tenderest parts of life,
His country was his children and his wife.
From justice' righteous lore he never swerv'd,
But rigidly his honesty preserv'd.
On universal good his thoughts were bent,
Nor knew what gain, or self-affection meant;
And while his benefits the public share,
Cato was always last in Cato's care.

Rowe's translation, 1714

His death was the weakness of a great soul, the
error of a Stoic, a stain upon his life.

Napoleon on Cato[1]

8

Heroism Transformed: Lucretia, Brutus, and Cato of Utica

In the first chapter of this book it was argued that the story of the rape of Lucretia and the story of Lucius Junius Brutus mirror and complement each other in a variety of ways, and that the stories together form one composite, coherent, and consciously ordered myth, purporting to explain the origins of the Roman Republic. By now it will also be apparent that there are remarkable similarities in the ways in which these closely related stories have been interpreted, criticized, and rewritten over the centuries: in the story of their stories. In classical times both Lucretia and Brutus were generally admired as models of heroic conduct. In Christian times, doubts gather, arguments commence, sharply divergent variants of the myth begin to proliferate. Alongside the tradition of the chaste and heroic Lucretia, other traditions develop: of the colluding, desperate, vainglorious Lucretia; while alongside the tradition of the heroic, superhuman Brutus, patriot extraordinary, there likewise appear the traditions of Brutus the political opportunist and Brutus the calloused and brutal tyrant. Still other variants of the myth emerge to counter these adverse interpretations; and both Lucretia and Brutus are transformed in various ways, sometimes into characters of deep passion, racked by secret loves and sorrows. These changes in the fortunes of the myth are related in a complex but significant way to other larger changes in thought and sensibility. And one of the most crucial of these changes is in attitudes to the idea of heroism.

Many societies regard the earliest period of their history as a heroic age, a period which subsequent generations must look back upon with pride, nostalgia, and a due sense of present inferiority, for the present age, it is assumed, can never hope to match the legendary accomplishments of the past. Refracted through the distance of time, the earliest heroes of a society take on a stature which may be out of all keeping with their actual achievements; their stories are enlarged and improved in countless ways, while the less attractive aspects of their lives are quietly forgotten. Often such heroes and their stories may be wholly imaginary, yet the spell of their imagined deeds may be no less powerful than those of heroes whose historicity is firmly vouched for. When the heroic past recedes too far into the remote distance, however, it may be regarded not merely with veneration but also in other ways: with scepticism or amusement or downright disapproval. Values change; and conduct which was considered noble and courageous in one epoch may be considered excessive or misguided or merely barbaric in another. The changing attitudes to the stories of Lucretia and Brutus outlined here form a small part of a larger and much more complex story of shifting values of just this kind: the story of Christian Europe's attempt to reconsider ancient heroic values in the light of Christian teaching and belief, and to transform the heroes of the past.

The telling of that larger story lies beyond the scope of this book. But it is worth recalling that the reinterpretations of Lucretia and Brutus surveyed here are not an altogether isolated phenomenon, and that many other stories from the ancient world have similarly complex histories of acceptance, rejection, and modification. Other figures are often closely associated with Lucretia and Brutus, and their fortunes sometimes run a parallel course to theirs. Lucretia is often compared and contrasted with other famous pagan women who took their own lives: with Dido, for example, and Cleopatra, with whom the artists also sometimes portray her – the two women in symmetrical poses, the one holding the asp to her breast, the other the dagger. Brutus is often discussed along with a variety of other Roman heroes, including (as we have seen) his alleged descendant, Marcus Junius Brutus, the assassin of Caesar: a single image also unites this pair, that of the liberator holding aloft the blood-stained knife. One Roman figure in particular is closely associated with the names of both Lucretia and Lucius Junius Brutus, and the story of his shifting reputation strikingly resembles theirs: Marcus Portius Cato, the hero of Utica. It is worth briefly sketching the story of Cato's fortunes in order to show how it resembles and intersects with the story we have been following so far. The analogy of Cato may also serve in a limited way to generalize the significance of what has gone before, opening up a broader view of changing ideas about the nature of Roman heroism.

I

Cato took his own life at Utica in 46 BC when facing certain defeat and possible humiliation at the hands of Julius Caesar. The story of Cato's suicide was a popular one, often retold and often elaborated.[2] On the last night of his life, it was said, Cato had talked at length over supper about questions of philosophy and had argued vigorously for the opinion of the Stoic philosophers, that only the good man is wholly free, and that the evil man remains a slave. Afterwards he gave his last instructions to the watch, embraced his friends and his son, and retired to bed to read Plato's account, in *Phaedo*, of the immortality of the soul. He then called for his sword, which his friends had apprehensively taken from the room; and later in the night stabbed himself in the stomach, tearing open the wound with his own hands while his friends struggled in vain to prevent him. For the manner of both his life and death, Cato was widely celebrated by classical writers. Like Lucius Junius Brutus, Cato was hailed as a father of his country, and as a champion of liberty.[3] The liberty which Cato struggled to attain was both political and personal: Seneca regarded Cato's suicide as a final assertion of freedom, an act which God himself might contemplate with admiration.[4] Cato's sword, with which he had defended Rome and finally taken his own life, could be seen as a symbol uniting these two concepts of liberty – like Lucretia's dagger, on which Brutus had sworn to liberate Rome. The early Fathers of the Christian Church also expressed admiration for Cato, and Cato's positive reputation –

like the positive reputation of Lucretia and Brutus – may be traced through the Middle Ages and Renaissance until at least the time of the Enlightenment. Cato was thought of as occupying an honoured place in the afterlife. Virgil imagines 'great Cato' in the next world living amongst the good and giving them laws. Dante places Cato not in Hell (along with other suicides and other enemies of Caesar) but in Purgatory, and implies that he will come in due time to Paradise. Filippo Strozzi the younger, in his suicide note in 1538, prayed that God might receive him 'into the place reserved for Cato and for those virtuous men who had also tried to take their own lives'. Like Lucretia, Cato was venerated as a kind of honorary saint, a Christian before his time.[5]

Yet an adverse tradition of interpretation also develops, as it does with Lucretia and Brutus, and exists alongside this positive reputation; and once again, this adverse tradition begins with Augustine. In the same part of *The City of God* in which he condemns Lucretia's suicide, Augustine also considers the case of Cato. Cato's death (says Augustine) is conventionally regarded as heroic; yet why should it be admired? Wasn't it an act of cowardice rather than of courage, of weakness rather than strength? Cato is said to have killed himself because he thought it shameful to live on under Caesar's rule; but why should life under Caesar have been reckoned a source of shame? If it was truly shameful, then surely Cato should have killed not merely himself but also his son, instead of telling him simply to trust to Caesar's kindness. Cato was not really motivated by a love of virtue, Augustine suggests, but rather by a love of glory, honour, and power, things which for Christians 'must be the consequences of virtue not its antecedents'. Augustine's sceptical analysis of the stories of Lucretia and Cato forms part of his larger reassessment of the values of pagan Rome, and of his fundamental distinction between true and false models of heroic conduct, between pagan ideas of 'greatness' and Christian ideas of 'goodness'. Even among pagan heroes, Augustine suggests, Cato can scarcely be regarded as an ideal model of heroic fortitude: a better example was set by Regulus, who honourably submitted to a death

16. Veronese, *Lucretia*, 1580–5.

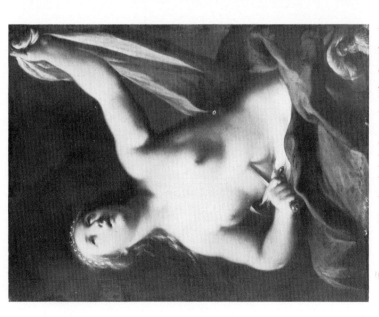

15. Francesco Trevisani (1656–1747), *The Suicide of Lucretia*.

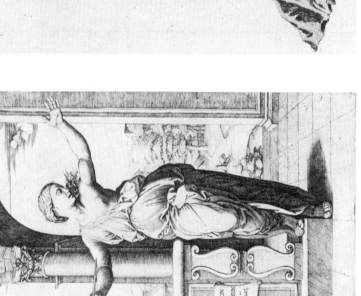

17. Marcantonio Raimondi, after a design by Raphael, *Lucretia*, c.1511–12.

18. 'It is but thus, and both are satisfy'd' (V. i): Mrs Yates as Calista in Nicholas Rowe's *The Fair Penitent* (frontispiece to 1777 edition).

19. Jacques-Antoine Beaufort, *The Oath of Brutus*, 1771.

imposed upon him by others rather than rashly deciding to take his own life. But Job and the Christian martyrs give finer examples of fortitude than any that can be found amongst the pagans; theirs is the true heroism, displayed in an infinitely finer cause.[6]

Augustine's remarks about Cato, like his remarks about Lucretia, mark the beginning of a divided tradition of commentary. Hero-worship is replaced by hero-controversy. During the Renaissance, writers such as Petrarch and Salutati agonized over Cato as they agonized over Lucretia and Brutus: were his actions splendid, or were they deeply flawed?[7] Petrarch in *De Remediis* set out the arguments for and against Cato's suicide, in much the same way in which Salutati set out the arguments for and against Lucretia's suicide in his *Declamatio Lucretiae*. It became common to debate the rights and wrongs of Cato's death, as it had become common to debate the rights and wrongs of Lucretia's. During the seventeenth and eighteenth centuries, one popular form for these debates was that of the 'Dialogues of the Dead' (deriving from Fontenelle and ultimately from Lucian), in which Cato, Lucretia, Brutus, and other great figures from the past were pitted in imaginary conversation against other figures, usually of different temperament and outlook, with whom they argued over the wisdom of their conduct while alive.[8] These Dialogues return constantly to a larger question, neatly posed, for example, by John Hughes in the preface of his English translation of Fontenelle in 1708: '*Where is the Respect due to Antiquity, and why must its Hero's be degraded?*' Hughes goes on to consider this question in relation to the case of Cato:

Is *Cato*'s death the more commendable in it self, because it has had the Applause of the Majority for seventeen hundred Years, and is it impossible that the Majority shou'd be (as they often are) in the wrong? 'Twoud be more proper to enquire what the Few of better Sense think of *Cato*'s Death, for such will not acquit him, because 'twas long ago, or because the Action has been greatly told, if it cannot be found agreeable to Reason – And if that had govern'd *Cato*, he certainly had not kill'd himself, but had subdu'd his surly

Temper, and accepted *Caesar*'s Pardon, tho' it had spoil'd a fine Story for the Tragedians.

Hughes concludes that there is no harm in stripping the death of Cato of its 'false Bravery'. 'These *Roman* Strains were only the Effect of a Bastard Virtue; not the Fortitude of a Hero, but the Cowardice of an uneasie Spirit that cou'd bear Life no longer, when attended with Disappointment; or the Rashness and Passion of a Gamester, that throws up the Cards when he ought to play out the Game.'[9]

The attitudes shown towards Cato in the eighteenth century, especially in England, are of special interest and complexity. It is usual to think of the eighteenth century as a time during which the values of Augustan Rome were warmly admired and emulated, especially in England; and it is principally the positive reputation of Cato throughout this period that has caught the attention of those who have written about eighteenth-century attitudes to pre-Christian Rome.[10] It is certainly true that Cato was much admired in the eighteenth century. One thinks of Jonathan Swift's verdict that Cato was 'the wisest and best of all the *Romans*' and one of the greatest figures of ancient and modern times; of Rousseau's similar verdict in his *Discours sur la vertu du héros* that Cato was the greatest of all the Romans, and the most virtuous of all men; of the firm association throughout the century of the name of Cato with the notion of political liberty; of Robespierre's naming of Cato amongst the great martyrs and benefactors of mankind; of the huge renown of Addison's tragedy of *Cato*, both in England and on the Continent; and of the many paintings and many operas which took the death of Cato as their theme.[11] Yet it is important to realize that Cato's reputation – like that of Lucretia and Brutus – was a very mixed one in the eighteenth century, and that the controversy aroused by his story (as by theirs) forms part of a much larger controversy about the nature of ancient and modern heroism.

The adverse view of Cato is well represented in eighteenth-century writings on the topic of suicide. J. Adams's *Essay Concerning Self-Murther*, published in London in 1700, is fairly typical in its attitudes. Adams concedes that throughout much of his life Cato showed probity, honour, integrity, and courage, even if he set 'too great a value upon his Actions' and was 'liable to something of vain Glory'. Yet he killed himself for a foolish reason, his hatred of Caesar, which 'drove him into those *strange Passions* which he fell into *before* be Stabb'd himself, and that *furious Rage* in which he Expir'd afterwards . . .' Though it is often said that Cato died in the cause of Roman liberty, that cause was not helped in any way by his death; nor did his death advance or represent 'liberty' ('a very doubtful Term') of any other kind. If Cato really believed in the Stoical paradox which he defended on the night of his death, that the good man alone is free and the evil man is a slave, why then did Cato (a good man) need to kill himself at all, when by definition he was already free? But in any case, Adams goes on, we can never know for certain whether an act is truly liberating, because we cannot foresee the consequences of every act; only God, the all-knowing, can tell what brings real liberty, and such decisions about life and death must finally rest with him. Lucretia's suicide, Adams argues elsewhere in his essay, was popularly admired because, like Cato's suicide, it seemed to represent a blow for liberty; yet this suicide, too, is a poor example of a truly free act, being merely the outcome of '*too severe* and *nice a sense of Honour*'. Adams is worried by the larger notion of heroism as it has come down from ancient times, and as it is celebrated in literature. '. . . what are many of the Heroes of Poetry', he asks, 'if stript of the Ornaments of Numbers, Wit and Eloquence, and consider'd in themselves?' And Adams goes on to criticize the behaviour of other figures from the ancient world: of Hercules, for example, and the heroes of Homer's epics.[12]

Other writers on suicide in eighteenth-century England argue in very similar terms. 'Men may flatter themselves from the Examples of *Cato*, *Lucretia*, and other *Heathens*, who ran into the embraces of Death, and became their own Executioners,' writes Thomas Knaggs in 1708, 'but the *Gospel* of Christ speaks other Things, and by that we shall be judg'd, and have our final Doom and Sentence.' The deaths of Cato, Lucretia, Marcus Brutus, Mark Antony, and Cleopatra are instances of the pursuit of false honour, writes John Prince in 1709, 'No nearer a-kin to true Honour, than a *Bristol*-Stone to a true Diamond . . .' Isaac Watts in 1726 takes a similar view, condemning the deaths of Lucretia, Cato, Curtius, Brutus, Otho, and other pagans:

They had many false and foolish Notions of *Courage, Greatness* and *Honour*, which betray'd them into real Iniquities. They sent forth their Armies to rob and plunder Nations to satisfy their own Ambition and Thirst of Honour; they could murder Thousands of Mankind in order to enlarge their Bounds of Empire, and for the Glory of their King or of their native City: 'Twas no wonder that Men of such Principles should *imbrue their Hands in their own Blood* under the Influence of such sort of Motives and Pretences. Besides this, they were animated with the Expectation of Fame after Death: Immortal Memory and Renown were the Rewards of what they called *Heroic Actions.* And thus the *Heathens* might *glory in their own Shame*, but they are not set up for our Guides or Patterns. A *Christian* must regulate his whole Conduct by the Law of his God, by the Rules of the Gospel, by the Views and Hopes and Fears of eternal Rewards or Punishments, which are reveal'd to him in a diviner Light.

Zachary Pearce in 1736 attacks those who admire Cato and place him 'at the Head of this false Heroism', pointing out that even amongst the Romans suicide was not universally approved. The anonymous author of *A Discourse upon Self-Murder* in 1754 condemns Cato along with Herod and 'others of former Ages' who were content to follow 'the Applause of Man, and therefore as they idolized themselves, and had 'no real Regard for God's Honour, he gave them up to the Conduct of their own Hearts, and suffer'd them to close their Days with the most dishonourable End, and so became the Contempt and Scorn of wise and good Men in all Ages'. Caleb Fleming in 1733 considers Cato's suicide to be 'the result of pride, distrust of providence, and an ungoverned passion in that Roman', condemning with equal severity the suicides of Cassius, Marcus Brutus, Decius Mus, and several of the Emperors, including Severus. Richard Hey in 1785 thinks that many who take their own lives do so because they consider suicide 'as a mode of expressing a sentiment of Heroism'. But it is foolish to admire such a man as Cato, Hey argues, who belonged to an age 'when Suicide, in *certain cases*, was by many accounted laudable'. What was exemplary conduct for a Roman in the first century BC is exemplary no longer for a Christian in the eighteenth century AD. 'He therefore who, in this more enlightened age, may give himself a mortal wound, imagining that he *imitates* Cato, is not unlike the person that should throw himself from a precipice, *in imitation* of a benighted traveller, to whom, for want of light, it had been fatal.'[13]

From the darkness of paganism into the light of Christianity: Hey's metaphor conveys a central feeling of his age – the age aptly called the Enlightenment – about the vexed question of heroic precedent.[14] The heroes of darkness may serve for those who walk in darkness, but not for the people who have seen a great light. The metaphor recurs in Charles Wicksted Ethelston's poem 'The Suicide: Occasioned by Reading "The Sorrows of Werter" ' in 1803. Ethelston contrasts pagan and Christian ways of regarding suicide:

> To die, with them, was greatness, and display'd
> A noble magnanimity of soul.
> But error's thick'ning mists obscur'd their sight:
> And will their tenets sanctify a crime,
> And justify a more enlighten'd soul?
> Or shall we err because a Cato err'd?[15]

'A more enlighten'd soul' needs more enlightened precedents. In 1713, Joseph Addison had attempted to present in his tragedy of *Cato* a hero who, on the point of death, illuminated by the first rays of the Enlightenment dawn, glimpses the possible folly of his own suicidal act:

> And yet, methinks, a beam of light breaks in
> On my departing soul – Alas, I fear
> I've been too hasty! . . . (*Dies*)[16]

The clumsiness of the dramatic moment betrays Addison's anxiety about the moral issue of Cato's suicide – a question he had examined more closely in the pages of *The Spectator*. In dramatizing the story of Cato's death, Addison attempts to present Cato as a man who is not altogether a benighted pagan, as a man who is in a limited sense illuminated, and capable of sharing with audiences of a more enlightened age grave doubts about the wisdom of the act which he himself nobly, but rashly, commits.

Addison's tragedy was by and large a resounding success; yet behind the general applause for the piece a groundswell of complaint was also to be heard: for Addison (it was alleged) has presented Cato's suicide in all too sympathetic a manner. 'We are sorry that self-destruction is placed in so fair a point of view,' wrote one commentator, 'and therefore think the catastrophe of this tragedy highly censurable because evidently pernicious.'[17] This complaint was often repeated. Those who asserted that the play had a baleful influence could point to a couple of spectacular case histories. In 1735, a Mr Thomas Beach, a merchant of Wrexham in Denbighshire, wrote an Epilogue to *Cato* for the benefit of 'the Scholars at Wrexham', arguing the rights and wrongs of Cato's suicide and concluding that while the action was 'brave and generous in a heathen view' it was not one which Christians should think of emulating:

> Our better sight restrains the horrid crime,
> And bids us wait the Sovereign Ruler's time;
> 'Tis his to give command, or to permit,
> 'Tis ours, with humble patience, to submit.
> In civil wars, or in domestic woes,
> The sacred precepts should our minds compose;
> Nor should we dare to antedate his will,
> Whose royal mandate runs, 'Thou shalt not kill'!
> What Cato faintly guess'd, we surely know,
> To hold our hand, and check the fatal blow . . .

Eighteen months later, Thomas Beach, evidently not wholly persuaded of his own poetic arguments, took his own life.[18] His was not the only suicide to follow in the wake of Addison's play. Just a few days before Beach's death Addison's cousin and associate, Eustace Budgell, after a series of financial and legal calamities, had filled his pockets with stones and jumped into the Thames, leaving on his desk a note which read

> What Cato did, and Addison approv'd
> Cannot be wrong —

Budgell's death was triumphantly cited by eighteenth-century writers on suicide as evidence of the corrupting effects of literature which attempted to celebrate the dubious heroic virtues of classical Rome.[19]

II

The fact that Cato had chosen to take his own life made him, for Christian commentators, a dubious hero; and those who criticized him on this score often associated him (as we have seen) with Lucretia. But Cato was also criticized on another score, and closely associated on this account with Lucius Junius Brutus. The problem this time was Cato's Stoicism. Was it possible to admire as truly heroic a man who was as cold and passionless as Cato appears to have been? Seneca in praising Cato had taken his suicide as an example of the way in which a truly virtuous man may exercise complete control over his passions; as a supreme exemplification and validation of the principles of the Stoics. Seneca's high praise of Cato was echoed by neo-Stoical writers in England and France in the seventeenth and eighteenth centuries. But by the early eighteenth century it had become a commonplace to say that Cato and other Stoical heroes had been misguided in attempting to stifle their natural feelings, and that it was indeed their refusal to acknowledge those feelings that made them poor models for imitation, false heroes rather than true. Addison himself voices such criticisms in a number of *Spectator* papers. In *Spectator* no. 397, he is sharply critical of the extreme doctrines and practices of the Stoics — their refusal to show concern for the misfortunes of others, and their supreme trust in 'indifference' rather than pity. In *Spectator* no. 169, Addison examines Sallust's account of Cato, and remarks that 'A Being who has nothing to pardon in himself, may reward every Man accord-

ing to his Works', adding that compassion, humanity, benevolence, and good nature are not much in evidence in Cato's
character. Cato, says Addison – invoking a favourite contrast
of the period – is a man 'rather awful than amiable'.[20] In
Spectator no. 349, Addison remarks with equal severity that
the 'indifference' which Cato showed at the close of his life 'is
to be looked upon as a piece of natural Carelessness and
Levity, rather than Fortitude'. As an example of better
fortitude, Addison instances a Christian hero, Sir Thomas
More, whose simple good humour at the time of his death was
of a piece with the natural cheerfulness and sanctity which he
showed throughout his life.

One way of attacking Cato's Stoicism was to describe it as
apathy or indifference. Another method of attack was to say
that Cato was not really passionless at all, but that he displayed
passions which were selfish rather than sociable. This tactic,
which originates with Augustine, has a remarkable effect on
the development of the story of Cato. Augustine suggests that
Cato might have killed himself not (as Seneca thought) because
he was the perfect master of his passions, but rather because he
was mastered by his passions; because he was impatient, or
afraid, or ambitious for worldly glory.[21] In putting these suggestions, Augustine is of course employing a measure of
fantasy; he is teasing out the possibilities of the story, asking
whether events might not have occurred for this reason rather
than for that. Augustine's later followers eagerly took up his
sceptical and speculative method, inventing further reasons –
all of them discreditable – why Cato should have taken his own
life. Montaigne in his essay 'Du jeune Caton' censures the habit
of guessing about the manner and motives of Cato's suicide,
yet during the seventeenth century this habit burgeons into a
popular philosophical sport. Cato is said to have killed himself
out of vanity, cowardice, despair, anger, pique, pusillanimity,
imbecility, envy of Caesar's fortunes, or a perverted wish for
self-gratification.[22] Under the pressure of moral attack, the
story of Cato – like the story of Lucretia and Brutus – is not in
any way diminished; on the contrary, it grows and flourishes.

Richard Steele's account of Cato's death in *The Christian*

Hero (1701) is a good example of the way in which this growth occurs. Steele's essay is an attempt to examine the lives and deaths of several well-known Roman heroes (Julius Caesar and Marcus Brutus also come within his scrutiny) in order to show the many ways in which the conduct of these pagans falls short of that which is expected of a Christian hero. Like Milton in his rejection of the themes of classical heroism at the opening of book ix of *Paradise Lost*, Steele is suggesting that there is another kind of heroism which better deserves celebration in literature and in life. Why did Cato kill himself? Steele's answer is simple: because he was afraid of Caesar. And Steele begins to retell the story of Cato's last night, generously elaborating here and there in order to blacken the picture as much as possible. Cato works himself up into a bad temper and goes off to bed to read '*Plato*'s Immortality, and Guesses at a future Life'. He behaves disgracefully towards those who are trying to restrain him from killing himself.

Among the rest, a fond Slave was putting in his Resistance, and his Affliction, for which he dash'd the poor Fellow's Teeth out with his Fist, and forc'd out of the Room his lamenting Friends, with Noise, and Taunt, and Tumult; a little while after had his Hand with which he struck his Servant dress'd, lay down, and was heard to Snore; but sure we may charitably enough believe, from all this unquiet Carriage, that the Sleep was dissembled, from which as soon as he awak'd, he Stabb'd himself, and fell on the Floor; His Fall alarm'd his wretched Dependants, whose help he resisted by tearing open his own Bowels, and rushing out of Life with Fury, Rage, and Indignation. . . . Thus did *Cato* leave the World, for which indeed he was very unfit. . . .[23]

Hence at the time when Addison began to write his tragedy of *Cato*, several sharply conflicting traditions about the man existed side by side. There was the heroic Cato, admired by such men as Swift. There was the cool Cato, judged to be sadly deficient in normal human feeling. There was the desperate Cato, possessed of 'Fury, Rage, and Indignation', who killed himself in a miserable panic. And there was the benighted Cato, who did as well as could be expected of him, but lacked the guiding beacon of Christianity. This multiplicity of Catos, like the multiplicity of Lucretias and Brutuses, was the source of many narrative possibilities, but also – as the example of Addison's tragedy shows – of many narrative and imaginative problems and pitfalls.

It is possible to imagine a tragedy on the subject of Cato which might express the mixed feelings which Addison shows in his various *Spectator* essays about him. Its hero might be a man admirable in his sense of duty, his self-discipline, his consistency to principle, but fatally lacking in warmth, humour, generosity, and, finally, in real knowledge of himself and of the motives that drive him to suicide. The hero of Addison's *Cato* is not, however, a man of this kind. Where he has found the historical Cato deficient, Addison has chosen not to expose this deficiency, but rather to change and soften the character. This is the kind of character that emerges; Cato's daughter, Marcia, is speaking:

> Though stern and awful to the foes of *Rome*,
> He is all goodness, *Lucia*, always mild,
> Compassionate, and gentle to his friends.
> Fill'd with domestic tenderness, the best,
> The kindest father! I have ever found him
> Easie, and good, and bounteous to my wishes.
>
> (V.iv)

Addison is attempting to transform the Cato of Seneca – and all of the early commentators – into an eighteenth-century Man of Feeling. Equally anxious to avoid the desperate Cato and the cold Cato, Addison gives us instead what might be called the tender Cato: Cato domesticated, Cato the kindly father of his family. The real Cato's domestic life was not, in fact, entirely above reproach, and Addison is forced to maintain a discreet silence about at least one aspect of this 'domestic tenderness'; 'Heroic, stoic Cato, the sententious/ Who lent his lady to his friend Hortensius' makes no appearance in Addison's play, as he was later to do in the less reverent pages of Byron's *Don Juan* (VI.vii).

Addison's transformation of Cato strikingly resembles the transformation of Lucius Junius Brutus which is effected by Madeleine de Scudéry and by the dramatists who deal with his

story in England and France in the late seventeenth and eighteenth centuries. All of these writers, faced with the problem
that their hero has been criticized for his callousness and
insensitivity, attempt to turn him into a more sympathetic and
deeply passionate character. All of them try to look behind the
public mask to find the private man. All of them surround their
hero with members of his family (often invented specially for
the occasion, often lavishly tearful and demonstrative in their
behaviour) and interlace the traditional, austere story with
new and surprising love plots. Plutarch reports that Cato was
accompanied to Utica by one son, Marcus Portius, who was
with him to the end. Adopting a trick that he had already
censured in other writers of tragedy, Addison attempts to
increase the pathos of this play by increasing the number of
Cato's children. He gives Cato two sons (whom he calls
Marcus and Portius) and a daughter, Marcia, all of whom
accompany him to Utica, attended by various lovers.[24] The
sub-plot which Addison created by the addition of these
characters is a curiously sentimental one, especially for a play
which seems to celebrate the conduct of a hero of the Stoics.
The sense of a proud family tradition of stoical conduct which
is found in Plutarch ('I am the daughter of Cato, and wife of
Brutus') is entirely absent.[25] Within seconds of the opening of
the play Portius is in tears as he realizes that he and his brother
Marcus are rivals for the hand of Lucia, and the sub-plot
continues on the same high note of hectic passion. As John
Dennis pointed out in his lengthy and hostile 'Remarks upon
Cato, A Tragedy', this whole area of the play is puzzlingly
contradictory, and a reader may well be unsure whether he is
being introduced to a 'Nest of *Stoicks*' or to a collection of
'whining Amorous Milk-Sops'.[26] A curious disjunction may be
felt to exist at the heart of Addison's play, similar to the
disjunction already noticed in Voltaire's *Brutus*. It is as though
Addison, like Voltaire, were trying to celebrate two quite
contradictory modes of behaviour, the passionate and the
austere. Cato's alleged tenderness is never allowed to compli-
cate his final decision to take his life; he moves boldly and (we
are told) smilingly to his death. The play's ideas about Stoicism

and sensibility are never brought into meaningful relationship with each other, but are simply allowed loosely and incongruously to coexist. For all his efforts, Addison has not been able to bring alive his somewhat abstract idea of the tender Cato; we are left instead with the cold Cato and his sentimental children. The play shows, in short, the same heroic schizophrenia that is to be found in Voltaire's *Brutus*, and certain other tragedies of the age.

One celebrated scene in the fourth act of *Cato* betrays some of the emotional uncertainties of the play, and at the same time associates it in a curious way with the story of Lucius Junius Brutus. Cato's son Portius enters hurriedly to announce to his father that his brother Marcus has just met his death in battle, bravely and against great odds. Cato's response is dry and short: 'I'm satisfy'd.' When Marcus' body is carried in, accompanied by weeping senators, Cato is still apparently unmoved, remarking only that he is sorry that it is possible to die only once for one's country. Then he turns to his weeping companions to deliver this rebuke, which serves in turn to bring on his own tears – not for his son, but for Rome:

> Alas, my friends!
> Why mourn you thus? let not a private loss
> Afflict your hearts. 'Tis *Rome* requires our tears.
> The mistress of the world, the seat of empire,
> The nurse of heroes, the delight of gods,
> That humbled the proud tyrants of the earth,
> And set the nations free, *Rome* is no more.
> O liberty! O virtue! O my country!
> *Juba (aside)* Behold that upright man! *Rome* fills his eyes
> With tears, that flow'd not o'er his own dead son.
>
> (IV.iv)

Cato's tears over Rome are attested by Plutarch.[27] The whole affair of the death of Marcus, however, is Addison's invention; as we have seen, no second son of Cato is known to have been present at Utica. Nothing in Plutarch's account suggests that Cato was a man insensible to personal grief; Plutarch remarks, indeed, at the death of his half-brother Caepio, Cato showed quite immoderate and extravagant lamentation.[28] Addison's

Cato, however, is a man who is at once preternaturally stoical about his private sufferings and preternaturally sensitive to the sufferings of his country; a balance of virtues which in some ways resembles that with which Swift was later to endow his Houyhnhnms. The whole scene resembles even more closely the legendary, dry-eyed judgement of his sons by that other father of his country, Lucius Junius Brutus, a man traditionally supposed to have been more deeply moved by the plight of Rome than the plight of his own family. It seems probable that Addison, in inventing this scene, allowed the stories of Brutus and Cato to coalesce in his mind. What is certain is that this scene, like Addison's play as a whole, made a deep impression upon Voltaire, and influenced in a number of ways his tragedy *Brutus*.[29] Thus the stories of the two Roman heroes became closely interwoven.

The words of Addison's Cato as he learns of the death of his son, 'I'm satisfy'd', were much admired in the period. Francis Gentleman found in them 'real dignity, mixed with paternal tenderness', and Laurence Eusden's verses suggest that the phrase drew tears from the women in Addison's audiences:

> Not so the fair their passions secret kept,
> Silent they heard, but as they heard, they wept,
> When gloriously the blooming Marcus dy'd,
> And Cato told the gods, I'm satisfy'd.[30]

Words like these had been uttered by Madeleine de Scudéry's Brutus – 'I die satisfied, so *Rome* be free, and *Lucretia* revenged' – and were to be echoed by Voltaire's Brutus – 'Thank heav'n! Rome's free; and I am satisfy'd' – and varied again by the Brutus of J. H. Payne: 'Justice is satisfied, and Rome is free!'[31] 'I'm satisfy'd': Addison's phrase is a curious example of what can only be described oxymoronically as sentimental Stoicism: a show of emotional restraint calculated to induce precisely the opposite effect in an audience ('Silent they heard, but as they heard, they wept'). Satisfying indeed though the scene as a whole evidently was to some members of the play's audiences, one or two critics were less easily pleased. Pope in his prologue to the play draws attention to the tears which Cato subsequently sheds over the plight of Rome:

> He bids your breasts with ancient ardor rise,
> And calls forth *Roman* drops from *British* eyes.
>   (ll. 15–16)

'*Roman* drops': these are special tears, noble, disinterested, patriotic. Yet Pope may also have been uneasily aware that the scene stirred other, more sentimental responses as well, and his verses 'On a Lady who P-st at the Tragedy of Cato' (if they are indeed by Pope) give an altogether more ribald view of the matter, humorously satirizing those secretly weeping audiences that Eusden had so reverentially invoked:

> While maudlin Whigs deplor'd their *Cato*'s Fate,
> Still with dry Eyes the Tory *Celia* sate,
> But while her Pride forbids her Tears to flow,
> The gushing Waters find a Vent below:
> Tho' secret, yet with copious Grief she mourns,
> Like twenty River-Gods with all their Urns.
> Let others screw their Hypocritick Face,
> She shews her Grief in a sincerer Place;
> There Nature reigns, and Passion void of Art,
> For that Road leads directly to the Heart.[32]

John Dennis attacked more openly what he saw to be the logical and emotional absurdity of Addison's scene. Why should Cato weep for Rome and yet not weep for the death of his son, he asked? When we weep for our country, Dennis argued, we do not weep for an abstraction but for the people who belong to that country; and it is only natural that we should care most for those people who are nearest to us. Thus 'for a Man to receive the News of his Son's Death with dry Eyes, and to weep at the same time for the Calamities of his Country, is a wretched Affectation and a miserable Inconsistency'.[33]

Dennis's commonsensical remarks were commended by Dr Johnson in his *Life of Addison*,[34] and it is tempting to think that Johnson was remembering and responding to this scene in *Cato* when he wrote in the eighteenth chapter of *Rasselas* of the philosopher who preached the virtues of 'rational fortitude' and enumerates 'many examples of heroes immovable by pain or pleasure', but who broke down inconsolably when told of the death of his daughter.[35] Possibly, too, *Cato* may form the link between this scene in *Rasselas* and a some-what similar scene in a novel which Johnson evidently never read: Fielding's *Joseph Andrews*.[36] In chapter eight of the fourth book of Fielding's novel, Parson Adams rebukes Joseph for being 'too much inclined to passion' – he cites Abraham's readiness to sacrifice Isaac as an example of the way in which the natural affections may properly be suppressed – when the news is brought in that his youngest son has just been drowned. Adams has been represented as a warm admirer of Addison's *Cato* – 'the only English tragedy I ever read' (iii.5) – a tragedy which he declares to be one of the only two plays 'fit for a Christian to read' (iii.11). Yet at the news of this seeming calamity ('seeming', for the boy in fact is not dead at all), Adams shows none of the stoical calm of his favourite hero of tragedy, but instead stamps vigorously about the room in grief, lamenting his apparent loss 'with the bitterest agony'. In their very different ways, both Johnson and Fielding appear to be reacting against the starker implications of Addison's *Cato*, and to be implying in turn that stoical ideas of 'rational fortitude', however fine they may be in principle, can often shatter as they come in contact with the world of actual human experience. For a moment, both Johnson's philosopher and Fielding's Parson Adams are glimpsed (so to speak) as anti-Catos, as men whose passionate reaction to the sudden news of bereavement is quite unlike the unflinching and tearless response of Addison's Cato: as distant transformations of the Roman hero, and of popular ideas about the ways in which his heroism expressed itself.

Fielding is especially sensitive to the precise implications of classical and neoclassical allusion, and his recall of heroic incident, whether mocking or serious, always has a moral watchfulness about it, as if Fielding were sifting out the precise value of the analogy he invokes. This habit of mind is evident, for example, in this passage from *Tom Jones* (v. 7), when Allworthy is told that he is unlikely to survive his present illness:

Mr. Allworthy, who had settled all his affairs in this world, and was as well prepared, as it is possible for human nature to be, for the other, received this information with the utmost calmness and unconcern. He could, indeed, whenever he lay himself down to rest, say with Cato in the tragical poem

> – Let guilt or fear
> Disturb man's rest, Cato knows neither of them;
> Indifferent in his choice, to sleep or die.

In reality, he could say this with ten times more reason and confidence than Cato, or any other proud fellow among the antient or modern heroes: for he was not only devoid of fear; but might be considered as a faithful labourer, when at the end of harvest, he is summoned to receive his reward at the hands of a bountiful master.

'Ten times more reason and confidence', because Allworthy is not taking his own life, but is meekly preparing to have it taken from him; and because he prepares to meet his death with the consolation not of Plato's *Phaedo* but of the Christian religion. Such fortitude as this, Fielding implies, is more worthy to be admired than the behaviour conventionally celebrated in heroic literature, ancient and modern; beside Allworthy, Cato is no more than a 'proud fellow'. Like Parson Adams, Allworthy is momentarily glimpsed as a new and transformed Cato, a greater hero than the Cato of Roman times, as celebrated in the tragedy of Addison.

Such was the fame of Addison's play that it stimulated other writers to think about the kind of heroism represented by Cato's life and death, and to produce other Catos, often more finely attuned to the changing sensibilities of the age. Two years after the first performance of Addison's tragedy, Nicholas Rowe's tragedy *Lady Jane Grey* was presented at Drury Lane (April 1715). In the fourth act of Rowe's play the heroine is discovered on the eve of her execution reading the same book which Cato studied on the night of his death:

> 'Tis Plato's *Phaedon*,
> Where dying *Socrates* takes leave of Life,
> With such an easy, careless, calm Indifference,
> As if the Trifle were of no Account,
> Mean in it self, and only to be worn
> In honour of the Giver.

The incident links Lady Jane in our minds not only with Socrates, but also – by its recall of Addison's play – with Cato. Socrates in his last hours had been forced to send away his shrewish wife Xanthippe, who 'cried out and said the kind of thing that women always do say' on such occasions; Socrates sees fit to die in the company of men. The implication of Rowe's play is that a woman is perfectly capable of showing the heroic courage normally associated with the names of Socrates and Cato; Lady Jane is a female Socrates, a female Cato. In a passionate final scene between Lady Jane Grey and her lover, Lord Guildford Dudley, Rowe shows also that the 'indifference' of which his heroine speaks is quite unlike the indifference of Socrates or Cato; her stoicism, Rowe suggests, is maintained only with difficulty, and is continually threatened by the force of her passion. As in the eighteenth-century rewritings of the story of Lucius Junius Brutus, so here it is possible to observe the entire concept of heroism undergoing a subtle but significant process of change. Stoicism is tempered by sensibility; 'virtue' is no longer thought of as a quality exhibited only by men. Such shifts of thought can be observed in other writings of the day. Lady Mary Wortley Montagu, who had read Addison's play in manuscript and made a number of detailed suggestions for its revision, later reflected upon the similarities and differences of heroic opportunity open to men and to women, pondering in particular the case of Cato:

as much greatness of Mind may be shewn in submission as in command [she wrote], and some Women have suffer'd a Life of Hardships with as much Philosophy as Cato travers'd the Desarts of Affrica, and without the support that the view of Glory afforded him and which is support enough for the Human mind that is touch'd with it, to go through any toil of Danger. But this is not the Situation of a Woman, whose virtue must only shine to her own recollection, and loses that name when it is ostentatiously expos'd to the World.[37]

As so often in her writings, Lady Mary's courage on such matters is possibly circumscribed by a lingering conservatism, yet the challenge is gently and firmly made: in her own way, it is suggested, a woman may show the same greatness of mind as

a Cato – possibly even a superior kind of greatness, less dependent upon worldly encouragement and applause.

One final, transformed, Cato may be noted. In the last act of
George Lillo's tragedy *The London Merchant* (1731), the
'prentice George Barnwell is discovered on the eve of his
execution reading not Plato, but the Bible, a work which – so
far from encouraging 'indifference' – drives him to more vehe-
ment passion: 'How shall I describe my present state of mind? I
hope in doubt, and trembling I rejoice. I feel my grief increase,
even as my fears give way. Joy and gratitude now supply more
tears than the horror and anguish of despair before.' (V.ii)

Barnwell meets his death not with the equanimity of a
Roman hero such as Cato, but with tears. The tears are not
tears of fear, nor are they tears of patriotic sentiment, like those
of Addison's Cato; they are the tears of grief, joy, and
gratitude, as he realizes both the consequences of his past
actions and the availability of Christian salvation. In his dedication to *The London Merchant*, Lillo speaks admiringly of
Addison's *Cato*, but goes on to remark that he himself has
attempted in his play to 'enlarge the province of tragedy'. Lillo
has attempted to enlarge not merely the traditional idea of the
station in life to which a tragic hero may belong, but also the
traditional idea of the kind and quality of fortitude which a
tragic hero may display at the point of death, and of the kind of
feeling which he may legitimately experience. He has transformed the Cato of Seneca – the hero of the Stoics, the 'Man
Without Passion' – into a tearful and penitent Christian Man
of Feeling; a new kind of hero, for a new kind of age.[38]

III

Lucretia, Brutus, and Cato were all venerated by the Romans
because of their readiness to sacrifice themselves or their
children for some larger cause: for an ideal of purity or justice
or liberty. The ideal of heroism which is implied here is built
upon the premiss that certain fates (sexual dishonour, political
betrayal, military defeat) are worse than death itself, and
cancellable only by death. Death, in this view of things, con-

verts possible defeat and shame into unquestionable triumph; it is the ultimate redeeming act. Christian heroism does not differ fundamentally from Roman heroism on this issue. Christianity shares the same belief in the transforming power of death, and in the importance of dying well. The central fact and symbol of Christianity is the crucifixion, a death forcibly imposed yet voluntarily undertaken; a death of a Son, permitted and approved by a Father. Despite the important shifts we have observed in ways of thinking about the question of suicide, both cultures equate the highest heroism with the idea of death; where they differ is in their estimation of the circumstances in which death may be warranted, and the motives from which it should spring.

It is therefore not surprising that the deaths of the great heroes of antiquity should become a topic of such fascination to Christian writers and artists, for such deaths are at once like and unlike the kinds of deaths which Christians must be prepared to undergo. Within the period upon which we have just been concentrating, for example, the deaths not only of Cato and Lucretia but of Virginia, Portia, Iphigenia, Socrates, Hector, Curtius, Regulus, Germanicus, Seneca, Septimius Severus, the sons of Brutus and of Manlius Torquatus (to name just a handful of popular examples) are celebrated and scrutinized in Christian art and literature with something of the same intensity as are the deaths of the Christian saints and martrys, and of Christ himself.[39] In the visual arts, the treatment of these subjects is, more often than not, confidently heroic; the moral doubts and ambiguities sometimes registered in contemporary discussions of these figures do not always find precise equivalents in visual terms. I have found no painting, for example, of a desperate, lascivious, or vainglorious Lucretia, or of a cowardly or irresolute Cato, though such figures are commonly found in literature. Most of the painters who tackle 'heroic' subjects of this sort seem to be in one sense more conservative than many of the writers; their interest seems to lie not so much in the possible moral ambiguities of the scenes they depict as in the flesh tones, the disposition of limbs, the folds of garments – in short, in the sensuousness or

pathos of the moment. The iconography of many legendary
acts of Roman heroism continues to flourish at a time when the
propriety of those acts is being sharply debated.[40] Even in the
visual arts, however, changing ideas about the nature of
ancient heroism often have a crucial influence upon the conception and style of composition, as we have had occasion to
see, for example, in the case of David's *Brutus*. In literature the
impact of these ideas is on the whole more marked, and the
hesitations and nuances of contemporary debate find some
equivalence of expression in the many literary variations and
transformations of older narrative which have been traced
throughout this book. The distance between the Lucretia of
ancient Rome and Clarissa Harlowe, between the dying Cato
of Utica and the dying Squire Allworthy, is the distance
between the old heroism and the new.

Between the 'new' heroism of the eighteenth century and
modern perceptions of heroism, another and equally
important distance may be felt to exist; though to describe this
sense of distance and indeed to describe modern ideas of the
heroic would be an altogether harder undertaking, for the very
concept is less dominant in our thinking, less clearly
articulated, and possibly less enthusiastically regarded than
once it was. Though we hear much of the anti-heroes of
modern literature, that term likewise is often used casually and
without precision: it defines itself, one might say, by negating
an unknown positive. We celebrate the 'heroes' of the sports
field and the world of entertainment more readily than the
heroes of the battlefield and the deathbed; the word is drained
of its moral sense. Nowadays, too, the heroes and heroines of
antiquity are less obviously before us; their stories are fading,
and to every generation the names of Lucretia, Collatinus,
Tarquin, and Brutus are less and less familiar. Centuries of
controversy did not kill the story of the rape of Lucretia:
controversy gave it new life. What has at last led to the story's
gradual disappearance from popular knowledge is not moral
disapproval, but neglect: the explanation lies in the modern
decline in classical knowledge and classical education.

But that, as Kipling would say, is another story.

NOTES

PREFACE

1. Mention must be made here of the one substantial previous study of the Lucretia story, Hans Galinsky's *Der Lucretia-Stoff in der Weltliteratur* (Breslau, 1932). Professor Galinsky broadly surveys literary treatments of the story, giving good coverage to German versions (which in the present study are comparatively neglected).

PART I. LUCRETIA

1. *Diderot's Letters to Sophie Volland*, a selection translated by Peter France (London, 1972), p. 85.

Chapter 1. The Shaping of the Myth (1)

2. William Painter, 'The second Nouell' in *The Palace of Pleasure* (London, 1566), p. 5 (contracted spellings expanded), from Livy, *Ab Urbe Condita*, i, 57–60. The story of Brutus continues in Livy's Second Book. Other translations of Livy used here are from B. O. Foster's Loeb edn. (Cambridge, Mass., and London, 1926) and the Penguin edn., trs. Audrey de Sélincourt, introd. R. M. Ogilvie (Harmondsworth, 1971).

3. Ovid, *Fasti*, ii. 721–852, at lines 761–2; Livy, i. 57. 11 (a touch omitted in Painter's version); Dio Cassius, *Roman History*, ii. 15, trs. E. Cary and H. B. Foster, Loeb edn. (London and Cambridge, Mass., 1954).

4. As a kinsman of Collatinus, Sextus Tarquinius might have claimed legal justification for such a killing: see Alan Watson, *Rome of the XII Tables: Persons and Property* (Princeton, New Jersey, 1975), p. 36. Sexual relations between a married woman and a slave were thought especially heinous: see Sarah B. Pomeroy, *Goddesses, Whores, Wives and Slaves: Women in Classical Antiquity* (New York, 1975), pp. 160–1. Servius in his commentary on *Aeneid*, viii. 646, calls the slave an Ethiope, and in Renaissance art the slave is sometimes depicted as black: see e.g. plate fourteen.

5. In Dionysius of Halicarnassus' account, Lucretia asks her father to 'send for as many of your friends and kinsmen as you can, so that they may hear the report from me, the victim of terrible wrongs, rather than from others'. 'The most prominent men' of Rome are present at the suicide, but Collatinus and Brutus are not. See *Roman Antiquities*, trs.

E. Cary and E. Spelman, Loeb edn. (London and Cambridge, Mass., 1939), iv. 64–82, at iv. 66–7.

6. Livy, i. 59. 1.

7. From the remarks of Dionysius of Halicarnassus (iv. 64. 3), we know that the story was treated by Fabius Pictor (born 254 BC). It was the subject of a *fabula praetexta*, or historical drama, by Lucius Accius (born 170 BC), perhaps his *Brutus*, of which fragments remain.

8. Plutarch, 'Life of Publius Valerius Publicola'; Diodorus of Sicily, x. 20–2; Valerius Maximus, vi. 1; Florus, *Epitome*, I. ii–iii; Dio Cassius, *Roman History*, ii. 13–20.

9. A. Alföldi, *Early Rome and the Latins* (Ann Arbor, [1965]). For a sceptical assessment of this thesis, see R. M. Ogilvie in *Classical Review*, n.s. xvi (1966), 94–8.

10. Ettore Pais, *Ancient Legends of Roman History*, trs. Mario E. Cosenza (London, 1906), ch. 10, 'The Legends of Lucretia and of Virginia and the Cults of the Prisci Latini'.

11. R. M. Ogilvie, *A Commentary on Livy Books 1–5* (Oxford, 1965; 2nd edn., 1970). See also P. G. Walsh, *Livy: His Historical Aims and Methods* (Cambridge, 1961).

12. The story of Brutus' assumed idiocy, for example, sits oddly with the idea that he also held the responsible office of Tribune of the Celeres. On Brutus, see Ogilvie, *A Commentary*, p. 216; Schur in Pauly-Wissowa, *Real-Encyclopädie der classischen Altertumswissenschaft*, Suppl. 5 (Stuttgart, 1931), pp. 356 ff.; and, for a more sceptical view as to his historicity, Einar Gjerstad, *Legends and Facts of Early Roman History* (Lund, 1963), p. 45, and Alföldi, *Early Rome and the Latins*, pp. 82–3.

13. Cf. e.g. Terence, *Heautontimorumenos*, 279–91.

14. Tibullus, i. 3. 83–94.

15. The traditional dating of the Lucretia story is, however, highly suspect: see R. M. Ogilvie, *Early Rome and the Etruscans* (London, 1976), ch. 7. On Harmodius and Aristogeiton, see also K. J. Dover, *Greek Homosexuality* (London, 1978), pp. 41, 62 f., 82, 191.

16. See Ogilvie, *A Commentary*, pp. 195, 476 ff. Livy says that the Decemvirate were contemptuously referred to as the 'ten Tarquins'; Appius Claudius' fatal error was to forget the moral of the story of Lucretia, as the people themselves did not:

> For this did Servius give us laws? For this did Lucrece bleed?
> For this was the great vengeance wrought on Tarquin's evil-seed?
> (Macaulay, *Lays of Ancient Rome*: 'Virginia'.) Cf. Florus, i. xvii.

17. Plutarch, *Mulierum Virtutes*, xxxvi (*Moralia*, 261e–262d).

18. *A General Dictionary, Historical and Critical . . . of the Celebrated Mr Bayle*, trs. (and enlarged) J. P. Bernard, T. Birch, and J. Lockman (London, 1738), vii, 217.

19. In some versions of the story deriving from Madeleine de Scudéry's *Clélie*, Tarquinius Superbus is also in hot pursuit of Lucretia, or Clelia, or both.

20. Seneca, *Epistulae Morales*, xii. 10, lxx. 14, lxxvii. 15; Hume's arguments on suicide were intended 'to restore men to their native liberty': 'On Suicide', *Essays Moral, Political and Literary* (Oxford, 1963), p. 587. The connection between suicide and other forms of apparent liberty is trenchantly discussed by J. Adams, *An Essay Concerning Self-Murther* (London, 1700), ch. 14; see ch. 8 below. The idea that there should be liberty of opinion on the question of suicide was of some importance during the French Revolution: see Hubert Beauclin, 'Le Suicide et la Révolution française', *La Révolution française*, Nouvelle série no. 16 (oct.-nov.-déc. 1922), pp. 289–314, reviewing Albert Bayet, *Le Suicide et la morale* (Paris, 1922). A cat, emblem of liberty, sits beside the suiciding Lucretia in one of the panels in the *Storia di Lucrezia* in the Ca' d'Oro in Venice.

21. Charles Gildon, *The Patriot, or the Italian Conspiracy* (London, 1703), Preface, sig. A3^v.

22. On the association between Sinon and Tarquin, the fall of Troy and the fall of the Roman kings, see T. W. Baldwin, *On the Literary Genetics of Shakespeare's Poems & Sonnets* (Urbana, Ill., 1950), pp. 144–5; D. C. Allen, 'The Rape of Lucrece', in *Image and Meaning* (Baltimore, 1968), ch. 4. In Hans Sachs's *Tragedia. Von der Lucretia* (1527), Tarquin is compared with Paris, carrying Helen off to Troy: see *Lucretia-Dramen*, ed. Horst Hartmann (Leipzig, 1973), p. 100.

23. Some of the links between military conquest and sexual conquest are documented by Susan Brownmiller in *Against Our Will: Men, Women, and Rape* (New York, 1975). See especially ch. 3, 'War'.

24. Simone de Beauvoir, *Le Deuxième Sexe*, I: *Les Faits et les mythes* (Paris, 1949), p. 220; *The Second Sex*, trs. and ed. H. M. Parshley (Harmondsworth, 1972), p. 162.

25. See, for example, Handel's *Lucrezia* cantata, probably composed around 1707.

26. Brownmiller, *Against Our Will*, pp. 78–86.

27. Augustine found it a 'detestable injustice' that Brutus, though related to the Tarquins, should have retained his consulship, while Collatinus should have lost his simply because he was surnamed Tarquinius: 'he should have been compelled to change his name, not his country'; *The City of God*, trs. Henry Bettenson, ed. David Knowles (Harmondsworth, 1972), bk. iii, ch. 16, p. 110.

28. See ch. 2, pp. 23–4.

29. Edward More, retelling the story in *A Lytle and bryefe treatyse called the defence of women* in 1560, seems actually to have assumed that Brutus was married to Lucretia: 'Alas good Brutus where wert thou? to succor then thy wife' (sig. B.ii). For Madeleine de Scudéry's romantically inflated version of the story, *Clélie*, in which Brutus is Lucretia's secret lover, see ch. 7 below.

30. For other naked Tarquins, see Tintoretto's *Tarquin and Lucretia* in the Depot of the Prado at Madrid (Detlev, Baron von Hadeln, 'Early Works by Tintoretto – II', *Burlington Magazine,* xli (1922), 278–9), Augustino Veneziano's engraving from a design by Raphael, in the Albertina in Vienna, and the engravings of H. Aldegrever (1553 and 1539) and Georg Pencz (Adam Bartsch, *Le peintre graveur* (Leipzig, 1854–70), vol. viii, 385.64, 384.63, 342.78).

31. See A. Pigler, *Barockthemen: eine Auswahl von Verzeichnissen zur Ikonographie des 17. und 18. Jahrhunderts*, Band ii, Verlag der Ungarischen Akademie der Wissenschaften (1956), pp. 386–90; Wolfgang Stechow, 'Lucretiae Statua', *Beiträge für Georg Swarzenski* (Berlin and Chicago, 1951), pp. 114–24. Thirty-five portrayals of Lucretia by Cranach are listed by Max J. Friedländer and Jakob Rosenberg, *Die Gemälde von Lucas Cranach* (Basel, Boston, Stuttgart, 1979), pp. 203–4. A copy by La Fresnaye of one of Cranach's Lucretias suffered the indignity of having a tunic painted over the nude body during the nineteenth century, to spare onlookers possible embarrassment; see M. Georges de Miré, *Connaissance des arts,* 15 juin 1953, p. 13.

32. Ovid, *Fasti*, ii. 834; cf. *Metamorphoses*, xiii. 479–80, and see ch. 6, p. 107 below.

33. Jocelyn Penny Small, 'The Death of Lucretia', *American Journal of Archeology,* lxxx (1976), 349–60.

34. Michael Jaffé, 'Pesaro Family Portraits: Pordenone, Lotto, and Titian', *Burlington Magazine,* cxiii (1971), 696–702.

35. Erwin Panofsky's discussion of the connotations of nudity and clothing in Titian's *Sacred and Profane Love* is particularly relevant here: *Studies in Iconology* (New York, 1939), ch. 5, esp. pp. 150–60.

36. '. . . s'appretant à annuler l'effet du viol qu'elle a subi, par un geste pareil'; *L'Âge d'homme* (Paris, 1939), pp. 142–3. Something of the same symmetry is to be found in Bandello's version of the story in which Lucretia says that she will stab herself in the breast, where Tarquin first placed his hand: M. Bandello, *Le Novelle*, 3 vols. (Bari, 1931), vol. iii, novella xxi, p. 69.

37. There is a symmetry here comparable to that which Marion Monaco finds in certain tragedies of Racine, whose heroes or heroines, metaphorically 'poisoned' by love, kill themselves by taking a literal poison. '. . . it seems that Racine is following a dramatic tradition, which he puts to use in his usual exhaustive manner. As Sophocles' Ajax kills himself with the sword which is the gift of his foe, Hector, or as Jodelle's Dido wants to burn and thus extinguish the flame of her love, so Racine seems to use Phèdre's poison as the exact counterpart of the ill which brought her misfortune. The poison which closes the eyes of Phèdre is a counterpoison for the "poison du fol amour".' 'Racine and the Problem of Suicide', *PMLA, Publications of the Modern Language Association,* lxx (1955), 441–54, at p. 453.

38. Tiepolo's painting may be compared with other depictions of Lucretia's suicide, especially that of Simon Vouet (formerly at Potsdam, now apparently destroyed), in which Collatinus supports Lucretia from behind – in much the same manner in which, in Tiepolo's painting, Tarquin threatens her. Palma Vecchio's *Lucrezia* in Vienna contains some of the same ambiguities as Tiepolo's painting.

39. On the more general aspects of this topic, see John Berger's acute study, *Ways of Seeing* (Harmondsworth, Middlesex, 1972).

40. On Artemisia Gentileschi, see R. Ward Bissell, 'Artemisia Gentileschi – a New Documented Chronology', *Art Bulletin* 1 (1968), 153–65; Rudolf and Margot Wittkower, *Born Under Saturn. The Character and Conduct of Artists: A Documented History from Antiquity to the French Revolution* (New York, 1969), pp. 162–4; Ann Sutherland Harris and Linda Nochlin, *Women Artists 1550–1950* (New York, 1976), pp. 118–23; Germaine Greer, *The Obstacle Race: the Fortunes of Women Painters and their Work* (London, 1979), pp. 189–207.

Chapter 2. The Questioning of the Myth (1)

1. Livy, ii. 58; trs. Aubrey de Sélincourt. 'Dant ordine omnes fidem; consolantur aegram animi avertendo noxam ab coacta in auctorem delicti: mentem peccare, non corpus, et unde consilium afuerit, culpam abesse. "Vos," inquit, "videritis, quid illi debeatur: ego me etsi peccato absolvo, supplicio non libero; nec ulla deinde inpudica Lucretiae exemplo vivet." Cultrum, quem sub veste abditum habebat, eum in corde defigit prolapsaque in volnus moribunda cecidit.'

2. *Roman Antiquities,* iv. 65–7.

3. See A. Berger, *Encyclopaedic Dictionary of Roman Law* (Philadelphia, 1953), '*Adulterium*'; G. W. Westrup, *Introduction to Early Roman Law* (Copenhagen and London, 1944), vol. i, part I, sect. i, ch. 4, 'Fidelity'; Ogilvie, *A Commentary,* p. 225. Ogilvie points out that the words *mentem peccare, non corpus* invoke a familar distinction

in Roman law between *peccata* committed *dolo malo* (i.e. with *consilium* or intention) and *sine dolo*. This in turn is overlaid by Greek philosophical ideas on the question of intention as opposed to act.

4. Mary Douglas, *Purity and Danger: An Analysis of Concepts of Pollution and Taboo* (London, 1966).

5. Hugh Downman, *Lucius Junius Brutus; or, the Expulsion of the Tarquins: an Historical Play* (London, 1779), p. 101.

6. *Boswell's Life of Johnson*, ed. R. W. Chapman, new edn. corr. J. D. Fleeman (London, Oxford, and New York, 1970), p. 393. William Wollaston in his *Religion of Nature Delineated* (1724) argues in a somewhat similar way that adultery is essentially an offence against property.

7. Later in Livy's lifetime a criminal action against the wife was made possible. Cicero, *De Legibis*, ii. 10, implies that there were no written laws in the time of Lucretia to punish a man who committed rape, but asserts that Sextus Tarquinius in raping Lucretia offended against the 'eternal law' which exists 'in the primal and ultimate mind of God'. It is curious to note that penalties against suicide, on the other hand, had been introduced by Tarquinius Superbus' father, Tarquinius Priscus: see Pliny, *Nat. Hist.*, xxxvi. 24.

8. Alan Watson, *Rome of the XII Tables: Persons and Property*, pp. 34–6. R. M. Ogilvie (private communication) suspects that this may be one of many stories in Roman history which are partly invented or partly reworked to illustrate aspects of Roman law. Cf. his *Commentary*, note on iii. 44–9.

9. Charles Appleton, 'Trois épisodes de l'histoire ancienne de Rome: Les Sabines, Lucrèce, Virginie', *Revue historique de droit français et étranger*, 4ᵉ série (1924), 193–271, 592–670.

10. M. D. Faber, 'Shakespeare's Suicides: Some Historic, Dramatic and Psychological Reflections', in Edwin S. Shneidman (ed.), *Essays in Self-Destruction* (New York, 1967), pp. 30–58; at p. 38.

11. In 1685, du Rondel argued that Lucretia killed herself for religious reasons, in order to offer a sacrifice to the Eumenides. Pierre Bayle's *Pensées diverses sur la comète de 1680* (1682) and his essay on Lucretia in his *Dictionnaire historique et critique* (1697) argue, on the contrary, that Lucretia killed herself for reasons of honour and glory, not religion. The idea of Lucretia's death as a religious sacrifice is prominent in some dramatic versions of the story, such as Delfino's *La Lucrezia* (in *Le tragedie di Giovanni Delfino* (Padua, 1733)).

12. *Against Jovianus*, bk. i, in *The Principal Works of St. Jerome*, trs. W. H. Fremantle with G. Lewis and W. G. Martley (London, 1893).

13. *Ad Martyras*, in *The Writings of Tertullian*, vol. i; *On Exhortation to*

Chastity and *On Monogamy*, ibid., vol. iii, *Translations of the Writings of the Fathers, Down to A.D. 325,* ed. Alexander Roberts and James Donaldson, vols. xi, xviii (Edinburgh, 1869, 1870).

14. *On Exhortation to Chastity,* ed. cit., p. 20.

15. Eusebius, Bishop of Caesarea, *The Ecclesiastical History and the Martyrs of Palestine,* trs. with an introd. by H. J. Lawlor and J. E. L. Oulton, 2 vols. (New York and Toronto, 1927), i. 273-4 (bk. viii, sect. 14). On this general topic, see Marina Warner, *Alone of All her Sex: The Myth and Cult of the Virgin Mary* (London, 1976), esp. ch. 5, 'Virgins and Martyrs'; W. E. H. Lecky, *History of European Morals from Augustus to Charlemagne,* 2 vols. (London, 1911), esp. ii. 19 ff.

16. *Butler's Lives of the Saints,* ed., rev., and suppl. by H. Thurston S. J. and D. Attwater, 4 vols. (London, 1956), ii. 510–11; Hippolyte Delehaye, *The Legends of the Saints,* trs. D. Attwater (London, 1962), pp. 150–5.

17. *Inferno,* iv. 118 ff.

18. *The Legend of Good Women,* ll. 1871–2, in *The Works of Geoffrey Chaucer,* ed. F. N. Robinson (2nd edn., Boston, 1957). W. W. Skeat points out that Ovid in *Fasti* tells Lucretia's story under a particular date, so that Chaucer believes Lucretia to have her own day, like a saint (*The Complete Works of Geoffrey Chaucer,* 7 vols. (Oxford, 1894–7), iii. 333). E. F. Shannon suggests that Chaucer may also be remembering the way in which Ovid's Brutus swears by Lucretia's spirit, which will become a divinity to him (*Chaucer and the Roman Poets* (Cambridge, Mass., 1929), p. 227; see *Fasti,* ii. 841–3).

19. Battista Dossi's *St. Lucretia* in the Samuel H. Kress collection of the National Gallery of Art, Washington D.C., may be intended as a compliment to Lucrezia Borgia; perhaps the subject is a minor fourth-century Spanish saint. See William E. Suida, 'Lucrezia Borgia, *In Memoriam',* *Gazette des Beaux-Arts,* ser. 6, xxxv (1949), 275–84; and, for the attribution to Battista rather than Dosso Dossi, Felton Gibbons, *Dosso and Battista Dossi, Court Painters at Ferrara* (Princeton, New Jersey, 1968), p. 235. Possibly the obscure figure in the niche behind the seated saint is intended to represent the classical Lucretia. On the quasi-Christian connotations of Lucretia during the Renaissance, see also Gustav Gluck, 'Mabuse and the Development of the Flemish Renaissance', *Art Quarterly,* viii (1945), 116–39.

20. Pierre Le Moyne, *La Gallerie des femmes fortes* (Lyons, 1667), pp. 191, 195; cf. Hebrews 6:6. For a thorough survey of French feminist writings in this period, see Ian Maclean, *Woman Triumphant: Feminism in French Literature 1610–1652* (Oxford, 1977).

21. 'O blessure impalpable! Mystérieuse; affreuse balafre': recalling and intensifying Shakespeare's 'O unfelt sore! crest-wounding, private

scar!' etc., *The Rape of Lucrece*, l. 828. The wound here is to reputation: see pp. 53–5 below. Obey's play was first performed on 12 March 1931 at the Théâtre du Vieux-Colombier by the Compagnie des Quinze.

22. The opera, first performed at Glyndebourne on 7 June 1946, is discussed in *The Rape of Lucretia: A Symposium*, by Benjamin Britten, John Piper, Eric Crozier, Ronald Duncan, Henry Boys, and Angus McBean (London, 1948).

23. 'Si adulterata, cur laudata; si pudica, cur occisa?' See Augustine, *The City of God*, trs. Henry Bettenson, ed. David Knowles (Harmondsworth, 1972), bk. i, ch. 19, pp. 29, 30.

24. Introduction of the Poems of Shakespeare in *The Complete Signet Classic Shakespeare*, ed. Sylvan Barnet (New York, etc., 1972), p. 1670.

25. Erwin Stengel, *Suicide and Attempted Suicide* (Harmondsworth, 1964), p. 60; J. M. Rist, *Stoic Philosophy* (Cambridge, 1969), ch. 13, 'Suicide'.

26. *The City of God*, bk. i, ch. 26, p. 37.

27. Ibid., bk. i, ch. 25, p. 36.

28. Ibid., bk. i, ch. 28, pp. 39–40. The complex question of the operation of the will in pre-lapsarian and post-lapsarian man (and woman) is discussed at greater length in bk. xiv.

29. Matthew 5: 28.

30. Robert Burton, *The Anatomy of Melancholy*, pt. I, sec. 4, mem. 1; Everyman edn., 3 vols. (London and New York, 1932), i.

31. John Case, *Speculum Quaestionum Moralium* (Oxford, 1596), lib. III, cap. vii, p. 161: *pugiunculus Lucretiae Lucretiam nec castam nec fortem fecit*. Robert Burton, *The Anatomy of Melancholy*, loc. cit. John Sym, *Lifes Preservative Against Self-killing* (London, 1637), p. 178. William Vaughan, *The Golden-groue* (2nd edn. enlarged, London, 1608), bk. i, chs. 24, 28; quotation at sig. F^v. John Donne, *Biathanatos* [1695], reproduced from the first edition, with a bibliographical note by J. William Hebel, Facsimile Text Society (New York, 1930), pt. II, dist. 6, sect. 8, p. 147. Jeremy Taylor, *Ductor Dubitantium or the Rule of Conscience*, 2 vols. (London, 1660), vol. ii, bk. iii, ch. 2, pp. 71–9; quotation at p. 73. J. Adams, *An Essay Concerning Self-Murther* (1700), ch. xiii, 'Of Honour', pp. 239–40. Lucretia's suicide is also disapprovingly discussed (along with that of Cato, as so often in these contexts) by Thomas Knaggs, *A Sermon Against Self-Murder* (London, 1708), by John Prince, *Self-Murder Asserted to be a Very Heinous Crime* (London, 1709), and in other eighteenth-century writings on suicide. See further S. E. Sprott, *The English Debate on Suicide from Donne to Hume* (La Salle, Ill. 1961); Lester G. Croker, 'The Discussion of Suicide in the Eighteenth Century', *ELH: A Journal of English*

Literary History, xiii (1952), 47–72; H. R. Fedden, *Suicide. A Social and Historical Study* (London, 1938); Louis I. Dublin, *Suicide. A Sociological and Statistical Study* (New York, 1963); A. Alvarez, *The Savage God* (London, 1971).

32. See, for example, Plato, *Phaedo*, 61–2; Cicero, *De Senectute*, xx. 72–3; and for a general discussion of this topic, Rist, *Stoic Philosophy*, ch. 13, and A. W. Mair, 'Suicide (Greek and Roman)', in James Hastings (ed.), *Encyclopaedia of Religion and Ethics* (New York, 1921), xii, 26–33.

33. Albert Bayet, *Le Suicide et le morale* (Paris, 1922).

34. E. R. Dodds, *The Greeks and the Irrational* (Berkeley and Los Angeles, 1951). Dodds borrows these terms from anthropology; see e.g. Ruth Benedict, *The Chrysanthemum and the Sword: Patterns of Japanese Culture* (London, 1947).

35. William Tyndale, 'The Obedience of a Christian Man' (1527–8), in *Doctrinal Treatises*, ed. H. Walter, Parker Society (Cambridge, 1848), pp. 183–4.

36. Jean François Senault, *Man Become Guilty* (London, 1650), p. 148, the English translation by Henry Cary, Earl of Monmouth, of *L'Homme criminel* (Paris, 1644).

37. Tyndale, p. 184, Senault, p. 148.

38. Prince, *Self-Murder*, pp. 26–7.

39. Bernard Mandeville, Remark (R) to *The Grumbling Hive*, in *The Fable of the Bees*, ed. F. B. Kaye, 2 vols. (Oxford, 1924), i. 209–10. The Second Dialogue of Mandeville's *An Enquiry into the Origin of Honour* follows a similar line of enquiry, suggesting that the female wish to preserve chastity, a wish contrary to natural inclination, can derive only from principles of religion or from 'the Fear of Shame, which has its Foundation in Self-liking'. See *An Enquiry into the Origin of Honour and the Usefulness of Christianity in War*, ed. M. M. Goldsmith (London, 1971), p. 58.

40. 'Astrea to Lysander', prefixed to *Seneca Unmasqued, or, Moral Reflections*, trs. 'Mrs A. B.' [Aphra Behn] (London, 1685), sig. X3.

41. See n. 46 below.

42. M. Bandello, *Le Novelle*, vol. iii, novella xxi, pp. 69–70.

43. G. Rivers, *The Heroinae: or the Lives of Arria, Paulina, Lucrecia, Dido, Theutilla, Cypriana, Aretaphila* (London, 1639), p. 67.

44. Jacques du Bosc, *The Compleat Woman* (London, 1639), p. 52; the English translation by 'N.N.' of *L'Honneste Femme* (2nd edn. corr. and enlarged, Paris, 1633–6).

45. Senault, *Man Become Guilty*, p. 147.

46. On Salutati's *Declamatio*, see Hans Baron, *The Crisis of the Early Italian Renaissance* (rev. one-vol. edn., Princeton, 1966), p. 115; and, for a somewhat different view, the useful discussion by Letizia A. Panizza in 'The St Paul Seneca Correspondence: Its Significance for Stoic Thought from Petrarch to Erasmus' (Ph.D. thesis, University of London (Warburg Institute), 1976).

47. Argument (Roman/italic reversed) prefixed to 'Lucretia to Collatinus', *Les Femmes Illustres or the Heroick Harrangues of the Illustrious Women* (Edinburgh, 1681). This is the English translation by James Innes of *Les Femmes illustres, ou les harangues héroïques* (Paris, 1642) by Georges (and, almost certainly, Madeleine) de Scudéry.

Chapter 3. *'A Theme for Disputation': Shakespeare's Lucrece*

1. See ch. 2, above. Quotations from Peter Alexander's edition of *William Shakespeare: The Complete Works* (London and Glasgow, 1951).

2. On the rhetorical elements in the poem, see Richard A. Lanham, *The Motives of Eloquence: Literary Rhetoric in the Renaissance* (New Haven and London, 1976), ch. 4.

3. On Shakespeare's handling of the political aspects of the story, see ch. 6, pp. 115–17 below.

4. William Tyndale, *The Obedience of a Christian Man* (1527–8), in *Doctrinal Treatises*, ed. Revd. Henry Walter (Parker Society, Cambridge, 1848), p. 183.

5. See pp. 58–9 below.

6. F. T. Prince, ed., *The Poems*, Arden edn. (London and Cambridge, Mass., 1960), p. 119, responding to Pooler in his edition of 1911.

7. See, for example, Hallett Smith: 'There is no temptation, no testing of Lucrece, except in the matter of honest fame; her good name and her husband's honour must be preserved, and her decision is a heroically simple one. The poem is an expansion of a simple situation in which a readily recognized and accepted ideal is outraged' (*Elizabethan Poetry* (University of Michigan, 1968), p. 116). Cf. Bickford Sylvester, 'Natural Mutability and Human Responsibility: Form in Shakespeare's *Lucrece*', *College English*, xxvi (1964–5), 505–11: 'each protagonist has before him a clearly-perceived ethical ideal which engages in a running debate with his fleshly weakness'. The issues are not as simple as either of these statements implies.

8. Supporting the 'poison'd closet' image are those of the impure 'chest' at ll. 760–1 and of the 'polluted prison' at ll. 1725–6.

9. Augustine, *The City of God*, trs. Henry Bettenson, ed. David Knowles, bk. 1, ch. 29, p. 40.

10. Sam Hynes, 'The Rape of Tarquin', *Shakespeare Quarterly,* x (1959),

451–3. Cf. Christopher Devlin, *The Life of Robert Southwell, Poet and Martyr* (London, 1956; repr. 1967), p. 272. J. Quarles's 'continuation' of Shakespeare's poem, *Tarquin Banished: or, the Reward of Lust* (appended to the 1655 London edn. of *The Rape of Lucrece*) makes much of the reflexive nature of the story. '*Lucretia*, ah *Lucretia*! thou didst finde/ A raped body, I a raped minde,' says the banished Tarquin, soliloquizing in a 'shadie grove'. Tarquin is visited by a flock of nightingales who proceed to sing him to death and then pick out his eyes: 'From which sad story we may well infer,/ That *Philomel* abhors a Ravisher' (pp. 10, 12). Quarles is not concerned, however, with the idea of spiritual retribution.

Chapter 4 *'Another Lucretia': Clarissa and the Dilemmas of Rape*

1. For Voltaire's play and its English imitations, see chs. six and seven below; for Richardson and *The Plain Dealer*, see T. C. Duncan Eaves and Ben D. Kimpel, *Samuel Richardson: A Biography* (Oxford, 1971), pp. 37–8.

2. 'Lucretia', in *A General Dictionary, Historical and Critical . . . of the Celebrated Mr Bayle*, trs. J. P. Bernard, T. Birch, and J. Lockman, viii, 217. For Augustine's arguments, see ch. 2 above.

3. *Pamela: or, Virtue Rewarded,* the Shakespeare Head Edition of the Novels of Samuel Richardson, 4 vols. (Oxford, 1929); references are to volume and page numbers. This edition follows the text of the 1742 edition. The first edition (1740) speaks only of 'blame', not 'shame', in the quoted passage: see *Pamela: or, Virtue Rewarded*, ed. T. C. Duncan Eaves and Ben D. Kimpel, the Riverside edn. (Boston, etc., 1971), p. 42.

4. *Clarissa: or, the History of a Young Lady*, the Shakespeare Head Edition of the Novels of Samuel Richardson, 8 vols. (Oxford, 1930); references are to volume and page numbers. This edition follows the text of 1751. In the passage quoted, Belford is actually speaking of death by duelling, 'the dreadfullest of all deaths, next to Suicide, because it gives no opportunity for repentance'. More than once in the novel Lovelace and Belford recognize that it would be natural for someone in Clarissa's situation to kill herself (i.251, vi. 283–4, 374), while towards the end of the novel (viii.144) Lovelace himself contemplates suicide.

5. See ch. 1, above. Margaret Anne Doody in *A Natural Passion*: *A Study the Novels of Samuel Richardson* (Oxford, 1974), p. 120, n. 3, compares Richardson's scene with that in James Shirley's *The Traitor* (1631), in which Amidea threatens to kill herself with her own knife rather than submit to the importunities of the Duke of Florence. What she does not notice is that on three occasions Amidea is explicitly compared with

Lucretia meeting Tarquin. The Lucretia story seems to lie behind Shirley's play, as it does behind a very similar scene in Ben Jonson's *Catiline*, II. 278 ff.

6. See ch. 1.

7. On this episode, see John A. Dussinger, 'Richardson and Johnson: Critical Agreement on Rowe's *The Fair Penitent*', *English Studies*, xlix (1968), 45–7. Dussinger's essay, 'Richardson's Tragic Muse', *Philological Quarterly*, xlvi (1967), 18–33, is also relevant here.

8. This chapter was written before I had read Leo Braudy's ingenious essay, 'Penetration and Impenetrability in *Clarissa*', in Phillip Harth (ed.), *New Approaches to Eighteenth-Century Literature*, Selected Papers from the English Institute (New York and London, 1974), pp. 177–206.

9. *A Natural Passion*, p. 171. Miss Doody concedes that the whole business is 'certainly a trifle mysterious'.

10. Contrast the fate of Mrs Gaskell's Ruth, finally carried off by typhoid after heroically nursing the man who had seduced her many years earlier. Ruth's work in the fever ward transforms her from outcast to saint; her death, like Clarissa's, marks the final stage of social redemption and apotheosis.

11. Anthony Kearney, *Samuel Richardson: Clarissa* (London, 1975), pp. 10, 27.

12. *A Masque Presented at Ludlow Castle*, 1. 662. Cf. Gillian Beer, 'Richardson, Milton, and the Status of Evil', *Review of English Studies*, n.s. xix (1968), 261–70.

13. Chaucer, *The Legend of Good Women*, 1. 1816; Gower, *Confessio Amantis*, bk. iv, 1. 4987. Other writers negotiate this difficulty in other ways. Pierre du Ryer, for example, in his tragedy of *Lucrèce* (probably first acted 1636), imagines that Lucrèce was physically overpowered by Tarquin, being given no opportunity to exercise choice. Shakespeare's Lucrece is 'dead' with fright before Tarquin (l. 1267), who finally appears to rape her by force.

14. Cf. Thomas Knaggs, *A Sermon Against Self-Murder*, p. 11: 'Our Prayer, whether in Sickness or in Health, in the day of Prosperity or Adversity, ought to be, *Not my will O Father, but thine be done*'.

15. See ch. viii of *Psychopathology of Everyday Life*, in *The Basic Writings of Sigmund Freud*, trs. and ed. A. A. Brill (New York, 1938).

16. *Selected Letters of Samuel Richardson*, ed. John Carroll (Oxford, 1964), p. 77 and note.

17. See John Carroll, 'Lovelace as Tragic Hero', *University of Toronto Quarterly*, xlii (1973), 14–25.

18. *Selected Letters*, ed. Carroll, p. 161.

19. Judith Wilt, 'He Could Go No Farther: A Modest Proposal about Lovelace and Clarissa', *PMLA*, xcii (1977), 19–32: a clever but wrong-headed article, which convincingly insists that Lovelace is victim as well as agent in his relationship with Clarissa, but misses or distorts some of the novel's more obvious events and ironies.

20. Robert Bage, *Mount Henneth, A Novel*, 2 vols. (Dublin, 1782; repr. New York and London, 1979), i. 233. See also R. P. Utter and G. B. Needham, *Pamela's Daughters* (London, 1937), p. 298.

21. Yet in Kleist's story *The Marquise of O*— the woman in question can say nothing at all about the matter. During a seige in northern Italy, the respectable Marquise is raped, while unconscious, by her apparent rescuer, a gallant Russian officer, into whose arms she has gratefully swooned. When she comes to, he is gone; months later, she is non-plussed to find herself pregnant. Clarissa's unconsciousness is less absolute: despite her drugs, she is able dimly to perceive what is occurring. Kleist's story (possibly based on an anecdote reported by Montaigne in his essay 'Of Drunkenness') deftly explores social reactions to the 'disgrace' of rape, as does Richardson's novel. The Russian officer's cry when wounded, apparently mortally, on the battlefield – 'Giulietta! This bullet avenges you!' – may be compared with Lovelace's final cry when mortally wounded in the duel with Morden: 'LET THIS EXPIATE!' (viii. 277). For Jean Giraudoux's variation upon the theme of the unconscious rape victim, *Pour Lucrèce*, see ch. five below.

22. Barbara Toner, *The Facts of Rape* (London, 1977), p. 174.

23. Thomas Holcroft, *Anna St. Ives*, ed. Peter Faulkner, Oxford English Novels (London, New York, and Toronto, 1970), pp. 423–4.

24. Thomas Hardy, *Tess of the d'Urbervilles: A Pure Woman*, the New Wessex Edition, introd. P. N. Furbank (London, 1975), p. 392; Mary Jacobus, 'Tess's Purity', *Essays in Criticism*, xxvi (1976), 318–38, at 320; see also W. Eugene Davis, 'Tess of the d'Urbervilles: Some Ambiguities about a Pure Woman', *Nineteenth-Century Fiction*, xxii (1967–8), 397–401.

25. On the idea of will in the novel, see J. T. Laird, *The Shaping of 'Tess of the d'Urbervilles'* (Oxford, 1975), pp. 45 ff. For a more recent fictional treatment of the dilemmas of rape and seduction, see Kingsley Amis's *Take a Girl Like You* (1960), a novel which in some ways reads like a modern version of *Clarissa*. Amis's Jenny Bunn is raped after she has passed out at a party at which she has been given too much to drink, but finds herself later very much alive and with no clear answers to the problems which now face her.

Chapter 5. Joking about Rape: The Myth Inverted

1. See ch. 7.

2. See ch. 2, pp. 36–7.

3. ' . . . je méditois . . . un plan de Tragédie en prose, dont le sujet qui n'étoit pas moins que Lucrece ne m'ôtoit pas l'espoir d'atterrer les rieurs, quoique j'osasse laisser paroitre encor cette infortunée, quand elle ne le peut plus sur aucun Theatre françois.' Jean-Jacques Rousseau, *Œuvres complètes*, Pléiade edn., i (Bruges, 1959), *Les Confessions*, ed. Bernard Gagnebin and Marcel Raymond, bk. viii, p. 394.

4. Rousseau, ed. cit., ii (Dijon, 1969), ed. Jacques Sherer, p. 1869. This overlooks Arnault's play. See also ch. 6 below.

5. [Jean-Jacques Bel], *Le Nouveau Tarquin, comédie en trois actes* (n.p., [1732]).

6. Arthur Melville Clark, *Thomas Heywood: Playwright and Miscellanist* (Oxford, 1931; reissued New York, 1967), p. 47, thinks that Heywood's play was probably written in 1606 or 1607. The play is itself glancingly parodied in Beaumont and Fletcher's *The Knight of the Burning Pestle* in 1613: see Clark, p. 211.

7. [William Hunt], *The Fall of Tarquin: or, the Distressed Lovers, a Tragedy* (Newcastle upon Tyne, 1713), Epilogue.

8. Thomas Southerne, *The Fatal Marriage: or, the Innocent Adultery* (London, 1694), Epilogue.

9. *Rape upon Rape; or the Justice Caught in His Own Trap*, in *The Complete Works of Henry Fielding Esq.*, ed. W. E. Henley, 16 vols. (London, repr. 1967), ix. 157–8.

10. *Jonathan Wild*, bk. iii, ch. 7, in Fielding, *Works*, ed. Henley, ii. 117.

11. *The Relapse*, IV. iii, in the Mermaid *Sir John Vanbrugh*, ed. A. E. H. Swain (London and New York, n.d.).

12. 'Che vi parse di Lucrezia? non fu ella matta a tor consiglio da lui [l'onore]? Era una galantaria il beccarsi la stretta datale da messer Tarquinio, e vivere.' Letter of 21 December 1537, to Malatesta; in *Tutte le opere di Pietro Aretino* (n.p., 1960), *Lettere: il primo e il secondo libro*, ed. Francesco Flora, p. 380. Aretino elsewhere refers to a courtesan who affectedly called herself Lucrezia (*Sei Giornate*, ed. Giovanni Aquilecchia (Bari, 1969), pp. 74, 82, 120, 126, etc.). Cf. Robert Burton, *The Anatomy of Melancholy*, pt. III, sec. 2, mem. 1, subs. 2 (Everyman edn., iii. 54): 'Aretino's Lucretia sold her maidenhead a thousand times before she was twenty-four years old'. Thomas Carew in his poem 'The Rapture', ll. 115 ff., imagines the Roman Lucretia reading the erotic works of Aretino, knowing 'as well as *Lais*, how to move/ Her plyant body in the act of love', and vigorously meeting the advances of Tar-

quin: *The Poems of Thomas Carew*, ed. Rhodes Dunlap (Oxford, 1970), p. 52. The notion of 'Lucretia turned whore' was sometimes associated with the tradition of 'the world upside-down': see E. R. Curtius, *European Literature and the Latin Middle Ages*, trs. W. R. Trask (London, 1953), p. 95. Benedetto Croce discusses a number of Italian jokes and parodies relating to the Lucretia story in his *Aneddoti di varia letteratura* (Bari, 1953), i, ch. 46.

13. English translation by Bruce Penman in his *Five Italian Renaissance Comedies* (Harmondsworth, 1978). Italian quotations from Niccolò Machiavelli, *La Mandragola, La Clizia, Balfagor*, ed. Vittoria Osimo (Rome, 1920).

14. Henry Paolucci, introduction to *Mandragola*, trs. Anne and Henry Paolucci (Indianapolis and New York, 1957). In *Pirandello's Theater* (Carbondale, Ill., etc., 1974), ch. 3, Anne Paolucci compares *Mandragola* with Pirandello's *Liolà*, relating both plays to the story of Lucretia.

15. *The City of God*, bk. i, ch. 26.

16. Paolucci translation.

17. Daniel C. Boughner, *The Devil's Disciple: Ben Jonson's Debt to Machiavelli* (New York, 1968), pp. 133–7, briefly examines the similarities (but not the differences) between the two plays, arguing that Jonson the 'omnivorous plagiary' may have imitated Machiavelli, and that Celia is to be regarded as 'a comic Lucrece'. Neither argument seems wholly persuasive.

18. *Pushkin on Literature*, sel., trs., and ed. Tatiana Wolff (London, 1971), pp. 272–3. For *Count Nulin*, see *Pushkin Threefold: Narrative, Lyric, Polemic, and Ribald Verse*, the originals with linear and metric translations by Walter Arndt (London, 1972), pp. 88–99, 326–47. Arndt finds 'the parodical intent so faint as to be nearly irrelevant', p. 88. See also George Gibian, 'Pushkin's Parody of *The Rape of Lucrece*', *Shakespeare Quarterly*, i (1950), 264–6.

19. *Pushkin on Literature*, p. 273.

20. *The Rape of the Lock*, the rape of Lucretia: Pope's title triggers a memory which is not otherwise explicitly recalled in the poem. 'Rape' was a popular word in the titles of many eighteenth-century parodies and burlesques, partly because of the success of Pope's poem: see Richmond P. Bond, *English Burlesque Poetry 1700–1750* (repr. New York, 1964), pp. 96–7. In Italy, Alessandro Tassoni's *La secchia rapita* (1622, 'The Rape of the Bucket') includes in its eighth canto a comic version of the story of the rape of Lucretia.

21. *Pour Lucrèce*, in Jean Giraudoux, *Théâtre*, iv (Paris, 1962). The play was first produced by Jean-Louis Barrault at the Théâtre Marigny in

1953. English quotations here are from Christopher Fry's (at times somewhat abridged) translation, *Duel of Angels*, in vol. i of Giraudoux, *Plays* (London, 1963).

22. H. E. Rollins in his New Variorum edition of *Shakespeare: The Poems* (Philadelphia and London, 1938), p. 416, mentions a dramatic parody of the Lucretia story entitled *Katydid. So What?*, produced by Mary Young at the Copley Theatre, Boston, on 5 November 1935, in which the sexual roles are reversed: Tarquin is a woman, and Lucrece a smug and virtuous husband, whose complaisance Tarquin manages to break down. This version, which I have not seen, appears to invert the story more radically than the other parodies and comic versions discussed in this chapter.

PART II. LUCIUS JUNIUS BRUTUS

1. Dryden's translation misses the sharpness and ambiguity of Virgil's original – but so (remarkably) do most of the better-known English translations. ' . . . patriotism shall prevail and love of / Honour' is C. Day Lewis's rendering on line 823. Voltaire, in quoting from (a variant of) this passage on the title-page of his tragedy *Brutus* in 1736, terminates the sentence at a significant point: '*Infelix utcumque ferent ea facta nepotes/ Vincet amor patriae.*'

Chapter 6. The Shaping of the Myth (2)

2. See Robert Rosenblum, 'Gavin Hamilton's "Brutus" and its Aftermath', *Burlington Magazine*, ciii (1961), 8–16. An anonymous Italian correspondent found that the subject had been treated by Hamilton 'd'une manière toute nouvelle'; Rosenblum (p. 11) agrees that Hamilton hit upon 'an entirely new interpretation of Lucretia's death'. See also B. C. Skinner, 'Hamilton's *Oath of Brutus*', *Burlington Magazine*, ciii (1961), 146; and Rosenblum's response; and Rosenblum, *Transformations in Late Eighteenth Century Art* (Princeton, 1967), pp. 68–9 and nn.

3. See Robert Rosenblum, 'A Source for David's "Horatii" ', *Burlington Magazine*, cxii (1970), 269–73. This article modifies some points made in Rosenblum's earlier article cited in the preceding note.

4. *The Discourses of Niccolò Machiavelli*, trs. Leslie J. Walker, S. J. (London, 1950), bk. iii, discourse 5[1]. Cf. bk. i, discourse 16[4]; bk. iii, discourse 2[1]; bk. iii, discourse 3[1].

5. Sir Thomas Elyot, *The Boke Named the Gouernour*, ed. from the 1st edn. of 1531 by H. H. S. Croft, 2 vols. (London, 1880), ii. 44–5 (bk. ii, ch. 5). Cf. i. 18 (bk. i, ch. 2). (The name 'Aruncius' or 'Aruns' is substituted for 'Sextus' in some versions of the story deriving from Florus.) Cf. Plutarch, *Publicola*, i. 3.

6.   'Chose singulière! ce n'est presque jamais la raison qui fait les choses raisonnables, et on ne va presque jamais à elle par elle.

Quand on sait comment ont été produits les beaux effets qu'on voit dans le monde, on en rougit pour le bon sens. Deux petites femmes de Rome, par leur petite vanité sotte, ne furent-elles pas cause que cette ville communique les honneurs aux Plébéiens et parvint par là à ce période tant vanté d'une république parfaite' [*Mes pensées*, x, 1199].

'Il est pourtant vrai que la mort de Lucrèce ne fut que l'occasion de la révolution qui arriva: car un peuple fier, entreprenant, hardi, et renfermé dans des murailles, doit nécessairement secouer le joug, ou adoucir ses mœurs' [*Considérations sur les causes de la grandeur des Romains et de leur décadence*].

Montesquieu, *Œuvres complètes* (Paris, 1964), pp. 995, 436. See also Sheila M. Mason, 'Livy and Montesquieu', in T. A. Dorey (ed.), *Livy* (London and Toronto, 1971), pp. 118–58.

7.   See Ogilvie, *A Commentary*, pp. 216, 219, 227, 232. In *Pro Sestio* (delivered in 56 BC), section 123, Cicero says that the spectators at a performance of Accius' *Brutus* took a verse of the second-century dramatist as referring to Cicero's own actions in the Catilinarian affair. Was Accius' own play (of which only fragments remain) itself shaped by contemporary political events? Accius was a friend of D. Junius Brutus Callaicus (consul in 138 BC), who took part in the killing (in 121 BC) of C. Gracchus; Gracchus had been accused by some of his opponents of trying to make himself a king (Professor H. Jocelyn, privately).

8.   Professor R. M. Ogilvie (private communication) thinks it likely that when a (plebeian) branch of the Junii rose to power in the fourth century they acquired the surname Brutus, claimed descent from the original Brutus, and cultivated a series of stories about his stupidity which were added to the much older Lucretia myth. Surnames of this kind are not firmly attested before the fourth century.

9.   Cicero, *Letters to Atticus*, xiii. 40; *Philippic*, ii. 26. Cf. *Philippics*, i. 6, iii. 4, iv. 3, x. 6; *Tusculan Disputations*, iv. 2; *Brutus*, 52–3. Cicero was fascinated by the larger shape of the story of the fall of the Tarquins, feeling that it demonstrated 'the regular curving path through which governments travel', 'that orbit of development with whose natural motion and circular course you must become acquainted from its beginning'. The reign of Tarquinius Superbus began and ended in crime: the murder of Servius Tullius, the rape of Lucretia. The symmetry of the story of the two Brutuses is part of that larger pattern of history. See *De Re Publica*, II. xxv. 45–6, trs. C. W. Keyes, Loeb edn. (London and New York, 1928). Dante (*Paradiso*, vi. 40–1) perceived a similar shape in the entire period of the Roman kings.

10. Ovid, *Fasti*, ii. 834; Suetonius, *Divus Julius*, lxxxii. 2. Both Ovid and Suetonius are probably remembering Euripides' description of the death

of Polyxena in *Hecuba*, 557–70 (though Polyxena in fact bares herself to the waist before indulging in this final act of modesty). See also ch. 1, p. 14 and n. 32.

11. *Philippic*, ii. 28–30. A similar parallelism is to be found in Shakespeare's *The Rape of Lucrece*, ll. 1734–6, and *Julius Caesar*, III. ii. 178–82.

12. Ogilvie, *A Commentary*, p. 227. Livy similarly sees in Tarquinius Superbus a prototype of Catiline, introducing into his account of Tarquin memories from Sallust and Cicero. Cicero had seen Catiline as a new Tarquin: see Ogilvie, p. 186. It is worth noting that both Livy's and Dionysius' accounts of Brutus were written during the principate of Augustus. Augustus assiduously maintained the cult of his murdered great-uncle Julius Caesar; his own regime would have been considered by many as an ill-disguised monarchy.

13. Heinrich Bullinger, Hans Sachs, *Lucretia-Dramen*, ed. Horst Hartmann; Derek van Abbé, *Drama in Renaissance Germany and Switzerland* (Melbourne, 1961), pp. 38, 42–4. The play was written *c*.1526.

14. Harold T. Parker, *The Cult of Antiquity and the French Revolutionaries* (Chicago, 1937), ch. 12.

15. Political writings from around this period which invoke the name of Brutus include *Lettre des deux Brutus au peuple Français* (Paris, year 3) and *Récit de la Révolution de Rome, sous Tarquin-le-Superbe* (Dijon, 1791).

16. Marvin Carlson, *The Theatre of the French Revolution* (Ithaca, N. Y., 1966), pp. 54–5; R. Pomeau, 'Voltaire et le héros', *Revue des sciences humaines* (Lille, 1951), pp. 345–51; Robert L. Herbert, *David, Voltaire, 'Brutus', and the French Revolution* (London, 1972) in the Allen Lane 'Art in Context' series, ed. John Fleming and Hugh Honour; Henri Welschinger, *Le Théâtre de la Révolution 1789–1799* (Paris, 1880), pp. 102–3. Georg Büchner's play *Dantons Tod* (1835) nicely catches the way in which the Roman play-acting in this period continued outside, as well as inside, the theatre.

17. *The Tragedies of Vittorio Alfieri*, trs. Charles Lloyd, 3 vols. (London, 1815), iii. p. xix; Vittorio Alfieri, *Memoirs*, the anonymous tr. of 1810, rev. E. R. Vincent (London, New York, and Toronto, 1961), p. 247.

18. A. V. Arnault, *Lucrèce, ou Rome Libre*, in *Œuvres, Théâtre*, i (Paris, 1824).

19. F. G. J. S. Andrieux, *Lucius Junius Brutus* (Paris, 1830), préface.

20. F. Ponsard, *Lucretia: A Tragedy* (London, 1848), 'To the Reader'; p. 27. Contemporary with Ponsard's play is that of S. P. Hill, published anonymously in Sydney in 1843, *Tarquin the Proud; or the Downfall of Tyranny*.

21. [William Fulbecke], *An Abridgement, Or rather, A Bridge of Roman*

Histories, to passe the nearest way from Titus Livius to Cornelius Tacitus (London, 1608), 'To the Reader' (dated 1600). On the problem of accommodating Roman Republican history to Tudor monarchical theory, see T. J. B. Spencer, 'Shakespeare and the Elizabethan Romans', *Shakespeare Survey*, 10 (1957), 27–38, and George K. Hunter, 'A Roman Thought: Renaissance Attitudes to History Exemplified in Shakespeare and Jonson', in B. S. Lee (ed.), *An English Miscellany Presented to W. S. Mackie* (Cape Town, etc., 1977), pp. 93–118.

22. Henry Cary, Lord Lepington (later second Earl of Monmouth), *Romulus and Tarquin* (London, 1637), Epistle Dedicatory.

23. *Mercurius Politicus*, 1650, in *The English Revolution*, iii, Newsbooks 5, vol. i (repr. London, 1971), *passim*; *The Complete Prose Works of John Milton*, Yale edn. (New Haven and London, 1971), v. 1649–59, Part ii, p. 495 and n.; iv. 1650–5, Part i, p. 682; cf. i. 1624–42, p. 640. I am indebted to Dr Christopher Hill and Professor R. L. Brett for drawing my attention to these passages. See also Zera S. Fink, *The Classical Republicans* (Evanston, Ill., 1945).

24. *The Poems of Richard Lovelace*, ed. C. H. Wilkinson, 2 vols. (Oxford, 1925), ii. 143.

25. Jonathan Swift, *A Discourse of the Contests and Dissentions Between the Nobles and the Commons in Athens and Rome*, ed. Frank H. Ellis (Oxford, 1967), pp. 101–2; *The Sentiments of a Church-of-England Man, With Respect to Religion and Government,* in *Bickerstaff Papers and Pamphlets on the Church* (Oxford, 1940), p. 23 (and on Brutus, cf. 'A Digression Concerning Madness' in *A Tale of a Tub*, ed. Herbert Davis (Oxford, 1939), p. 111). Rousseau's admiration for Brutus is evident in the *Confessions*; see also Denise Leduc-Fayette, *J.-J. Rousseau et le mythe de l'antiquité* (Paris, 1974). Arthur Mainwaring in 1690 played yet another variation on the story in his *Tarquin and Tullia*, a verse satire on William and Mary.

26. From the suppression order for the play, 11 December 1680; quoted by Allardyce Nicoll, *A History of Restoration Drama 1660–1700* (Cambridge, 1923), p. 10, n. 4. Quotations from the play are taken from *Lucius Junius Brutus*, ed. John Loftis, Regents Restoration Drama Series (London, 1968). See also Frances Barbour, 'The Unconventional Heroic Plays of Nathaniel Lee', *University of Texas Studies in English* (1940), 109–16.

27. Charles Gildon, *The Patriot, or the Italian Conspiracy*, p. 55. In his first rewriting of Lee's play, Gildon retained Lee's original names and setting, but the Master of the Revels refused to approve it in this form: see Preface, sig. A3.

28. [William Hunt], *The Fall of Tarquin: or, the Distressed Lovers, a Tragedy*. In the preface to the edition of the play published in York in the

same year Hunt further stresses his loyalty: 'My Intention in publishing [the play] is very remote from reflecting upon that glorious Constitution with which Providence has bless'd us, and the Loyalty of my Heart flatters me with the Hopes that *Tarquin* will be read without an ill-natur'd Application.'

29. *The Tuscan Treaty: Or, Tarquin's Overthrow.* Written by a Gentleman lately deceased, Revised and Altered by W. Bond, Esq. (London, 1733); J. H. Plumb, *Sir Robert Walpole: The King's Minister*, 2 vols., ii (London, 1960), 266. John Loftis thinks the play 'had only such political relevance as was implicit in a tyrant's fall': *The Politics of Drama in Augustan England* (Oxford, 1963), p. 122. The play was acted at Covent Garden on 20 and 21 August 1733: see *The London Stage, Part 3: 1729–1747*, ed. Arthur H. Scouten (Carbondale, Ill. 1961), pp. 311–12.

30. William Duncombe, *Junius Brutus, A Tragedy* (London, 1735); *Memoirs of Viscountess Sundon*, ed. Katherine Thomson, 2 vols. (London, 1847), i. 394–6, at 394; *Letters by Several Eminent Persons Deceased. Including the Correspondence of John Hughes, Esq.*, ii (London, 1772), 295–301; J. J. Lynch, *Box Pit and Gallery: Stage and Society in Johnson's London* (Berkeley and Los Angeles, 1953), p. 248.

31. J. H. Payne, *Brutus; or the Fall of Tarquin* (London, 1818); Grace Overmyer, *America's First Hamlet* (New York, 1957), pp. 159–72.

Chapter 7. The Questioning of the Myth (2)

1. *Henry V*, II. iv. 38.

2. Livy, i. 56; Zonaras, vii. 11, etc.

3. Bk. iii, discourse 2.

4. Livy, ii. 5; de Sélincourt's translation.

5. Dionysius of Halicarnassus, v. 8.

6. 'The Life of Publius Valerius Publicola', *Plutarch's Lives of the Noble Grecians and Romans Englished by Sir Thomas North*, Anno 1579, introd. George Wyndham, vol. vii of The Tudor Translations, ed. W. E. Henley (London, 1895), i. 255.

7. Cf. Alan Wardman, *Plutarch's Lives* (London, 1974), p. 108. At the outset of his 'Life of Marcus Brutus', Plutarch contrasts Lucius Junius Brutus' 'sower stearne nature, not softned by reason' with Marcus Brutus' more gentle and civilized temperament: *Lives*, vi. 182.

8. *Aeneid*, vi. 822–3, trs. H. Rushton Fairclough, Loeb edn. (London and Cambridge, Mass., 1965); *The City of God*, trs. Bettenson, bk. iii, ch. 16, pp. 109–10. Virgil's ambivalence about Brutus is based upon political, as well as moral, considerations: a supporter of the Augustan regime could not whole-heartedly admire this enemy of kingship.

9. Livy, viii. 34.

10. *Inferno*, xxxiv. 64 ff.

11. For Caesar's affair with Brutus' mother Servilia, see Suetonius, *Divus Julius*, 1; the notion of Caesar's fathering Brutus is developed by Plutarch in his 'Life of Marcus Brutus', *Lives*, vi. 185. When Plutarch's Brutus finally strikes Caesar he gives him 'one wounde about his privities', 'The Life of Julius Caesar', *Lives*, v. 68. Suetonius' account of Caesar's words as Brutus strikes – 'You too, my child?' (καὶ σὺ τεκνον;) – possibly strengthened the idea of parricide: *Divus Julius*, lxxxii. It is curious to note that another Brutus, the legendary great-grandson of Aeneas and the first king of Britain, was also said to have killed his father.

12. Coluccio Salutati, *De Tyranno*, ch. 5; in Ephraim Emerton, *Humanism and Tyranny: Studies in the Italian Trecento* (Cambridge, Mass., 1925), p. 111. On the debate about the younger Brutus, see also D. J. Gordon, 'Giannotti, Michelangelo and the Cult of Brutus', in Stephen Orgel (coll. and ed.), *The Renaissance Imagination: Essays and Lectures by D. J. Gordon* (Berkeley, Los Angeles, and London, 1975).

13. Hans Baron, *The Crisis of the Early Italian Renaissance*, rev. one-vol. edn. (Princeton, 1966), pp. 114–19; quotation at p. 118.

14. Ibid., p. 166. For Petrarch on the Brutuses, see also his *Exhortation to Cola di Rienzo and to the Roman People (Epistolae Variae*, xlviii, summer 1347), in *Petrarch: A Humanist Among Princes*, ed. David Thompson (New York, Evanston, Ill., and London, 1971), pp. 69 ff.

15. Bk. iii, discourse 3.

16. N. Hooke, *The Roman History, From the Building of Rome to the Ruin of the Commonwealth*, 3rd edn. (London, 1757), p. 122.

17. Robert Jephson, *Roman Portraits, A Poem, in Heroick Verse* (London, 1794), ll. 227–36.

18. [Madeleine de Scudéry], *Clelia, an Excellent New Romance*, pts. i–iii, trs. John Davies (1659), pts. iv–v, trs. G. Havers (1677) (London, 1678), pt. ii, bk. 3, p. 315.

19. Ibid., pt. ii, bk. 3, p. 325.

20. Ibid., pt. iii, bk. 2, p. 284.

21. C. Bernard, *Brutus, Tragédie* (Paris, 1691), préface.

22. Voltaire, *Discours sur la tragédie*, in *Brutus*, rev. and corr. edn. (Paris, 1736), pp. xxii–iii. See also R. S. Ridgway, *Voltaire and Sensibility* (Montreal and London, 1973), esp. pp. 113–14.

23. Antonio Conti, *Giunio Bruto*, prefazione, in *Le Quattro Tragedie* (Florence, 1751), pp. 31–2.

24. 'William Duncombe', in *The Dictionary of National Biography*.

25. *The Sybil, or the Elder Brutus. A Tragedy*, Act V, in *The Posthumous Works of the late Richard Cumberland, Esq.*, 2 vols. (London, 1813), i. 61.

26. J. H. Payne, *Brutus; or the Fall or Tarquin* (1818), Act V. Payne gave instructions to Kean in a letter of 3 December 1818 concerning the way this scene should be played: see Overmyer, *America's First Hamlet*, p. 164.

27. Andrieux, *Lucius Junius Brutus*, préface, pp. xv ff.

28. G. Wilson Knight, *The Golden Labyrinth* (London, 1965), pp. 165–7. See also David M. Vieth, 'Psychological Myth as Tragedy: Nathaniel Lee's *Lucius Junius Brutus*', *Huntington Library Quarterly*, xxxix (1975–6), 57–76: an ingenious analysis, which does not always distinguish between elements in the traditional story and those invented by Lee.

29. The main source for the incident is Plutarch's 'Life of Publicola'; though possibly Lee is remembering also Livy's discussion (ii. 2) of the office of the 'king of sacrifices', and the Catilinian conspirators' sacrament of blood in Jonson's *Catiline*, Act I.

30. See *OED* 'bowel', *sb.*, † 5, 'offspring, children'. Cf. IV. 288, 312, V. i. 120, V. ii. 38, etc.

31. Dionysius of Halicarnassus, iv. 82.

32. 'Life of Marcus Brutus', *Lives*, vi. 194.

33. Robert L. Herbert, *J. L. David: Brutus*, Appendix, pp. 127–8. See also Rosenblum, *Transformations in Late Eighteenth Century Art*, pp. 76–81.

PART III. AN EPILOGUE – AND AN ANALOGUE

1. 'Sa mort fut la faiblesse d'une grande âme, l'erreur d'un stoïcien, une tache dans sa vie': cit. Albert Bayet, *Le Suicide et la morale* (Paris, 1922), p. 742.

Chapter 8. Heroism Transformed: Lucretia, Brutus, and Cato of Utica

2. The principal classical accounts of Cato are those of Lucan, *De Bello Civili*, Plutarch, *Life of Cato Minor*, and Sallust, *Bellum Catilinae*, lii–liv.

3. Lucan, *De Bello Civili*, ii. 388; cf. ii. 297–303.

4. Seneca, *De Providentia*, ii. 10. Addison quoted Seneca's words in *Spectator* no. 237, and later attached them as a motto to his tragedy of *Cato*.

5. Virgil, *Aeneid*, vi. 841, viii. 670; Dante, *Purgatorio*, i. 31 (Cato as warder at the entrance to Purgatory); Eugène Müntz, *Histoire de l'art pendant la Renaissance*, ii: *Italie, l'âge d'or* (Paris, 1891), p. 22.

6. Augustine, *The City of God*, bk. i, chs. 22–4; bk. v, ch. 12.

7. Baron, *The Crisis of the Early Italian Renaissance*, pp. 118–19.

8. Fontenelle's *Nouveaux dialogues des morts* appeared in 1683 and were translated into English in the same year by 'J.D.', *New Dialogues of the Dead* (London, 1683). The fourth dialogue of part one concerns Cato, the sixth dialogue of part three, Lucretia. See also *Fontenelle's Dialogues of the Dead*, [trs. John Hughes] (London, 1708) (the first dialogue, by Hughes himself, concerns L. J. Brutus); [William Weston], *New Dialogues of the Dead* (London, 1762) (the fourth dialogue concerns Lucretia); [Lord Lyttleton], *Dialogues of the Dead* (London, 1760) (dialogue nine concerns Cato); and Frederick M. Keener, *English Dialogues of the Dead: A Critical History, an Anthology, and a Check-List* (New York and London, 1973), *passim*.

9. *Fontenelle's Dialogues of the Dead*, preface, pp. xviii–xx.

10. J. W. Johnson, *The Formation of English Neo-Classical Thought* (Princeton, 1967), pp. 95–105 (a pioneering account); Denise Leduc-Fayette, *J.-J. Rousseau et le myth de l'antiquité* (Paris, 1974), ch. 2. I have discussed the ambivalence of eighteenth-century attitudes to Cato in my essay 'Cato in Tears: Stoical Guises of the Man of Feeling', in R. F. Brissenden (ed.), *Studies in the Eighteenth Century* (Canberra, 1973). The present chapter draws upon, and adds substantially to, that essay. Eighteenth-century English attitudes to Augustan Rome were decidedly mixed: see Howard Weinbrot, *Augustus Caesar in 'Augustan' England: The Decline of a Classical Norm* (Princeton, 1978).

11. Jonathan Swift, *The Sentiments of a Church-of-England Man*, in *Bickerstaff Papers and Pamphlets on the Church* (Oxford, 1940), p. 2 (cf. *Gulliver's Travels*, iii. 7; *Miscellaneous and Autobiographical Pieces*, ed. Herbert Davies (Oxford, 1969), p. 84; *Irish Tracts 1720–1723*, ed. L. Landa (Oxford, 1948), p. 249; Johnson, *The Formation of English Neo-Classical Thought*, pp. 101–2; and M. M. Kelsall, '*Iterum Houyhnhnm*: Swift's Sextumvirate and the Horses', *Essays in Criticism*, xix (1969), 35–45); J.-J. Rousseau, *Œuvres complètes*, ed. Michel Launay, ii (Paris, 1971), p. 122; *Lettres de Maximilien Robespierre* (Paris, 1792), p. 334. On Addison's *Cato*, see esp. Peter Smithers, *The Life of Joseph Addison* (Oxford, 1954), pp. 250 ff.; M. M. Kelsall, 'The Meaning of Addison's *Cato*', *Review of English Studies*, n.s. xvii (1966), pp. 149–62; and – for eighteenth-century translations and imitations of the play – *The New Cambridge Bibliography of English Literature*, ii: *1660–1800*, ed. George Watson (Cambridge, 1971), cols. 125, 176, 191, 211. On the play's ambiguous political significance, see John Loftis, *The Politics of Drama in Augustan England* (Oxford, 1963), pp. 56–61. The 'Cato' letters of Thomas Gordon and John Trenchard which appeared in the *London Journal* and *British Journal* between 1720 and 1723 played upon the political associations of Cato's name.

For operas on the subject of Cato, see Leduc-Fayette. There are eighteenth-century paintings of the death of Cato by Lethière, Boucher, Guérin, Le Brun, and others.

12. J. Adams, *An Essay Concerning Self-Murther* (1700), chs. 11–14, *passim*.

13. Thomas Knaggs, *A Sermon Against Self-Murder* (London, 1708), p. 14; John Prince, *Self-Murder Asserted to be a Very Heinous Crime* (London, 1709), pp. 25–6; Isaac Watts, *A Defense Against the Temptation to Self-Murder* (London, 1726), pp. 22–4; [Zachary Pearce], *A Sermon on Self-Murder* (London, 1736), p. 7; *A Discourse upon Self-Murder . . . in a Letter to a Freethinker that despis'd Life*, 2nd edn. corr. (London, 1754), p. 10; Caleb Fleming, *A Dissertation upon the Unnatural Crime of Self-Murder* (London, 1773), p. 5; Richard Hey, *A Dissertation on Suicide* (Cambridge, 1785), pp. 13, 3–5.

14. The metaphor of 'enlightenment' is, of course, not a new one in the eighteenth century, but is found extensively in earlier Christian writings.

15. Charles Wicksted Ethelston, *The Suicide: with other Poems* (London, 1803), p. 40.

16. 'This sentiment is not in character,' noted Bishop Hurd in his edition of Addison, 'but the amiable author, ever attentive to the interests of religion and virtue, chose, for the sake of these, to violate decorum': *The Works of the Right Honourable Joseph Addison*, with notes by Richard Hurd, D. D., 6 vols. (London, 1811), i. 294. There is a similar touch in Hugh Downman's *Lucius Junius Brutus* (1779), after Lucretia's suicide: 'Rash action!' says her husband.

17. [F. Gentleman], *The Dramatic Censor* (London, 1770), p. 454.

18. *Letters from the Late Most Reverend Dr Thomas Herring, Lord Archbishop of Canterbury, to William Duncombe, Esq., deceased, From the Year 1728 to 1757* (London, 1777), pp. 54–5, 195–7.

19. T. Cibber, *The Lives of the Poets of Great-Britain and Ireland* (London, 1753), v. 13; Caleb Fleming, *A Dissertation . . .* , p. 5.

20. Cf. David Hume, 'An Enquiry concerning the Principles of Morals', Appendix iv, in Ralph Cohen (ed.), *Essential Works of David Hume* (New York, Toronto, and London, 1965), p. 287. Hume, like Addison, is discussing Sallust's comparative account of the characters of Caesar and Cato. Professor Claude Rawson points out to me that the contrast between 'awful' (or 'admirable') virtues and 'amiable' virtues is to be found in several places in Fielding's work. On the general question of anti-Stoical writing in this period, see R. S. Crane's classic account, 'Suggestions towards a Genealogy of the "Man of Feeling" ', *ELH: A Journal of English Literary History*, i (1934), 205–30.

21. *The City of God*, bk. i, chs. 23, 24; bk. v, ch. 12.

22. See, for example, Jean-François Senault, *Man Become Guilty* (the English translation by Henry Cary, Earl of Monmouth, 1650, of *L'Homme criminel*, 1644), p. 153; Jacques Abbadie, *The Art of Knowing One-Self: Or, an Enquiry Into the Sources of Morality* (the English translation by 'T.W.', Oxford, 1695, of *L'Art de se connoitre soy-meme, ou la recherche des sources de la morale*, 1692), pp. 263–4; William Ayloffe, *The Government of the Passions* (London, 1700), pp. 93–4; Antoine Le Grand, *Man Without Passion: Or, the Wise Stoick, According to the Sentiments of Seneca* (the English translation, 1675, of *Le Sage des Stoiques ou l'homme sans passions. Selon les sentiments de Seneque*, (1662)), pp. 250–1.

23. Richard Steele, *The Christian Hero: or No Principles but those of Religion Sufficient to make a Great Man*, ed. Rae Blanchard (London, 1932), pp. 20–1. Blanchard's introduction is helpful on the background to Steele's work. For Steele's change of mind about Cato, see *The Guardian*, xxxiii, 18 April 1713, and *The Englishman*, xxv, 1 December 1713, and xxxiv, 22 December 1713.

24. See *Spectator* no. 44. It is not known precisely how many children the real Cato had; by his first wife, Atilia, he had one daughter, Portia, and one son, Marcus Portius Cato; by his second wife, Martia, he had one son (? Lucius Portius Cato) and two daughters. Plutarch (*Cato Minor*, lii. 3) tells us that when Cato decided to follow Pompey into exile, he took with him his elder son, sending his younger son (apparently not yet adult) to Munatius in Bruttium for safe keeping, and leaving his daughters with his wife Martia, whom – after Hortensius' death – he had just remarried. (I am grateful to Dr Beryl Rawson for guiding me, here and elsewhere, through the intricacies of Cato's family relationships.)

25. See p. 140 above.

26. *The Critical Works of John Dennis*, ed. E. N. Hooker, 2 vols. (Baltimore, 1943), ii. 41–80, at p. 54. 'All Stoicism is undramatic', declared Lessing in *Laokoon*, and Dennis (p. 50) was not the only critic to notice the problems inherent in a tragedy about a stoical hero: see Edward Young's *Conjectures on Original Composition*, in *The Complete Works, Poetry and Prose, of the Reverend Edward Young L. L. D.* (London, 1854), ii. 576; William Guthrie, *An Essay Upon English Tragedy* (London, n.d), p. 24; Dennis, *Critical Works*, ed. cit., ii. 452.

27. *Cato Minor*, liv. 7, lxiii. 6. Lucan in his account of the African journey speaks of 'Sorrows that might tears, ev'n from Cato, gain,/ And teach the rigid Stoic to complain': *De Bello Civili*, ix. 47–50, Rowe's translation.

28. *Cato Minor*, xi. i.

29. Voltaire, *Discours sur la tragédie*, in *Brutus*, rev. and corr. edn. (Paris, 1736), p. xi.

30. *The Dramatic Censor*, p. 450; Addison's *Works*, ed. Hurd, i. 203.

31. *Clelia*, trs. John Davies, pt. iii, bk. 3 (in the French, '*ie meurs content, pourueu que Rome soit libre, & que Lucrece soit vangée*'); *Brutus*, trs. Francklin, 1761 (in the French, '*Rome est libre: il suffit . . . Rendons grâce aux dieux!*'). Voltaire's line was also to become a famous one: see Robert L. Herbert, *Brutus*, p. 70.

32. Pope, *Minor Poems*, ed. N. Ault, J. Butt, Twickenham edn. of the *Poems of Alexander Pope*, vi (London and New Haven, 1964), pp. 96–100. Pope reported to Caryll in February 1712/13 that Addison's play 'drew tears from me in several parts of the fourth and fifth acts' while he read it in manuscript: see *The Correspondence of Alexander Pope*, ed. George Sherburn (Oxford, 1956), i. 173.

33. Dennis, 'Remarks', p. 67.

34. Samuel Johnson, *Lives of the English Poets*, ed. G. B. Hill (Oxford, 1905), ii. 135–6.

35. Gwin J. Kolb has shown that it was common in neo-Stoical writings of the time to remark that a particular fortitude was necessary to endure the death of a close friend or relative, 'The Use of Stoical Doctrines in *Rasselas*, ch. XVIII', *Modern Language Notes*, lxviii (1953), 439–47. This advice is also to be found in other writings, e.g. Jeremy Taylor's *The Rule and Exercise of Holy Living*, ch. ii, §vi, in *Works* (London, 1839), iv. 133 ff. Yet not even Seneca, who had declared that 'to Lament the Death of a Friend, is both Natural and Just', had taken such an extreme view as Addison implies in this scene (Roger L'Estrange, trs., *Seneca's Morals by Way of Abstract*, 9th edn., 1705, p. 266).

36. *Boswell's Life of Johnson*, ed. G. B. Hill, rev. L. F. Powell, ii. 174. O. F. Emerson, in his edition of *Rasselas* in 1895 (p. 160), noted the possibility that Fielding has in mind Cicero's allusion in *Tusculanae Disputationes*, iii. 28. 70, to the hero Oïleus (in a lost tragedy by Sophocles) who, having consoled Telamon for the death of Ajax, breaks down when he hears of the death of his own son. It is in the same section of this work that Cicero describes Cato the Censor's fortitude on hearing of the death of his son. For Fielding's views on bereavement and Stoicism, see his essay 'Of Remedy of Affliction for the Loss of Our Friends', in *Works*, ed. Henley, xvi: *Miscellaneous Writings*, iii. 97–109, and Henry Knight Miller's *Essays on Fielding's Miscellanies. A Commentary on Volume One* (Princeton, 1961), pp. 254–71 and *passim*.

37. *The Nonsense of Common-Sense*, 24 January 1738, in *Lady Mary Wortley Montagu, Essays and Poems and 'Simplicity', a Comedy*, ed. Robert Halsband and Isobel Grundy (Oxford, 1977), p. 133; cf. p. 231, and *The Complete Letters of Lady Mary Wortley Montagu*, ed. Robert

Halsband, 3 vols. (Oxford, 1965–7), iii. 208, 219, 220. For Lady Mary's critique of *Cato*, see *Essays and Poems*, pp. 62–8, and Halsband, 'Addison's *Cato* and Lady Mary Wortley Montagu', *PMLA*, lxv (1950), 1122–9.

38. William H. McBurney sees another echo of Addison's famous scene in Lillo's *Fatal Curiosity*, II. iii: see his edition of the play for the Regents Restoration Drama Series (London, 1967), p. 35. The scene in Gay's burlesque play *The What D'Ye Call It*, in which Timothy Peascod tearfully reads *Pilgrim's Progress* while awaiting execution, was thought to parody Addison's scene in *Cato*: see Pope, *Correspondence*, ed. Sherburn, i, 290–1.

39. See Robert Rosenblum, *Transformations in Late Eighteenth Century Art*, esp. ch. 2.

40. Cf. S. E. Sprott, *The English Debate on Suicide from Donne to Hume* (La Salle, Ill., 1961), p. 13.

INDEX